"Very timely! Tells us how to succeed in this crazy new environment, without betting the ranch at every turn. Must reading!"

—DAVID R. HOLMES, Chairman of the Board,
The Reynolds & Reynolds Company

"Nobody thinks about strategy like D'Aveni. Provides innovative ways for companies to create spheres of influence to tip the balance of power in their favor. Read it and learn how to gain an edge and defend your position."

—BRUCE A. PASTERNACK, Senior Vice President and
Member of the Executive Committee,
Booz•Allen & Hamilton, and Managing Partner,
Strategic Leadership Practice

"Stimulates reexamination of one's business assumptions and strategies. . . . A practitioner's roadmap to evolving strategy. . . . A lively dialogue between reality and theory, reflecting on which can make a huge difference to your strategy."

—RAHUL BAJAJ, Chairman and Managing Director,
Bajaj Auto Ltd., India

"Finally . . . powerful tools for building and defending a global enterprise. A rich toolkit for the corporate leaders charged with this complex and challenging task."

—JAMES HAYMAKER, Corporate Vice President,
Strategy and Business Development, Cargill, Inc.

"Provides for a mindset that will trigger change in your strategic thinking and create a dynamic vision for leadership in your industry."

—HADDO MEIJER, Chairman Executive Committee,
P&O Nedlloyd, The Netherlands/UK

*f*P

STRATEGIC SUPREMACY®

How Industry Leaders Create Growth,
Wealth, and Power through
Spheres of Influence

Richard A. D'Aveni

With Robert Gunther and Joni Cole

THE FREE PRESS

NEW YORK   LONDON   TORONTO   SYDNEY   SINGAPORE

THE FREE PRESS
A Division of Simon & Schuster, Inc.
1230 Avenue of the Americas
New York, NY 10020

Strategic Supremacy is a registered trademark.
For information about special
discounts for bulk purchases, please contact Simon & Schuster Special Sales:
1-800-456-6798 or business@simonandschuster.com

DESIGNED BY LISA CHOVNICK

Manufactured in the United States of America

10   9   8   7   6   5   4   3   2   1

Library of Congress Cataloging-in-Publication Data

D'Aveni, Richard A.
Strategic supremacy : how industry leaders create growth, wealth, and power through spheres
of influence / Richard A. D'Aveni with Robert Gunther and Joni Cole.
p.   cm.
Includes bibliographical references and index.
1. Strategic planning.   2. Competition.   3. Wealth.   4. Power (Social sciences)
5. Spheres of influence.   I. Gunther, Robert E.   II. Cole, Joni.   III. Title.

HD30.28.D376 2001
658.4'012—dc21   2001051068
ISBN 0-684-87180-7 (alk. paper)

The author gratefully acknowledges permission from the following sources to reprint material in their control:

Academy of Management Review for a figure from Volume/Edition 16.1 by Christine Oliver that appears as exhibit
  4.4 in this book. Copyright © 1991 by Academy of Management. Reprinted by permission of the publisher
  via Copyright Clearance Center.
Academy of Management Review for a figure from Volume/Edition 16.1 by Christine Oliver that appears as exhibit
  4.5 in this book. Copyright © 1991 by Academy of Management. Reprinted by permission of the publisher
  via Copyright Clearance Center.
Academy of Management Review for a figure from Volume/Edition 21.1 by Ming-Jer Chen that appears as exhibit
  6.1 in this book. Copyright © 1991 by Academy of Management. Reprinted by permission of the publisher
  via Copyright Clearance Center.
EC Media Group for table "Preemptive Strategies" from Journal of Business Strategy, 1983, Vol. 4, that appears as
  exhibit 3.2 in this book. Copyright © 1983 by EC Media Group, Eleven Penn Plaza, New York, NY 10001.
Oxford University Press for a graph located in Contemporary Economic Policy, Vol. 18, No. 3, July 2000, page 312,
  by Joseph A. Clougherty, that appears as exhibit 6.10 in this book. Copyright © 2000 by Oxford University Press.
Prentice-Hall, Inc., for an excerpt by Ian MacMillan titled "Seizing Competitive Initiative" on page 274 of the
  January 1, 1984, edition of Competitive Strategic Management by Robert B. Lamb that appears as exhibit 3.3
  in this book. Copyright © 1984 by Lamb, Robert B. Reprinted by permission of Prentice-Hall, Inc., Upper
  Saddle River, NJ.

A Dedication

To my hero, my father, Pfc. Anthony Rosario D'Aveni, who landed with the 9th Infantry Division as part of the second wave of the D-Day (June 6, 1944) invasion of Europe. Awarded the Purple Heart with Oak Leaf Cluster. For the benefit of mankind, you and your fallen friends completed a cross-channel invasion, something that had not been done since William the Conqueror in A.D. 1066. Historians may remember the generals, but I will never forget that history is made by men like you.

And a Tribute

Out of respect and love, I have published your August 26, 1998, letter to me in Appendix A of this book. Your humility would never have allowed this, so please excuse the surprise. The world and your grandchildren should know your bravery and sacrifice. And you should know my pride in being your son.

"Where there is no vision, the people perish."

PROVERBS *29:18*

"You've got to be very careful if you don't know where you're going, because you might not get there."

YOGI BERRA

Many people have contributed to the development of this book. First and foremost, I want to thank my colleague, executive assistant, and friend, Tracy Flynn-Scott; my secretary at the Tuck School of Business at Dartmouth College, Pat Hunt; and the research staff at Dartmouth's Feldberg Library, including Sarah Buckingham, Jim Fries, Karen Sluzenski, and especially Bette Snyder. They put endless hours into the research and production of this book. Without them, this book would have never existed.

I am grateful to countless business leaders who have shared their experiences and insights with me (and sometimes with my students) during the last five years of research, consulting, and speaking. The executives (and their titles at the time of my discussions with them) include: Jim Abegglen, Founder of Gemini-Japan; Doug Atkins, CEO, Instinet (Reuters); Jim Bailey, Executive Vice President of Citicorp; Paul Batchelor, Managing Director of Coopers & Lybrand Europe; J.T. Battenberg, III, CEO, Delphi Automotive Systems; Hans Beckerer, CEO, John Deere; Steve Beebe, CEO, J.R. Simplot Co.; Larry Bossidy, CEO of Allied Signal; Yale Brandt, Vice Chairman of the Board, Reynolds Metals; Edward Brennan, CEO of Sears; Rudie Bryce, CEO, Schering-Plough International; William Burke, Vice President of Boston Technologies; Peter Campanella, CEO, Corning Consumer Products; Lt. General (ret.) Paul Cerjan, President of the National Defense University and NATO Command; Alison Corcoran, Vice President and General Manager, Polaroid Corporation; Karen Dawes, Senior Vice President, Marketing and Sales, Bayer Pharmaceuticals; David Della Penta, President and CEO, Fischer Scientific; Tom Doorley, Founding Partner of Braxton Associates; Douglas Dunn, Vice President of AT&T Multimedia Services; David Ehlen, CEO of Wilson Learning; Michael Eisner, CEO of Disney; Jerry Elson, Vice President of General Motors; Dom Esposito, CEO, Grant Thornton; Bob Forte, Vice President, Marketing, Fischer Scientific; John Foster, CEO, Foster Investments; William Gaither, Chairman of the Board of The Heafner Group; Jim Haymaker, Vice President of Strategy and Business Development, Cargill; David Holmes, CEO of Reynolds and Reynolds; David Jarvis, Co-head of Global Financial Institutions, Salomon Smith Barney; Guy Jillings, retired Head of Strategic Planning of Royal Dutch Shell; Phil Koerner, Chairman and CEO, National Grange Mutual; Charles Leighton, CEO, CML (Nordic Track); David Martin, Executive Vice President of Texas Instruments; Kevin McGrath, CEO of Hughes Communications; Richard Measle, Worldwide Managing Partner of Arthur Andersen & Co.; Haddo Meijer, Chairman Executive Committee of P & O Nedlloyd, The Netherlands/UK; John Miller, Head Strategy Officer, AT&T Network Systems (now Lucent); Hans Morris, Co-head of Global Financial Institutions, Salomon Smith Barney; Loay Nazer, Vice Chairman, Nazer Group (Saudi Arabia); Terry Neil, Managing Director of Andersen Consulting–Europe; Jonathan Newcomb, CEO, Simon & Schuster; Ken Noyes, CEO, Schwan's Food; Tom Peters, Founder of The Tom Peters Group; Jim Preston, CEO of Avon Products; Robert Purcell, Jr., Executive in Charge of Corporate Strategy at General Motors; Tony Ridder, Chairman and CEO of Knight-Ridder; Matt Rightmire, Vice President and General Manager, Yahoo! Inc.; Anthony T.G. Rogers, Managing Director of Zeneca Ltd.; Joan Rothman, Senior Vice President, Marketing, Dun & Bradstreet; Peter Shreer, President of Philip Morris–Latin America; Andy Sigler, CEO of Champion International; Ted Simplot, Chairman, J.R. Simplot Co.; Dan Simpson, Vice President of Strategy & Planning for Clorox; Adrian Slywotzky, Founding Partner, Corporate Decisions, Inc.; Terri Taylor, CEO, Dun & Bradstreet; Walter Thoma, CEO of Philip-Morris–Europe; April Thornton, Vice President Marketing, Armstrong Industries; John Tormondsen, Managing Director, Fixed Income Securities Trading, Goldman Sachs & Company; Alex Trotman, CEO of Ford Motor Co.; Paul Walsh, CEO of Pillsbury; Wolf Schmitt, CEO of Rubbermaid; Roy Vagelos, CEO of Merck & Co.

I would also like to thank the following Tuck and Dartmouth students who have worked as research assistants for me: Rebecca Adams, Brent Ahrens, Tamara Brock, Greg Capitolo, Fernando R. Chaddad, Tracy Dorsey, Tracey Fudge, Lutz Goedde, Heather Grace, Jeffrey Halpern, Eric

Harnish, Jack Herrick, Andrew Hirsch, Rebecca Joffrey, Derrick Johnson, Clinton Kendall, Ilmars Kerbers, Matthew Kunkle, Alexandra Y. Latypova, Eugene Lowe, Steve Mendola, Stuart Murray, Robert Lynch, Sameer V. Nadkarni, Terri E. O'Connor, Chris Pears, Michael J. Perera, Igor Popov, James Rice, Brett Rome, Kathy Schaider, Michael Sexton, Gary Smith, James Sole, Yancey Spruill, Karin Stawarky, Stephen Wilson, Brittany Windsor, Barry Winer, Paul Whiting, Jr. Their efforts and ideas have made a big difference to the accuracy and depth of the book.

I also thank all the students who took my seminars. They suffered through early drafts, and their critiques and feedback held me to a high standard and pushed me toward ever more refined ideas. These students are listed by course:

SEMINAR ON BUSINESS POLICY STUDENTS: Susan M. Chargin, Jan C. Faller, Debra Ann Gerardi, Jeffrey Goodman, Brian T. Hansen, John C. Harpole, Edward B. Hill, Daniel T. Myers, Mark A. Peterson, Steven D. Ritchie, Jeffrey Saunders, Michael Schultz, Robert Stallings, Joseph E. Villa, Per-Arne Weiner.

INDUSTRY AND COMPETITIVE ANALYSIS OLIGOPOLISTIC INDUSTRIES STUDENTS: Marshall Bartlett, Greg Belonogoff, William Bennett, Dave Block, Oliver Boulind, Derek Calzini, Fernando Chaddac, Yong Choi, Tom Christenson, Marco Di Liberto, Nat Fisher, Dan Givens, Patrick Halas, Elizabeth Harris, Kristiana Helmick, Mark Hess, Rebecca Jackson, Peter C. Johnson, Chad Johnston, Tom Leverton, John Levine, Steve Meade, Lee Modesitt, Rob Petrie, Miriam Plavin, Bill Pond, Peggy Reid, Mark Russell, Ben Shaw, John Smith, Tiffany Smith, Bernd Spitz, Todd Stern, Tracy Thomas, Steven Tran, Jean Tsai, Frans Van Camp, Amanda Vineyard, Shane Young, Chris Zepf.

Very significantly, I want to thank the many strategy scholars whose works have been helpful in the preparation of this book. These include: Philip Anderson, Chris Bartlett, Maikel V. Batelaan, Joel Baum, Warren Boeker, William Bogner, Ming-Jer Chen, David Collis, William N. Evans, Kathy Eisenhardt, Walter Ferrier, Syd Finkelstein, Javier Gimeno, J. Goodstein, Sumantra Ghoshal, Vijay Govindarajan, H.R. Greve, Curtis

Grimm, Don Hambrick, Gary Hamel, Heather Haveman, Connie Helfat, Mike Hitt, David Jemison, William Joyce, Aneel Karnani, Ioannis Kessides, Bruce Kogut, Rita McGrath, Ian MacMillan, Joe Mahoney, Cynthia Montgomery, Karl Moore, Lynn Nonnemaker, Margie Peteraf, Joe Porac, Michael Porter, C. K. Prahalad, James Brian Quinn, John T. Scott, Ken G. Smith, Jeff Sonnenfeld, Alva Taylor, Howard Thomas, Birger Wernerfelt, and Carolyn Woo. Their work on corporate strategy, chaos theory, complex adaptive systems, portfolio strategy, multimarket contacts, leadership, and the dynamics of strategic interactions is the foundation that this book rests upon. Because of their insights and empirical findings, the theoretical underpinnings of this book are more secure, and the credibility of the strategies that I have developed in this book is improved greatly.

Last, but far from least, I want to thank Bob Wallace of the Free Press. His editorial guidance proved invaluable. He challenged me to throw away an entire (ninth) draft and start over. He helped me fine tune my concepts, hone in on a clearer audience, and get the proper balance between history and business. Without his help, this book would have been a mere whisper compared to what he pushed me to produce.

CONTENTS

The Art of Strategy

In my view, business strategy scholars have developed an inferiority complex. In our struggle for academic legitimacy, we have been co-opted by scientific methods—data collection, statistical analysis, and modeling—as a way to gain not only results, but credibility and respect. Scientific thought has contributed greatly to the field, but in our strident efforts to quantify strategy to prove our worth, we have lost sight of an important principle—strategy is an art as much as it is a science. At its most fundamental level, the field of strategy is one of the humanities. After all, great strategies come from experience, intuition, insight, and inspiration—from seeing the big picture and viewing the world as a canvas on which to paint the next big picture.

In my twenty-plus years as a strategy consultant and scholar, I have witnessed a gradual de-legitimization of the use of the humanities in our field. The knowledge contained in the long history of human experience has been ignored by strategy professors for too long, resulting in some unhealthy side effects. As the old joke in medicine goes, the operation was a success but the patient died. In converting strategy to cold science, we have inadvertently extracted the heart and guts that give strategy its life—and its genius.

The field, in my opinion, needs resuscitation. As strategy scholars, consultants, and practitioners, we need to look beyond science to other sources of inspiration and creativity. In my case, inspiration came in 1996 as I walked through the Winter Palace of Peter the Great (now the Hermitage Museum) in St. Petersburg, Russia, with the excitement of a child in a forbidden place. I was on the way to a ballet in the Czar's private theater. As I watched the dancers on stage, I was transported back to a time of pre-communist, imperial splendor. I felt the still-present aura of the czars, and couldn't help but think about how this once-great nation held supremacy over a vast portion of the world. Sitting in that historic theater, I began considering Russia's power and place in world politics before Lenin interrupted history. From the reign of the Romanovs to the Russian Revolution, to the ruin of the USSR, here was an empire that had gone from the center stage of geopolitics to a nation waiting in the wings to find its place in history once again. It seemed almost unfathomable that an American tourist such as myself could now be sitting in a theater that was once the private domain of a dynasty.

Later that evening, my thoughts extended to other great powers throughout history. As a scholar of business strategy, I was struck by the analogy between multinational empires and global corporations, and the similarities in how nations and companies struggle for territory and power. This analogy raised a compelling question—what can today's business leaders learn from the experiences of potentates and presidents through-out geopolitical history? It was then that I realized that many of the most important issues related to corporate strategy—the geographic positioning of firms, the scope of an enterprise's borders, and the use of its power—have been addressed for millennia.

And so I began my quest "back to the future," a five-year journey that took me from Caesar to cyberspace, and culminated in *Strategic Supremacy*. I explored the rise of the Ancient Roman and Greek Empires, as well as the more recent French, Spanish, Russian, British, Soviet, and American empires. My research also crossed the border into the world of multinational business enterprises, including the twenty most admired global firms (according to *Fortune*), and twenty large global companies that declined.

I analyzed the commonalities among these great powers' growth strategies, alliances, geopolitical or geo-product positioning, and their foreign policies or global strategies. Because my focus was to understand how multinational enterprises cope with chaotic environments and adapt by creating patterns and structures that define their competitive and cooperative relationships, I looked at history through the lenses of chaos theory and complex adaptive systems. My goal was to discover and revitalize strategies relevant to the giants of modern business competing in a chaotic and complex world.

In the chapters that follow, I have greatly pared down the dusty details of my research, including only a limited number of historical highlights to illustrate and motivate the business discussions. Despite their brevity, these historical summaries add both drama and depth to our understanding of corporate enterprises—how they maneuver, interact, project their power, and evolve over time.

Admittedly, my perspective while writing this book was not that of an historian. While this book is based on what I learned from history, this is not a book about history. It is not even a book about business history. It is about *making history.*

Some might argue that lessons from past potentates and presidents are irrelevant in helping people make history in an era of rapid change. But it is precisely because we live in a fast-paced world that we must look to history. Over the millennia, history has already answered many of the questions about how great powers survive and thrive in periods of rapid change, revolutions, and seismic shifts.

It seems ironic that the field of strategy, which was pioneered by famous business historians such as Pulitzer prize winner Alfred Chandler, Jr., is now resistant, even shocked, by the suggestion that the lessons of history deserve a place in our scholarly journals. I hope this book will inspire my younger academic colleagues to consider the effects this detour has had on the direction and heart of our field, and to re-legitimize the notion of strategy as a humanity. Otherwise, I fear that our profession—rather than making history—will become history.

I also hope that managers reading this book, especially those at the helm of multinational businesses, will be as inspired as I was by the strategies that history has revealed. May you use the timeless principles presented in this work to make history in your own right, and in your own day.

RICHARD D'AVENI
Hanover, New Hampshire
April 8, 2001

Strategic Supremacy

Remember the old joke about the patient who went to the doctor and said, "Doctor, every time I bend over backwards it hurts." And the doctor's response was, "So, don't do that."

Today, managers of are being told to bend over backward to adopt the latest trends in business strategy: disruption; revolution; chaos. There are hundreds of books—including my own previous work, *Hypercompetition*—that advocate strategies for disrupting the status quo, leading the revolution, and managing on the edge of chaos. Many agile firms have made a lot of money with these high-risk strategies, particularly those with the flexibility to bend over backward by abandoning their current strengths and constantly jumping to new ones.

But this is only part of the story. Large and multinational corporations with diverse and dispersed organizations are already leaders in their industries and rightfully question the wisdom of inciting chaos and revolution to topple the established order. For these firms, disruption, revolution, and chaos could unnecessarily bend their organizations to the breaking point. Many companies have experienced "initiative fatigue" that demoralizes and exhausts their managers and workers, and causes unnecessary turnover and costly turmoil that weakens their position. Given the organizational constraints and the cost of changing the work force in a large corporation, perhaps these firms should follow the advice of the doctor in the old joke and, "stop doing that."

After writing *Hypercompetition,* I spoke with executives in hundreds of successful companies and discovered that, far from being revolutionaries, these industry leaders want to take a path more suitable to their situation and advantages. They want to offer better, risk-adjusted returns than the thousands of revolutionaries who promise the moon and the stars, but fade out in the light of day. These managers know that, as the established leaders, it is downright inadvisable to be a revolutionary, particularly given the fact that, as history shows, most revolutions fail and most revolutionaries are hanged. While revolutions grab the headlines, profits and prosperity most often come from *stability and orderly change.*

In February 2001, Peter Brabeck, CEO of Nestlé—the world's largest food company—said: "Big change is fine for a crisis. . . . But not every company in the world is in crisis all the time. Many companies are like us—not as big, of course—but they are performing well. Growing, innovating, and so forth—good and fit. Why should we manufacture dramatic change? Just for change's sake? . . . Big disruptive change programs are anything but [pragmatic]. You cannot underestimate the traumatic impact of abrupt change, the distraction it causes in running the business, the fear that it provokes in people, the demands it makes on management's time. . . . Evolution can happen if you believe in it. You can have slow and steady change, and that is nothing to be ashamed of. Our market capitalization in 1997 was CHF 55 billion (Swiss francs), and today [2001] it is CHF 150 billion. It happened without frenzy, without bloodshed. . . . Our company is more like a 40-year-old, someone who is strong and trim, and who can easily run 10 miles without being pushed or pulled. We will see how all these [revolutionary] 'technology' companies are performing in ten years. I wonder, I wonder. I can tell you Nestlé will still be here."[1]

Even the revolutionaries, once they become successful, want to restabilize the industry into a new order that places them at the center. Former revolutionaries like Dell, Cisco, or AOL now want to keep upstarts and existing powers from destroying their leadership positions in their markets.

The establishment doesn't have to take revolution and disruption lying down. Often, they control potential chaos by embracing and molding the revolutionaries. Media and publishing giant Bertelsmann cleans up the wild-eyed MP3 revolutionaries of Napster and brings them into the fold of BMG and the music establishment. Similarly, Bertelsmann brings

Barnes and Noble.com into its publishing empire in order to stabilize its position in the publishing world.

These industry leaders live in an age when the maps of their business world are being redrawn. Corporate great powers are carrying their banners into new territories around the globe, and others are retaliating by entering their core territories. Alliances and megamergers such as Citibank–Travelers–Salomon Smith Barney and AOL–Time Warner–Netscape are reshaping their companies and their industries' playing fields.

Because managers of these firms must win on their global playing fields, they are left with unanswered questions about critical strategic issues:

- How do I respond to all the rebellions going on in the thousands of geo-product markets where my company competes?
- What if my company is an elephant that can never learn to dance?
- Rather than disrupt my industry, how do I cooperate with my competitors in order to create the alliances necessary to reach global markets and acquire new competencies?
- How can I increase my firm's profits, growth, and power without provoking retaliation from global giants with massive resources?
- How can I create a clear vision for my company's portfolio of businesses when it is spread over so many geographies and products?

All of these questions feed into two major challenges that managers confront every day: How should I position my geographic and product (geo-product) portfolio and allocate my resources against competitors without instigating a global competitive conflagration? And how should I do this without getting distracted by too many brushfires?

To help managers address these challenges and achieve new heights, I have written *Strategic Supremacy*. This book is for firms in industries where it is impossible to pull off the high-risk margins and skyrocketing growth standards promised by the hype of hypercompetition and revelations of revolutionaries. This book is not only for the superstars in hot industries, but also for those firms who are in mature industries that aren't necessarily glamorous, hip, or innovative. In short, this book is for the managers of firms who prefer evolution rather than revolution. And it is for those who must fight for every piece of turf, inch by inch.

While chaos and change cannot be prevented, the most enduring corporations have found ways to use these forces of change to redraw the maps of competition to create a favorable world around themselves. They create periods of dynamic stability and shape a world to their benefit. Throughout history, great powers have built and reshaped their territory, absorbed or deflected revolutions, and managed their relations with other great powers with one overriding aim: strategic supremacy.

Whether you are already a leader in your industry, or leadership is your destination, the principles of strategic supremacy offered in this book will hit home. These strategies have been proven throughout history—in the realms of both business and nations—to conquer chaos and fashion a favorable world. Regardless of your industry, they can help you deal with rapid change and overcome an onslaught of challenges to your leadership, all while satisfying the insatiable demands of your shareholders for more growth and profits.

CONQUERING CHAOS AND FASHIONING A FAVORABLE WORLD

World and industry leaders—whether multinational ancient empires or modern global corporations—have always engaged in tussles over turf. At corporate headquarters, managers work to stake out their corporation's position on the global "playing field," a competitive space delineated by geographies, and by a company's products and services (see Exhibit I-1). At corporate and divisional headquarters or within marketing departments, managers work to stake out their product positioning on parts of the geo-product space. No matter whether you are CEO or brand manager, you compete and cooperate to win the most attractive geo-product markets, and you do so as part of a larger system comprised of many rivals with varying amounts of strong and weak territories, and hence varying degrees of power.

For companies with diverse and dispersed holdings, the playing field is all too often a chaotic space, a complex competitive arena where even "winning" the tussle over turf can have an adverse affect on your financial performance. Sometimes, the cost of winning an attractive market that everyone wants exceeds the benefits. At other times, you may succeed in ac-

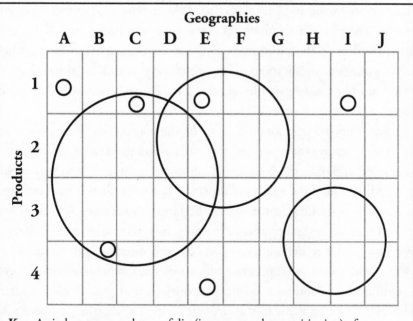

Key: A circle represents the portfolio (i.e., geo-product positioning) of a company on the geo-product "playing field" (i.e., its positioning within the competitive space). Each box represents a zone within the larger competitive space. Other market divisions can be used to define zones within the space. Instead of geographies, the competitive space can be divided into customer segments or distribution channels. For the sake of simplicity this book will limit itself to geographies and/or products to define "zones" within a competitive space.

Exhibit I-1: The Competitive System—A Struggle for Turf and Power

cumulating strong positions in a collection of attractive markets that leverage your core competencies, but you may still end up with a geo-product portfolio that lacks cohesion and vision. For example, your geo-product portfolio may leave you poorly positioned against other competitors because they control geo-product markets that surround your collection of attractive markets, thus giving these rivals numerous launch pads into your turf.

Because of the inherent chaotic nature of the competitive playing field, a geo-product portfolio focused on attractive markets and core competencies is not enough to create the power needed to protect your future.

Winning on your industry's playing field demands a special kind of power—the power not only to stake out your own turf on that field, but also to influence the positioning and maneuvering of your rivals. This power gives you the ability to define the playing field as a way to conquer chaos and fashion a favorable world. I have labeled this power "strategic supremacy."

Firms with strategic supremacy define the playing field by establishing the borders around their own territory and around the territory of competitors. In other words, they establish a "sphere of influence," and they mold the borders around the spheres of others. Spheres of influence may overlap, but only to a limited degree before the borders disappear. What's more, spheres with strategic supremacy determine how those borders will change over time, and even delimit the borders of the competitive space itself.

In essence, strategic supremacy offers a framework for envisioning how a multiproduct, multilocation firm successfully and proactively interacts with other leading firms in the struggle for turf *and* power. Sometimes, only one firm in an industry has strategic supremacy. In other cases, several firms share supremacy. And in other cases, no one has achieved supremacy yet, though many are pursuing it. Even small- and moderate-sized firms can gain strategic supremacy over a region of their competitive space. In all these cases, building and using a strong sphere of influence is at the heart of capturing, preserving, or usurping strategic supremacy.

The Heart of Strategic Supremacy: The Sphere of Influence

A sphere of influence is your company's geo-product portfolio on steroids. Your sphere is centered on a core market that you "own." This is the market where you have established value leadership. This means you set the expectations of customers and rivals when it comes to quality, price, and performance, and you also set the standards that everyone else benchmarks.

The sphere of influence is not a portfolio of "core competencies." It is based on a *core market,* but that is only the beginning. Your sphere's core market is surrounded by your presence in other geo-product markets, each of which serves a specific strategic intent. Some markets are vital interests that increase the power of your core using traditional shared competencies and economies of scale and scope. Your sphere also includes markets that serve as buffer zones that protect your power by helping you defend against rivals that surround your core and vital interests. Pivotal zones in your sphere capture power vacuums, allowing you to improve your sphere's power through indirect, rather than head-on, competition. Pivotal zones can also serve as bets on the future, positioning you in markets that may become so important they could shift the balance of power. Your sphere of influence also includes forward positions in rival spheres. These positions allow you to counterattack competitors, signal your strategic intentions, and even establish tacit alliances with rivals. (See Chapter 1 for more on how to construct a cohesive sphere of influence.)

A gestalt of powerful proportions, a sphere is greater than the sum of its parts, creating a competitive arsenal that can be used to influence rivals and customers in a way that defines the playing field. Because each zone plays an important strategic role, a cohesive sphere protects your present. It also positions you for the future—even in the event of a seismic shift in your industry. And it allows you to utilize your entire company as a platform for building competitive advantage.

In essence, the sphere of influence provides a new logic for your portfolio, one that recognizes that your firm's power can derive from much more than core competencies. One example: Many successful spheres create positions in markets where they have no strengths and no chance of winning, all in the service of the larger strategic purpose of increasing their power relative to rivals, in order to define the playing field. To the unenlightened eye, spheres with strategic supremacy may look illogical today, but they won't when the Monday morning quarterbacks see how they were used to shape the future.

A cohesive sphere of influence achieves strategic supremacy by helping your firm:

- *Circumvent the competitive compression on your sphere.* When rivals try to contain, constrict, strip, or domino their way into your sphere, you can use your sphere to buffer your core against the power of other spheres. You can restructure your sphere to create a platform for growth around the compression. And you can use your sphere to turn the tables by applying competitive compression on a rival's sphere. (See Chapter 2 for more insights on natural growth patterns that will help your firm counter or circumvent competitive compression.)

- *Create a vision for routing resources around your portfolio.* Rather than being subject to momentary market fluctuations and internal conflicts over funding, adhering to one of four proven paradigms for resource allocation within your sphere gives you a long-term vision for your sphere's accumulation of wealth and power. (See Chapter 3 for more on paradigms that will increase your sphere's wealth and power.)

- *Cope with a multitude of rebellions.* You can't ignore the hundreds of ambitious smaller challengers in your numerous geo-product markets. And you can't respond to every disruption everywhere. Using the power of a cohesive sphere, you can absorb some blows, counter the revolutions that rise to the top, and work with others to proactively keep the lid on chaos and stabilize your industry structure. (See Chapter 4 for more on dealing with disruption by ambitious lesser powers.)

- *Cooperate and compete to tip the balance of power in your favor.* Powerful spheres configure the other big players in their competitive space into "triangles"—great power relationships consisting of two allies and one target sphere. The alliances in these triangles achieve alignment using several strategies. By focusing multiple triangles on the same goal, your firm can gradually influence your industry's structure and gain preeminence for your company's "world view" of the competitive playing field. (See Chapter 5 for more on how your firm can configure other great powers to tip the balance of power in your favor.)

- *Guide your industry to a more profitable future.* A sphere with supremacy can use competitive pressure to intervene in its industry's power system, stabilize the power hierarchy, or redistribute power. Stabilizing mechanisms allow you to create a "dynamic stability," or you can apply "pressure cascades" to guide the transformation of an industry in transition and mold order amidst the chaos. (See Chapter 6 for more on how you can influence the future playing field by measuring, mapping, and redirecting patterns of competitive pressure and power.)

If you want strategic supremacy for your firm, you must create a powerful sphere and use it to structure the geo-product space in a way that tips the distribution of power in your favor. Therefore, the tussle over turf translates into a struggle that ultimately affects your position in the "power hierarchy" of your industry. Consequently, firms can't choose their portfolio of businesses without thinking about how their position in the geo-product space influences the power system within their industry. They must beware that they do not create impotent portfolios by occupying only niche markets and maneuvering in ways that provide no power to influence the behavior of their rivals. While profitable, such portfolios cannot redistribute or direct the flow and balance of power within an industry.

THE UNIQUE NATURE OF STRATEGIC SUPREMACY

Most large corporations think of their power in terms of massive size, global reach, and the authority or trust assigned to firms that have longevity. But these don't equate to strategic supremacy. For example, a large, widely diversified conglomerate with global reach has power and resources. It survives by spreading its risks over a large number of businesses. But a conglomerate cannot influence the borders of others because it faces too many rivals. It doesn't own a core that is strong enough to build a cohesive sphere around because it is too diffuse. And it competes not so much by shaping the playing field but rather by reshaping itself.

Strategic supremacy is a special kind of power that transcends size, reach, and longevity. It's not what you have, so much as how you use it. The attributes I just listed give firms the potential for strategic supremacy, but firms with massive size, reach, and longevity cannot achieve strategic supremacy without first understanding that they only have power over others if others believe they do. Throughout history, there are striking examples of this truth. George Washington and Mahatma Gandhi faced an empire with overwhelming size, longevity, and global reach. Yet they refused to buckle under the pressure and used guerrilla tactics, passive resistance, and leadership skills to render what appeared to be a formidable force useless. They simply recognized that British military power was not enough to create strategic supremacy over America and India.

Because of this reality, the unique nature of strategic supremacy is defined by three principles: the power of perception; the power to capture the hearts and minds of core customers; and the power to fashion a favorable world by using different combinations and patterns of competition and cooperation. These three principles are the tools for constructing a "social reality" without using the force of deep pockets, monopoly power, or illegal collusion.

The Power of Perception

Much like drawing borders on a map of the world, the lines around a company's sphere of influence are as much about perception as they are about reality. When the astronauts first photographed the earth from orbit, the photos looked very different than the maps. There were no borders on earth, and no territories under the control of one nation or another. The map was not the territory. The borderlines existed only because others perceived them and agreed to abide by them.

Even industry boundaries are based on shared beliefs. "Mental maps," developed by managers over years of experience, define who is seen as a competitor, in effect delimiting the competitive space. Every border you establish—from the lines around your sphere to how you delineate geo-product markets based on grouping geographies and products into categories, to how you delimit the competitive space—is, in effect, a socially constructed reality. Each can be reshaped, destroyed, or reconceived.

Strategic supremacy is, therefore, about creating a social reality that is shared among competitors within a competitive space. Signaling and strategic maneuvering for position on the playing field can be used to influence the perceptions of rivals, direct their attention toward a specific market, or change their intent away from other markets. This is how firms "negotiate" the borders of their spheres.

When one or more great powers achieves strategic supremacy, the borderlines that they have chalked become the accepted reality. Through many interactions with many rivals, a firm with supremacy gains preeminence for its "world view" of the competitive space. Over time, this world view becomes the mental map that others follow. In business, as in world politics, the power of perception cannot be underestimated. As Winston Churchill said, "the empires of the future are the empires of the mind."

Capturing Hearts and Minds

Given the power of perception, strategic supremacy starts with capturing the hearts and minds of customers in core markets. Typically, firms do so by offering customers much greater quality and service at lower prices. They set the standards that customers expect and rivals must benchmark, thus writing the rules of competition. To have supremacy, firms must offer value that is so superlative that they figuratively own their core markets.

In the 1970s shaving market, for example, Gillette had supremacy until BIC captured the hearts and minds of numerous Gillette customers by offering them low cost and disposable convenience. BIC redefined the playing field by creating and growing the disposable razor segment worldwide. Gillette quickly learned to play in this high-growth disposable razor market and eventually became the leader in the U.S. disposable market. But it was a Pyrrhic victory. This low-margin world—in which BIC was much better prepared to compete because of its strength in low-cost manufacturing of plastic goods—drained profits from the research-intensive Gillette and weakened its sphere by cannibalizing the company's long-term, higher margin core market in cartridges. Clearly, BIC had imposed its world view on the competitive space.

Gillette regained strategic supremacy when it took control of the playing field through the creation of its Sensor razor. The company recaptured the hearts and minds of customers by rewriting the rules of competition, offering significantly better shaving closeness, backed by the laser-welding technological expertise necessary to manufacture the Sensor. Rewriting the shaving rules allowed Gillette to restructure the playing field by owning a new core market in "shaving systems." This core grew at the expense of BIC's core disposable market and Gillette's old core in cartridges, such as the Atra and Atra II. The borders of Gillette's playing field changed as well, becoming global with Gillette's massive international launch of the Sensor.

Gillette teaches a good lesson about strategic supremacy. The struggle for supremacy is a dynamic process involving the continual creation of superlative value for your core customers. Failure to do so gives rivals the opportunity to invade your core with a better product, or to entice customers away from your core and accept a substitute product. Gillette, which had held leadership in the shaving market since World War I, forfeited its supremacy to BIC and was almost bought up in a hostile takeover because of its declining fortunes.

Since its brush with BIC for control of the shaving industry, Gillette learned it had to write the rules of the game in order to own a viable core. The company continued to write new rules for value in its new core with the Mach3 shaving system. It also continued to control the definition of the playing field by appealing to the women's market with a Sensor that was designed to meet their specific safety needs, rather than simply making a pink version of the original. Previously, Gillette had marketed the Sensor as "The best a man can get." Yet by seizing control of this new dual-gender playing field, the best a man can get—at least for Gillette— got a whole lot bigger and better.

Fashioning a Favorable World through Forms of Co-opetition

One of the interesting results from the struggle for power between BIC and Gillette was that each firm ended up redefining its sphere. BIC's sphere had been centered on low-cost manufactured plastic disposable products such as razors, lighters, and pens. After Gillette won in the razor market, BIC reduced its emphasis on razors, focusing on lighters and pens. Around the same time, Gillette exited the disposable lighter market. So the competition between the two companies ultimately encouraged a form of tacit cooperation over the redefinition of the borders of their spheres. In essence, Gillette and BIC legally fashioned a more favorable world by mixing competition and cooperation.

By competing over spheres of influence, competitors position themselves in different parts of the geo-product space naturally and without illegal, overt, and explicit agreements to divide up the markets into monopolies. This process allows competitors to differentiate themselves and avoid getting spread too thin by trying to compete across the entire playing field. During this process, firms with strategic supremacy use different combinations and patterns of competitive and cooperative actions and relationships—in other words, co-opetition—to fashion a favorable world. While firms using co-opetition can conceivably cross the line into monopolistic or collusive behavior, this rarely happens for three good reasons.

First, no sphere—even one with strategic supremacy—can completely eliminate competition because cooperation plants the seeds of its own destruction. Cooperation inherently involves compromise and restrictions, so it always results in a restless, dissatisfied, or ambitious party. These parties are typically: the "low firm on the totem pole"; the revolutionary who wants to disrupt the cooperative environment; the firm with new alliances that give it new technologies, shifting the balance of power in its favor; or the sphere that simply loses too much power because the cooperative environment restricts its full potential. While any or all of the "cooperative" firms may agree to peace, that doesn't necessarily mean they are happy about it. Thus, cooperation always lays the groundwork for the next dissatisfied firm to start the struggle for power all over again.

A second reason that spheres of influence don't stamp out competition is because even spheres that dominate their markets can't act like monopolists if they want to maintain their supremacy. Monopolists rely on overpricing and underserving customers to make a profit. In contrast, strategic supremacy involves owning your core market by continually creating superlative value for your core customers. If you don't create this value, you can kiss your core, and all the power of your sphere that goes with it, good-bye.

Third, even when spheres of influence have negotiated a peaceful coexistence, they still compete indirectly by defining and pursuing interests that do not clash. This may involve mining the unique core markets of their own sphere for growth or focusing on growing into markets that don't infringe on a competitor's spheres. One sphere could shift the balance of power in its favor by moving into power vacuums that give it superior growth and wealth. Over time, the new advantages can give the sphere enough power to invade a rival's sphere. While this form of competition is indirect, it still can be very intense.

Strategic supremacy gives you the power to create competitive and cooperative relationships among spheres of influence. It is easy to think that supremacy comes from simply balancing competition and cooperation, as

if firms can create some playing fields with more competition than cooperation, and others with more cooperation than competition. This is an
oversimplification, however, because of the dynamic way strategic supremacy really works. Cooperation does not eliminate competition; it
changes its form and nature. What's more, intense competition creates cooperation. Thus, competition and cooperation are not opposites. They are
two sides of the same coin and they drive constant action on the playing
field.

History has shown that no competitive contest can be won without cooperating with some rivals to prevent being attacked from all sides. And
no cooperative environment can be maintained without using competitive actions to enforce the peace. Thus, collusive environments are often a
mirage because cooperation engenders new forms of competition, and
competition engenders new forms of cooperation. (For more about effective and legal strategies based on different forms of co-opetition, see
Chapters 4, 5, and 6.)

THE SUPREMES: TODAY'S GLOBAL GREAT POWERS

Strategic supremacy seems like such a tall order. Can corporations really
define the playing field, delimit the borders of rival spheres, and lead the
evolution of their industry, even if their market is a global one? Nations
have done it for millennia. Through empires and alliances, they have created the equivalent of powerful spheres of influence and used those
spheres to establish borders and a system of international power politics.
Great powers throughout history, from Ancient Rome to the relatively
young United States, have all achieved the ability to spread their world
view throughout their competitive space despite centuries of change and
disruption. But do corporations really have the same influence as powerful nations?

The answer is a definitive yes. Compare the budgets of nations to the
revenues of today's global corporations. You'll see that global businesses
have resources that rival those of modern nations. In fact, only 57 national
governments are in the same ballpark as the *Fortune* 500 companies. And
the *Fortune* 500 outrank 134 of the 198 governments of the world in rev-

enues. The top six corporations have bigger gross receipts than the combined budgets of 64 governments representing 58 percent of the world's
population. The combined revenues of the top 14 global corporations ex-
ceed the revenues of the government of the United States. All in all, of the
one hundred largest enterprises in the world, 66 are corporations and only
34 are national governments.[2]

Even if you consider the size of the national economies that back national governments, some corporations still are in the same ballpark as
most nations. In 1999, each of the top five largest global firms had revenues that approximated the Gross Domestic Product (GDP) of Russia or
Turkey. The top five combined had the economic power of the United
Kingdom or France. They exceeded the GDPs of Italy, China, Brazil, and
Saudi Arabia. The top twenty had total revenues that approximated Germany's GDP.[3]

In business, imagine what can be achieved with revenues that approxi-
mate the GDP of Italy, Saudi Arabia, or even Germany. As I wrote earlier,
size isn't everything, but it does help create the potential for supremacy.
Just like nations that have achieved great power status, corporations that
have reached this level of influence over their competitive spaces are also
"great powers." And the relationships among these great powers of business look no different than modern nations engaged in international relations. With massive resources at their disposal, great power corporations
have the same capabilities as great power nations to build spheres of influence, form alliances, and establish borders on the map of the competitive
space—all in the ongoing pursuit of achieving strategic supremacy.

Today, corporations (both large and small) are clearly more oriented
toward strategies focused on accumulating attractive markets and leveraging core competencies. Most executives think in terms of deep pockets,
portfolios, and rivalry. They do not think in terms of "strategic supremacy" or "spheres of influence," or "power hierarchies." Indeed, the
very notion of pursuing power is not a topic for polite conversation.

But the truth is that many of today's most successful firms are *already*
oriented toward the principles of strategic supremacy, if not in the language they use, then in their actions. Why? Because the pursuit of strategic supremacy emerges naturally from corporate competition and the

ambition for growth, wealth, and market power. Today's leading firms are shaping their portfolios into competitive arsenals of many strategic intents. Whether small or large, they try to own their core markets and use their strength to influence the behavior of rivals to define the playing field around them. And, most importantly, their actions reinforce one of the most compelling principles of strategic supremacy—that its unique power derives not from absolute dominance, size, deep pockets, or wiping out the competition, but rather it comes from creating win-win situations for customers and shareholders alike.

The principles offered in this book can be used to guide your portfolio strategy, your product marketing strategy, your merger strategy, your alliance strategy, your market entry strategy, your resource allocation, and your competitor-selection strategy. They can help you devise surprising, counterintuitive strategies such as entering markets where you have no synergies and no chance of winning, all to the greater good of influencing the behavior of rival spheres. They can help you understand that the choice of your geo-product battlefields is *the* battle, determining who wins the struggle for power. And they can help you realize your firm's full potential to conquer chaos and fashion a favorable world. The goal is not to revolutionize your industry, but rather to lead it.

In today's volatile business environment, no corporation can avoid risk completely. But with strategic supremacy you can be an industry leader without leading the revolution. And you can push your corporation, without pushing it over the edge. *Strategic Supremacy* is a book about vision, value, and vigilance. As Woodrow Wilson once said, "To conquer with arms is to make only a temporary conquest; to conquer the world by earning its esteem is to make a permanent conquest."

Chapter 1

The Sphere of Influence

Rethinking Your Product Portfolio to
Achieve Strategic Supremacy

OVERVIEW

For firms in dynamic industries, traditional portfolio models that focus primarily on core competencies and synergies can be dangerously shortsighted. Great powers throughout political and business history have demonstrated that a far more effective means of achieving growth, wealth, and power is to frame your organization as a cohesive sphere of influence. *The sphere is your* competitive arsenal, *serving as your offensive, defensive, and reserve artillery. It not only consists of your* core *geo-product markets and* vital interests, *but also* buffer zones, pivotal zones, *and* forward positions, *each serving a specific strategic intent. From its center to its far-flung borders, a cohesive sphere of influence gives your organization the power and the critical ammunition to achieve and sustain strategic supremacy.*

VENI, VIDI, VICI

The Roman Empire rose to power out of the chaos of the declining Etruscan Empire. This power vacuum allowed Rome to establish its own supremacy within the Italian peninsula, using other Italian city-states as buffers against rival powerful empires centered in Carthage and Greece.

With Italy as a secure base, Rome gradually expanded its sphere of influence far beyond the aspirations of the Etruscans. During its early growth period from approximately the sixth to the second century B.C., Rome captured Spain and created forward positions in Sicily, where it faced both Carthage and Greece. It skillfully defeated Carthage completely before turning to the domination of Greece, avoiding overstretching its resources by fighting on only one front at a time.

As Rome continued to expand to the height of its empire (from approximately the first century B.C. to the end of the second century A.D.) it established extensive buffer zones, vital interests, and forward positions reaching to Northern France and Southern England. Each conquest satisfied a particular strategic need of the empire. Some territories were acquired because they were targets of opportunity, resulting from power vacuums. Others satisfied Rome's need for buffers against competing empires in the Middle East or powerful Germanic tribes to the north. Still others provided vital supplies, such as food, soldiers, metals, or trade goods. Much of Rome's growth was obtained by force (after all, Rome was a warrior nation). But as the empire grew in scope, the Roman ideology—embodied in its citizenship and system of governance—played a role just as important as its legionnaires in controlling its vast empire (see Exhibit 1-1).

At the death of Augustus in A.D. 14, Rome was the largest political, economic, and monetary entity to exist in the western world until it was overtaken by the expansion of the United States and the Russian Empire in the mid nineteenth century. Moreover, Rome spread its wealth fairly well for its time, with the Roman distribution of income in A.D. 14 looking approximately the same as in England in the early nineteenth century.[1] While some may view the story of the Roman Empire as ancient history, many of today's most successful modern global businesses have used similar strategies to achieve strategic supremacy.

Like Rome, industry leaders have achieved strategic supremacy—the power to conquer chaos and to fashion a favorable world by shaping the playing field. Rome did so by defining its territorial borders, the borders of its rivals' territories, and even the boundaries of the "civilized" world. Like Rome, these companies have built their strategic supremacy in physical space and cyberspace by identifying a center of interest or core market and then staking out different interests around that core—vital interests,

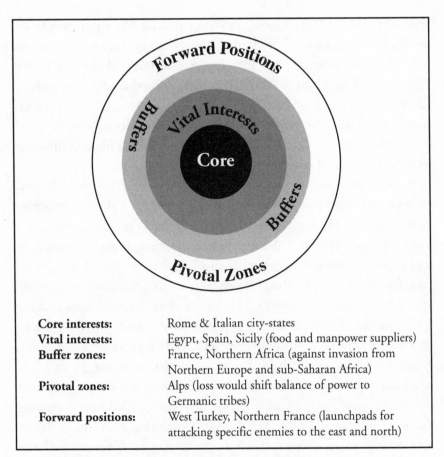

Core interests:	Rome & Italian city-states
Vital interests:	Egypt, Spain, Sicily (food and manpower suppliers)
Buffer zones:	France, Northern Africa (against invasion from Northern Europe and sub-Saharan Africa)
Pivotal zones:	Alps (loss would shift balance of power to Germanic tribes)
Forward positions:	West Turkey, Northern France (launchpads for attacking specific enemies to the east and north)

Exhibit 1-1: The Roman Sphere of Influence at Its Height—133 B.C.–A.D. 200

buffer zones, pivotal zones, and forward positions. By building a cohesive sphere of influence, these great powers clarify their corporate-wide strategy, specifying their strategic interests in each part of their portfolios and assigning a clear role for each of those parts in competing with rivals.

Microsoft is but one example of a modern firm that parallels Ancient Rome's development and use of a sphere of influence. While Rome's sphere was built around a capital city, Microsoft's sphere was built around a core market—the desktop operating system and graphical user interface. The company created its own software applications to buffer its core against potential invasion by application software providers. Microsoft also built its portal website, Microsoft Network (MSN), to buffer itself against attacks by AOL, Yahoo!, and other portals. Microsoft used Internet Explorer as a forward position against Netscape, bundling it for free with Windows in an attempt that appeared so imperial that the Justice Department found it to be "anti-competitive." Microsoft has also built vital interests in the critical networking and personal digital assistant software markets using Windows NT and CE. These positions were designed to capture growth markets vital to setting the standards for operating systems in the personal computing world (see Exhibit 1-2).

More recently, even as Microsoft contends with the aftermath of the government's antitrust case against it, Bill Gates and his legions are working hard to regroup and regenerate Microsoft's sphere of influence. Just as the Roman Empire regrouped and regenerated its sphere through migrating its core to Constantinople, Microsoft is migrating its core from desktop operating systems and graphical user interfaces to an integrated desktop-Internet operating system and interface. This would allow users to access desktop applications and Web content or applications seamlessly and to exchange data between the desktop's hard drive and Web sites with greater ease and speed. Rome's migration helped it to sustain its power longer than any other political empire in history. Many think that Microsoft's migration will do the same for Bill Gates because they believe Microsoft is creating the next "Windows" on the Web. In addition, during 2001, the company is increasing its presence on the Web, converting *MSN* from a buffer to a "pivotal" zone. Microsoft is beginning an MSN growth campaign to counter the rise of new threatening great powers such as the Godzilla that resulted from the merger of AOL and Time Warner (especially in light of the fact that AOL has already swallowed Microsoft rival Netscape).

Despite 2,000 years separating Microsoft and Ancient Rome, the sphere of influence concept offers a critical common framework for understanding how both these great powers have achieved strategic supremacy. The world may look different today, but the sphere of influence as a framework has stood the test of time. Companies and businesses that become great powers, that achieve strategic supremacy, do so by shaping a coherent sphere of influence. In essence, the sphere is a *competitive arsenal,* with different zones of the sphere serving as offensive, defensive, or reserve artillery for the future. In business as in politics, some zones in the sphere are wholly owned and contribute directly to its financial coffers. Other zones may not be directly owned or contribute directly to economic success of the core; nevertheless they play an important strategic role.

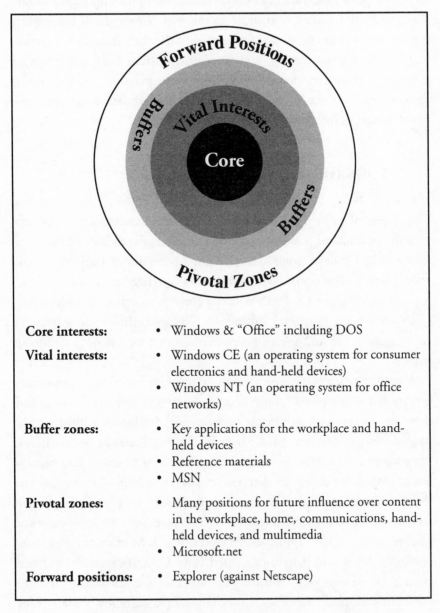

Core interests:	• Windows & "Office" including DOS
Vital interests:	• Windows CE (an operating system for consumer electronics and hand-held devices) • Windows NT (an operating system for office networks)
Buffer zones:	• Key applications for the workplace and hand-held devices • Reference materials • MSN
Pivotal zones:	• Many positions for future influence over content in the workplace, home, communications, hand-held devices, and multimedia • Microsoft.net
Forward positions:	• Explorer (against Netscape)

Exhibit 1-2: Microsoft's Sphere of Influence—1997–2000

A great power's sphere is more than a portfolio with synergies. It is a gestalt of powerful proportions because a great power's sphere of influence is much greater than the sum of its parts when the sphere is cohesive. Every zone of a sphere that surrounds its core—from its buffers to its far-flung territories—must contribute to the overall strength of the sphere, even if the zone has no direct synergies with the core. Indeed, in political empires throughout history, and in industries from computer chips to corn chips, the player that enjoys strategic supremacy or preeminence in the competitive space has been the company with the strongest, most cohesive sphere of influence.

LOOKING BEYOND TRADITIONAL PORTFOLIOS TO SPHERES OF INFLUENCE

The sphere of influence concept offers a richer framework for building growth, wealth, and power than traditional portfolio models. Traditional frameworks for developing a corporation's portfolio of businesses typically define a good portfolio as a collection of related businesses or solid niches in several geo-product markets, primarily designed to achieve synergies among the portfolio's businesses. Synergies come from leveraging core competencies and selecting new markets that are related to your core market.

However, when managers create this type of portfolio, they do not necessarily establish a powerful presence in the larger competitive space, and they tend to overlook significant opportunities (and threats) to the company's strategic interests that lie beyond the parameters of the portfolio. For example, managers may overlook threats posed by competing portfolios or growth opportunities that don't appear to be immediately related to the company's businesses. Would a synergy-based portfolio approach have seen the opportunity for Morton to shift its core from the low-profit salt market to the high-margin rocket market (which Morton has done successfully)? Or would it have prevented Penn Central's powerful railroad portfolio from meeting an untimely demise? Did Kodak's strategy of sticking to its core competence in photochemical photography prepare it for the threats of the digital age? Seemingly remote threats and opportunities can actually tip the balance of power away from your company to a competitor that has built a strong sphere of influence.

Related diversification appears to avoid some of the drawbacks of unrelated business groups, but the research is inconclusive. For example, a global study of more than eight hundred business groups spanning fourteen countries found affiliates of these highly diversified groups had *higher* returns than their peers in several countries.[2] The study's findings run contrary to the traditional American wisdom that unrelated diversification depresses profitability, and that unrelated business groups are only useful in countries with inefficient financial markets.

Corporate history is also far from clear on this point. Coca-Cola has created a lasting billion-dollar empire around a single core. But Motorola stuck close to its core in analog cellular phones and infrastructure and, yet, lost the leadership of its market. Motorola found that it made a lot of money for a while but, over the long run, this core-competence-based portfolio milked the company's present resources at the expense of the future. Perhaps the best example of a firm that violates traditional American wisdom concerning relatedness, synergies, and leveraging core competencies is General Electric. It has been one of the biggest wealth creators in the stock market over a period of more than one hundred years. Yet, GE's portfolio—an empire ranging from light bulbs to financial services—is thriving.

Why are the senior managers of so many industry leading firms diversifying their portfolios in ways that buck conventional wisdom? Where are the synergies in many of the global mega-mergers we see today? Is there any valid strategic reason that justifies why Daimler-Benz and Chrysler merged, given the difficulty of combining their vastly different corporate cultures and the contradictions created by putting the Mercedes brand name under the same roof as the Neon? Can Citicorp really take advantage of synergies between Citibank, Traveler's Insurance, and Salomon Smith Barney?

In most cases, large firms cannot capture synergies. Their internal cultural differences are too great, and the costs of coordinating diverse and dispersed subunits are too high. So, are the senior managers of these diversifying firms simply crazy egomaniacs on a lucky streak? Or have they tapped into some greater strategic purpose for their diverse interests—one that goes beyond related or unrelated diversification—as a framework for shaping their companies' global position relative to other global players?

There is obviously much more at play here than the relatedness of the elements of the portfolio. It is equally, if not more, important to consider *how* the elements of a portfolio are going to be used competitively. Of course these elements must be used to create wealth in the near term—making the profit-enhancing benefits of synergies, core competencies, and relatedness with your core markets important. But the elements of the portfolio can also be used to serve long-term purposes. For example, parts of your portfolio can be used for maneuvering against competitors to stake out a superior position in your competitive space, and to signal others about which parts of the space they should occupy. Other parts of your portfolio can be used to enter markets unrelated to your core, but which match important trends or which may become safehavens beyond the reach of aggressive competitors. These often ignored, larger competitive purposes of a portfolio are the focus of the sphere of influence concept.

The sphere of influence concept helps you examine the roles of each part of your sphere of influence and how these different parts interact. There are different defensive and offensive roles for each part of your portfolio that have to be considered. Because your environment is constantly being shaped by your customers and by your competitors, your portfolio is in dynamic motion. Traditional portfolio models can be too static or focus too closely on the present, hence risking your future strategic supremacy. They can also narrow your perspective too much, underutilizing your company as a platform for growth and for building the power you will need to survive the many struggles you will have with other global giants.

When facing off against global corporations with massive power, the key to success is to think of your portfolio as a sphere of influence, in which each piece serves as a source for your power. A diversified company's power must *start* from a secure core and synergies around it. But its presence in other zones can serve to enhance its power by projecting its sphere into unoccupied geo-product markets that threaten a competitor. In addition, its presence in other zones can position the sphere to defend itself against rivals seeking to build platforms for invasion.

Rather than the issue of relatedness, *spherical growth* focuses on more meaningful issues: How can you protect your present turf? How can you absorb new wealth and power while expending fewer resources than you gain? How can you avoid contact with more powerful players as you fortify and expand your own sphere? How and where must your sphere interact with rivals in order to achieve your ambitions or thwart another's drive for supremacy? And where should you position your sphere for the future in the event of a seismic shift in your industry?

By shifting from synergistic portfolio models to the richer sphere of influence framework, your company can enjoy a much broader and more insightful view of the competitive playing field. Quickly it becomes much clearer what areas—both inside and outside your company's holdings—can contribute to your wealth, power, and growth.

In the sphere of influence framework, your company does not have a single strategic intent. Your portfolio is actually revealed as a portfolio of *many* intentions that make up a cohesive whole. This is a new logic for portfolios—one that recognizes your firm's power can derive from much more than core competence. By looking beyond the narrow perspective of core competencies, relatedness, and synergy-based approaches, you can discover and take advantage of the many counterintuitive, even (at first) seemingly illogical, opportunities. These opportunities can benefit your sphere of influence and help you establish preeminence within your sphere and ultimately in the larger competitive space.

The sphere of influence framework offers a number of advantages over traditional portfolio approaches for developing power and supremacy over your world, as summarized in Exhibit 1-3.

CONSTRUCTING YOUR SPHERE

No great power has enough resources to achieve preeminence in every zone in its competitive space (not even Rome or Microsoft). Therefore the

Number One or Bust	Sphere of Influence
Premise: Build a portfolio only of businesses that are number one or two in their industries. **Holes:** Undervalues the importance of noncore zones of the sphere (such as buffers to protect the company from attack by a rival, or pivotal positions where it hopes to build its future); overlooks potential threats lurking in the periphery. **Case in Point:** In the late 1980s, Ralston Purina was number one in several segments of pet food in supermarkets but failed to see the threat of new channels such as veterinarians and pet superstores.	Promotes leadership in the core, but also recognizes the strategic need for developing a full and coherent sphere of interest that supports and defends the core, attacks rivals, and positions the company for future growth and profits.

Every Tub on Its Own Bottom	Sphere of Influence
Premise: Force every business unit to stand on its own financially. **Holes:** Diminishes the overall sphere to a collection of independent units. Fails to see the interrelationships between different parts of the sphere (for example, one business unit may serve as a buffer or vital interest for another unit, so it shouldn't be expected to sit on its own bottom). Opens the empire to "stripping" by competitors who pick off these independent sub-units one at a time and eventually capture the whole empire. **Case in Point:** General Motors—long run by financial managers from the company's treasury department—dismissed the small car market because it lacked strong margins . . . and opened the door for Japanese automakers to infiltrate this important marketplace.	Recognizes that the overall system needs to produce value, but not every part must stand on its own financially. Capitalizes on the coordinated competitive use of each part of the firm's entire sphere. Recognizes that losses may be incurred in some zones for the larger offensive or defensive strategy of the sphere, and allows for cross-subsidization (by moving resources from one place to another to support the overall sphere's strategy).

Exhibit 1-3: Traditional Portfolio Models vs. Sphere of Influence

Risk Reduction through Diversification	Sphere of Influence
Premise: Create a broad set of unrelated businesses in diverse parts of the globe (popular during the merger wave of the 1970s and among family-held companies). **Holes:** Makes the firm susceptible to stripping; oversimplifies the real issues: How does the empire define and divide the overall playing field of competition? What is the overall purpose of the company's sphere of influence? What is the role of each part of the sphere in the larger sphere's efforts to create supremacy? **Case in Point:** Richard Branson's complex Virgin empire—with positions in airlines, music retailing, and diverse other areas—leverages a common brand image. But without a sphere of influence solidly crafted around a core product, the company has not established strategic supremacy. It is a niche player in a wide range of areas but master of none.	Reduces risk through building a unified and interrelated sphere, not fragmentation. Creates greater value and security for the company by flexing its cohesive power in the face of potential marauders. Uses diversification to defend the core and attack opponents so firms can get "focus without being narrowly focused."

Traditional BCG Matrix	Sphere of Influence
Premise: Use resources from the company's cash cows to invest in the high-growth stars of the future. **Holes:** Opens the door for the periphery to become a burden on the sphere, milking the core of its vital juices; indiscriminately advocates the sale of "dogs," those companies that aren't immediately profitable. Assumes resources flow from cash cows to stars, when in fact, the flows between subunits can be more complex and vary over time. **Case in Point:** Pepsi's foray into fast foods seemed like a way to move its resources from its core soft drink business into a high-growth periphery, but ended up being a drain on its core business and created a "negative synergy" by attacking some of its fast food customers.	Looks beyond the reallocation of resources to the synergy of the entire sphere to create value. Recognizes that every "dog" has its day—some low-margin markets may indeed serve as important pivotal positions in the future. Provides critical alternatives to the BCG matrix to create value and allocate resources within the portfolio.

Exhibit 1-3 (Continued): *Traditional Portfolio Models vs. Sphere of Influence*

Leveraging Competencies	Sphere of Influence
Premise: Leverage core competencies by taking knowledge and assets from the core into the periphery. **Holes:** Overlooks the richness of the sphere of influence and the fact that noncore competencies and resources can be used for deterrence of rivals as well as for stopping attackers in the buffer zones. Focuses on core competencies rather than core product markets, where the battles for customers are being fought. **Case in Point:** Motorola leveraged its competencies in analog devices and radio frequency technology to create dominance in cellular phones, cellular infrastructure, and emergency two-way radios. Then along came Nokia and Ericsson in the 1990s. With their digital wireless technology and stylish designs, they quickly obsoleted Motorola's core competence and seriously threatened its leadership.	Recognizes that a great power's supremacy hinges on maintaining leadership in its core product market. Focuses on product markets (rather than core competencies) which can then be used as building blocks to create new competencies or obsolete traditional competencies. Enhances a company's portfolio beyond markets that rely on a core competence (enabling it, if necessary, to compete in other product markets that rely on different competencies). Recognizes that the portfolio can be used as a competitive arsenal to deter rivals and stake out turf within the competitive space. Creates another logic for a portfolio and sees the sphere as a guide for playing the global chess match.

Exhibit 1-3 (Continued): *Traditional Portfolio Models vs. Sphere of Influence*

key to strategic supremacy is to be very clear what part of the competitive space (i.e., which geo-product markets) you want supremacy over, and how the other parts of your sphere work together to contribute to its overall power. As a successful great power moves outside its core, each potential new zone in its sphere is viewed with a specific eye toward how it helps the firm achieve one of the following four critical purposes:

- To create preeminence over lesser powers within your own sphere
- To create a defense against other great powers in nearby territories
- To create a platform for shifting the balance of power within the competitive space
- To provide a mechanism for sharing and spreading wealth and technology throughout your sphere

Typically, to achieve these purposes, a strong sphere of influence contains the following zones: core or center of interest, vital interests, buffer zones, pivotal zones, and forward positions.

Core or Center of Interest

This zone is the capital of a political great power or the core product market of a great power in business. It is the part of the sphere of influence that the company must "own" to survive because it is a very significant source of the company's revenues and profits. It is the most important product and geographic market where the firm sets the rules of the game. While leadership of the core market typically requires a set of core advantages and a specific organizational subunit to serve that market, the core market (like the other zones in a sphere) is not the core competencies used in that market or the subunit responsible for serving that core market. The sphere of influence concept is focused on geo-product markets (or zones) within a competitive space. It is about using leadership over a core market and maneuvering for better position in and around that core to gain influence over rivals within the larger competitive space. For Microsoft, the core or center of interest began as operating systems for PCs and expanded to include Windows, and Office. For Disney, the core zone was originally animated children's entertainment, but it has spread over time to include theme parks. For Toyota, the core is small cars in Japan. For General Motors, it was originally large cars in North America, but is expanding over time to include light trucks.

Vital Interests

These are geographic or product zones that provide the core with economic strengths. Vital interests include markets that are highly interconnected with success in the core. They also include complements. (Complementary products are those that make your core product more useful or valuable. For example, sugar is a complement that improves the value of coffee; more sophisticated and complex software makes increasingly powerful chips more valuable.) In addition, vital interests can include key markets that strengthen the home base by providing critical resources, such as key components, unique know-how, raw materials in short supply, or low-cost skilled labor. For Microsoft, its network (NT) and portable device (CE) operating systems are vital interests that support or complement its core desktop operating system and graphical user interface. Disney's vital interest in Touchstone Pictures gives its empire access to leading stars whose voices are used in its popular animated movies for children.

Buffer Zones

These defensive zones provide insulation against attack by another great power, much the way Poland offered a buffer against NATO powers for the former Soviet Union. Buffer zones are expendable (if battles must be fought and territory lost, better to bloody the buffer than the core). Buffer zones also protect against expansion by known and unforeseen rivals who could leverage their position in a nearby market to enter your core markets. For example, by moving into PC applications, Microsoft is prepared to cope with potential incursions by "killer" applications companies that could bundle operating systems with their applications and KO Microsoft's operating system or Windows graphical user interface—the core of the company's business. Another example of the buffer defense is Disney's foothold in children's book publishing. This foothold keeps the fight over a future Mickey Mouse in the book world and out of Disney's core turf of children's movies and theme parks (because movies and theme parks typically build on the success of book characters and stories).

Pivotal Zones

These are markets that could shift the balance of power over the long run to an opposing great power. These are a bet on the future, although not necessarily with a specific rival in mind. In both politics and business, the People's Republic of China serves as a pivotal zone because of its enormous economic potential. Microsoft maintains positions in a wide range of pivotal zones that it does not "own" yet. These include Internet-connectivity software as well as gaming and hand-held devices. Disney's sphere includes positions in potentially pivotal markets such as movies for adults, toy manufacturers, sports teams, and video game manufacturers.

Forward Positions

These are offensive, front-line positions, typically located near the vital interests or core of an opposing great power. For Microsoft, a forward position against AT&T (which owns the largest cable TV company in the United States, TCI) might include access to cable TV signal distribution through a set-top box using Microsoft software. This move gives Microsoft the capability of introducing Internet telephony if AT&T starts providing set-top boxes that access the Internet without Microsoft software or if it introduces voice-activated interfaces that replace graphical user interfaces (like Windows). (Note that, if AT&T ever actually pulls off the proposed breakup, which would separate cable and telephony into different companies, Microsoft would lose the ongoing capability to use a forward position in cable access against AT&T. But Microsoft still gains an advantage by bundling complimentary services that AT&T can't.) Disney's forward positions in digital and other distribution channels counter powerful competitors such as Toys "R" Us, which might use its influence over distribution channels to expand further into children's programming and characters.

Putting the Pieces Together

In contrast to creating a nicely synergistic portfolio, the goal of a sphere is to use the pieces of your portfolio to create power over your rivals and the larger competitive space. To have a sphere of influence that will make you a "great power" in your competitive space, you must have preeminence in some parts of the competitive space so that you can extend your influence into other parts of that space. Consequently, a sphere of influence is a particular type of portfolio, requiring your firm to have substantial market power in your core and vital interests. In other zones—beyond your core and vital interests—you may enjoy only a partial degree of influence, or you may have very little influence. Nevertheless, these zones are important to your sphere because you may become interested in influencing them in the future, or you may want to use them to change the interests of rivals, create respect for the boundaries of your sphere, and fashion a favorable world around your sphere.

If you can define your interests and consequential strategic intentions for each zone in your sphere, you'll recognize the truth in what Britain's former prime minister Lord Palmerston once said about his country's empire: "We have no eternal allies and we have no perpetual enemies. Our interests are eternal and perpetual, and those interests it is our duty to follow."[3]

ASSIGNING STRATEGIC INTENT TO EVERY ZONE IN YOUR SPHERE

The first critical step in creating a strong and cohesive sphere of influence is to understand how each zone of your sphere fits into one of the five general categories (core, vital interests, buffer zones, pivotal zones, and forward positions). But there are many types of vital interests, buffer and pivotal zones, and forward positions, and it is important to know what your intention is for each zone with even greater specificity. Do the strategic intents assigned to each zone fit together with the strategic intents of all the other zones? To determine this, you can analyze the role of each zone in your sphere of influence based on answers to the following important questions:

- What is the attractiveness of the zone (growth potential, profitability, and size)?
- What is your company's relative strength in the zone?
- What is the strategic relationship between the zone and your core?
- What is the strategic relationship between the zone and a rival sphere's core?

These questions provide a set of criteria for determining your key interests in each of the zones being considered for your sphere (see Exhibit 1-4). Of

Relative Market Strength within the Zones Being Considered

		Weak	Strong
Market Attractiveness	High	Forward Positions	Center of Interest (Core)
	Low	Expendable Zones or Buffer Zones or Forward Positions	Vital Interests
	Potentially High	Power Vacuum (if no other rival is strong)	Pivotal Positions

Exhibit 1-4: One Method for Determining Your Key Interests

course, many variations on these criteria are also possible, especially depending on how you wish to use your sphere to influence rivals.

For example, the strongest core possible is a zone that is very attractive, is located where your company has a very strong position, and is devoid of any major rivals. The markets in which the company has a strong position but are not as attractive can be used as vital interests. Vital interests are markets of high strategic importance because they are used to build the core's power.

The role of buffer zones in your sphere of influence depends on your rival's position, especially if the rival has a strong position in a zone near your sphere's core. Zones that are good candidates for buffers include:

- Any nearby geographic locations that offer your rival the ability to extend distribution into your core or vital interests
- Any zone where a major rival produces or sells products that are similar to, and that are substitutes for or complementary to, your products in your core or vital interests
- Any zone where a major rival produces or sells products or services relying on the same core competency (skills, brand name, technology, etc.) that you rely on
- Other zones where players have some advantage that can be used to attack your core or vital interests

Why are buffer zones so important? One reason is that they often will pin down rivals and avert attack of your core market. While you hold power in a core market a rival may feel too threatened to make a go of attacking there. However, over time, a rival can build up its competencies or infrastructure by occupying geo-product zones that have similarities to your core. Eventually, however, that rival can recombine its competencies from the various markets and extend its infrastructure until it reaches a critical mass that does enable it to make a credible attack in your core. Buffer zones enable your firm to fight it out with this rival before that scenario can play out.

Buffer zones also serve another strategic purpose. They allow you a way to bundle products or services with your core products. This can serve as a defensive move against others that may someday grow their own core product markets at your expense by bundling their core product with a free version of your core product or service.

Successful great powers also designate some zones as pivotal positions. These are zones that will be attractive in the near or long term for various reasons, but in which the company is currently weak. These zones are used for growth or long-run competitive purposes and include:

- High potential strategic target markets. These are markets where the firm is capable of building great strength, or where the firm intends to migrate its core in the long term.

- A market that is in untapped or undiscovered space and provides a great growth opportunity.

Last, but hardly least, companies can take forward positions near a competitor's sphere to achieve several different intents. A forward position can interfere with another great power's access to key resources—for example, threatening the United States by tying up oil resources in the Middle East. Forward positions can also pin down a competitor in a prolonged and fruitless use of resources to defend the zone (drawing the United States into war in Vietnam), or to enhance a great power's influence in a relatively neutral part of the world (the Soviets in Angola). Forward positions can be used as "flanking positions" around an opposing firm, "thorns" to irritate an opponent, or "diversions" used to distract an opposing great power. They also may be used to block a specific opponent's moves with the potential of changing the balance of power in an important region in the world. Forward positions also can be used to test and improve strategies or the latest weapons (new products) before entering a broader market. Finally, forward positions can serve as beachheads, where companies can land and then mount a larger offensive against a competing sphere. Like Britain's use of Hong Kong for access to China, a company might take, for example, territory near a competitor's sphere in preparation for a larger offensive in an adjacent market. In summary, forward positions serve a company's sphere by providing:

- A foothold position in a rival's core or vital interests, to keep them occupied at home
- A signal to a competitor to back off of your core markets
- A first step in a full-scale invasion of an opposing sphere
- A way to "soften up" an opponent before you attempt to acquire it

In addition, to create a cohesive sphere with enough power to create strategic supremacy, you need to structure it to signal a clear competitive direction. This direction must indicate where your priorities lie (core), how far you will go to support those priorities (vital interests), what your biggest potential threats are (buffers), whom you specifically wish to engage proactively (forward positions), and your alternative positions for the future (pivotal zones). When done properly, a clear sphere provides purpose to your portfolio, direction for your merger strategy, and guidance for your internal allocation of resources. It also gives you power over the world in and around the sphere. Taken in conjunction, a well-rounded sphere of influence is made up of the strategic intents for several zones with a single clear overarching purpose—to fashion a favorable world by influencing specific competitor behaviors and positioning.[4]

That said, the sphere must not be conceived as a monolithic set of strategic intents cast in stone. Your interests and strategic intentions for each zone may shift over time, rendering some zones more or less important.

In addition, a single zone may be core to your firm, a buffer to a rival, and a forward position to still another rival. As rivals push or change their interests in each zone, your desired intent in those zones may change as well. Moreover, you may find one zone playing dual roles for your sphere. The zone may buffer against one set of rivals and be a forward position against a specific competitor. For example, Microsoft's interests in speech recognition software may buffer against IBM's and other software companies' potential entry of the user interface market. At the same time it may be a forward position against AOL that provides a voice-activated interface with the web.

One caution, however, use of a single zone for dual intents may cause confusion about the goals for that market. In Microsoft's voice recognition case, it must be sure to resolve the conflicting goals of a buffer zone and a forward position regarding growth, resource needs, and competitive aggressiveness.

Positioning Your Sphere for the Future: Ugly Ducklings, Power Vacuums, and Outcasts

A cohesive sphere is not only constructed to achieve preeminence in its chosen zones today, but also to position the company for preeminence in the future. Therefore, when considering the strategic intents of the zones in your sphere, you also need to take into account factors such as potential shifts in a zone's attractiveness, or a change in the competitive positioning of your organization.

While you can hardly be expected to read the future, you do need to keep an eye on zones that may not be attractive now, but may have the potential to turn from an ugly duckling to a swan. Even in these ugly duckling zones, you may want to open a position as a means of creating an "option" in case it takes off.

Power vacuums are another type of market that can help your company bet on the future. Power vacuums are untapped growth opportunities where no one player has established a stronghold yet. Great powers often seek to bolster their competitive position in a power vacuum (if they have the resources) so as to preempt entry by a rival who seeks to use it as a launching point for an attack in the future. What's more, racing into power vacuums represents one of the best ways to use your pivotal positions to absorb new territory and wealth into your sphere, while expending *minimal* resources. But, as with any race, timing is of the essence when you move into unoccupied or newly created territory. Like nature, business abhors a vacuum. This means your window of opportunity to absorb that new wealth without shelling out big bucks in a fight is only as big as the time it takes for the first racer to cross the finish line and incorporate the power vacuum solidly into its sphere.

In addition to ugly ducklings and power vacuums, a cohesive sphere of influence might even include positions in zones located in the low attractiveness–weak position box shown earlier in Exhibit 1-4. In portfolios created from traditional strategic theories, these outcast zones are dismissed wholesale. Yet a strong sphere of influence doesn't overlook the potential of these zones, perhaps as future buffers for the sphere's core, or even as forward positions or options if the marketplace shifts. So, despite the advice of the traditional BCG matrix—which would say divest businesses in these zones—firms with strategic supremacy carefully consider outcasts in this inauspicious corner of the matrix, and classify them based on their larger role in the firms' spheres of influence.

Moreover, some traditional portfolio models suggest a different relationship between the core and the periphery of the portfolio. For example, the BCG matrix, a commonly used method for portfolio planning, depicts cash cows (low-growth, profitable zones) as the means to fund a company's future stars (high-growth, low-profit zones)—in other words, the core market funds pivotal zones. But successful great powers rarely operate so unidirectionally. In fact, some successful growth-oriented spheres may be based on a growing core that is fed by the peripheral vital interests, and protected by the outer ring of buffers and forward positions. In other cases, a zone may switch from being the supplier of resources to a forward position. Thus the vision for the sphere's future must drive the relationship between the zones.

EMPIRES OF THE MIND: THE ROLE OF IDEOLOGY IN CREATING A COHESIVE SPHERE

Thus far, I've discussed the sphere as a set of zones, each serving a unique purpose in enhancing the firm's present power, as well as securing its fu-

ture. But in addition to these "tangible" zones that reflect actual products
or services and markets, there is yet another, less tangible component that
plays a critical role in establishing a preeminent sphere. That component
is ideology, the glue that holds many parts of the sphere of influence together. Ultimately, strategic supremacy is as much about the conquest of
the mind as it is about the conquest of territories. As noted in the introduction, Churchill once said, "The empires of the future are the empires
of the mind."[5]

What exactly is a sphere's ideology? By definition, ideology is "a set of
closely related beliefs, ideas, or even attitudes characteristic of a group or
community."[6] In politics and business, ideology takes the form of a proposition that provides value to the great power's citizens or customers. For
example, the United States offers this value proposition to its citizens: "All
men are created equal." Business examples include the Body Shop's value
proposition to its customers—"Good for you and good for society"—and
General Electric's "We bring good things to life."

While countless companies have worthy value propositions, the company with strategic supremacy enjoys *value leadership* in its core and vital
interests. These preeminent firms are the ones that set the expectations of
customers and rivals when it comes to quality, price, and performance. To
have preeminence in your sphere you must have enough value leadership
to "own" your core and vital interests.

Here I must make two important distinctions. First, value leadership is
not the same as market share. Cadillac still has the largest market share in
luxury cars, but Lexus holds the value leadership position. Second, value
leadership is more than an ideology that creates a strong internal culture
within a firm. The company with value leadership is the one whose ideology—or value proposition—holds the most sway with the hearts and
minds of customers. It is the company whose ideology is adopted by, and
becomes a benchmark for, all other competitors. In short, it is this company's ideology against which all others are weighed. It is this company's
ideology that controls the standards, or norms of behavior—the rules of
competition—within core markets and vital interests.

For example, as mentioned in the introduction, the value leadership in
shaving might be the closeness of shave and experience of manliness em-

bodied in Gillette's "The best a man can get," as well as the research, production, and marketing expertise to deliver on that proposition. Schick often competes by following Gillette's lead and imitating its value proposition, rather than following BIC's competing value proposition based on disposability and low cost. Can a firm survive without value leadership in its core and vital interests? Yes. But can it have strategic supremacy over the geo-product space that makes up its sphere of influence? No. BIC, for example, is still profitable and surviving in the shaving market, but it is clearly a lesser power in this space. Gillette rules with its widely preferred Mach3 and Sensor products.

Why is value leadership so important in creating a preeminent sphere? To put the question another way, why can't a powerful company simply rely on force—takeovers, lawsuits, deep pockets, switching costs, forced tying agreements, and price wars—to control parts of the sphere? The answer is this: Force alone is not enough to achieve and maintain preeminence. Certainly, force can be a powerful tool in creating, defending, and expanding a sphere of influence, but defending a sphere of influence in this heavy-handed manner is tremendously difficult and inefficient, particularly as your sphere expands. Ultimately, relying strictly on force is likely to spark a revolt by customers, or in the case of political empires, a revolution among its citizens. As U.S. president Harry S. Truman commented, "All throughout history it's the nations that have given the most to the generals and the least to the people that have been the first to fall."[7]

Rather than focusing solely on force to advance and secure its sphere of influence, the successful great power relies just as heavily—if not more so—on the formidable, but less expensive, power of ideology to grow and sustain (and justify) its power. Why was the mighty General Motors vulnerable to the onslaught of a few relatively small but radical Japanese automakers in the 1960s and 1970s? How did fifty thousand British troops defeat the Moghul Empire and control hundreds of millions of Indians for three centuries? How could Mahatma Gandhi, without any military force, overthrow the colonialism of the British Empire? The empire builders that created General Motors and the British and Moghul empires were not outgunned, they were outvisioned.

As Exhibit 1-5 illustrates, some parts of a sphere are held by force, some

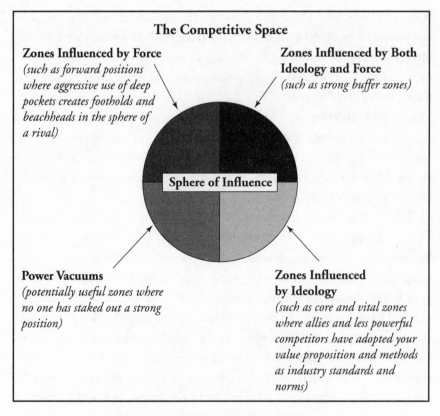

Exhibit 1-5: Controlling a Sphere of Influence

by ideology, and some by a combination of the two. The most efficient and long-lasting spheres rely more on ideology than force. As the exhibit also demonstrates, a sphere of influence can sometimes be a broader entity than a portfolio. Power vacuums frequently make up an important zone of your sphere, but not your current portfolio. In addition, you may not yet occupy some zones, but you may influence them through the power of your ideology or your strong presence in an adjacent market. Even when a company may not have the resources available to gain preeminence in a power vacuum, it is often in the company's best interest to enter that power vacuum, if only to discourage other players from establishing a strong presence there.

POWER PROJECTION: USING YOUR
POWER TO BEGET POWER

By establishing value leadership in your core and vital interests you then gain the ability to project your power into new areas. For example, you can use your value leadership in the core to leverage the company's power into new vital interests and forward positions that will enhance your profitability. How? By reshaping the profit pools of the rivals within the competitive space. You can do this by using your core and vital interests to drive up profitability in your buffers, pivotal zones, and forward positions, or by using your buffers and forward positions to reduce a rival's profitability in selected zones.

One way to reshape the profit pools within a competitive space is through quasi-forward or backward vertical integration. Coca-Cola has done this successfully. Using the contacts and influence it gained through its leadership in syrup production, Coca-Cola acquired and consolidated many of its local bottlers, then spun them off as regional bottlers. This power projection helped Coke combat the advantage PepsiCo had gained from its fully owned single system of bottlers, which were able to serve multi-city supermarket chains better than Coke's local bottlers. In this way, Coke projected its power over distributors and retailers, which gave it the ability to both shape and influence the profits along PepsiCo's value-added chain. Coke reduced Pepsi's ability to generate profits and market share from its supermarket distribution services.

Home Depot and Wal-Mart are two other examples of companies that have used their power to influence the profit pools of rivals. Establishing exclusive deals and other arrangements with selected suppliers based on their purchasing power with those suppliers, these companies get more variety, better deals (prices), unique product selection, and better service (delivery, displays, co-op ads, etc.) than their rivals. The net result is that rival retailers are motivated to look for new product categories where profits are still available.

Another way companies project their power to shift the profit pools of rivals is by negotiating with other firms to bundle their products together, or to acquire new products and services that complement their own cores.

For example, a company may bundle two products together, with each product enhancing the other's value. Intel's core is microprocessor chips, so it invests in applications that will increase the need for powerful microprocessors. Hewlett-Packard bundles its personal computers with its computer peripherals (such as printers) to provide "one stop shopping" to its small business customers. Microsoft integrates its browser (Explorer) with Windows. IBM bundles software and hardware to provide "solutions" to customers' problems. GM autos are bundled with GMAC financing, OnStar satellite equipment, and monthly service fees. GM credit cards give points toward the purchase of a new car to increase customer loyalty, accelerate payment for the car, and entice people to use the credit card. Bundling can influence the profitability of those who lack the ability to create similar bundles of equal quality, motivating them to look for new profit pools.

A third way companies project their power to shift the profit pools of rivals is by absorbing or decreasing the power of rival spheres. To do so, they use their forward positions as launching pads for encircling or invading their opponents' core and vital interests. In this way they decrease the preeminence of a rival by undermining the center of its power.

As the above examples illustrate, companies have many ways to project the power of their cores in order to build their spheres or attack rival spheres. And once you have built your sphere into a competitive arsenal that enables you to project your power, you then have the ability to achieve preeminence, not just within your sphere, but in the larger competitive space as well.

The Sphere and Preeminence in the Greater Competitive Space

No sphere of influence is an island. Empires carve out their spheres and take charge of them within the greater universe of the competitive space. The purpose of the sphere is to own or occupy a significant portion of the attractive markets within your competitive space so that even those players outside your sphere are influenced by your behavior. In addition, each of the different zones of your sphere plays a different role in gaining strategic supremacy over others in the larger competitive space. The core is your power source, and hence it must be relatively secure. Within your core, there can be lesser powers but no other great power can be a significant player. Your vital interests enhance the power of your core relative to other great powers. Your buffers, pivotal zones, and forward positions further enhance that power by providing your sphere with offensive and defensive tools to complete your arsenal.

Consider the competitive space within supermarkets. While Procter & Gamble doesn't "own" (in a legal sense) any supermarket shelf space, it informally owns some shelf space because of its power over the supermarkets in selected product lines. The extensive use of coupons and other price-based promotions in P&G's core markets all contribute to P&G's power. Thus, P&G sometimes influences parts of its sphere by force—the use of its deep pockets to aggressively "own" part of the shelf space—especially in its core and vital interests. However the core and vital interests of P&G's sphere are also influenced by P&G's ideology—its value leadership. P&G establishes this leadership through its excellent branding and advertising capabilities coupled with its capabilities to create new value-added products. Allies and rivals have adopted P&G's methods of creating value (e.g., service to supermarkets, use of brands) and its value propositions (product standards and characteristics in P&G's core and vital markets). Rival great powers outside P&G's sphere are often deterred from entering P&G's core and vital interests by its many buffer zones (see Exhibit 1-6). P&G can turn these buffer zones into more aggressive forward positions for the purpose of retaliation if these rivals go too far in P&G's important zones. P&G also uses its value leadership in its core to influence the nature of competition both within its sphere and in the larger competitive space. For example, it uses its power over retailers to command dedicated shelf space and to block others from getting on the shelf.

Outside the sphere of influence itself, there is a universe of the entire competitive space. This area is usually not a focus of interest, but it should be a focus of attention because other great powers will stake out their interests in this space and unsuspected attacks can come from this area.

For example, P&G's foray into over-the-counter drugs calls into question whether the packaged goods giant paid attention to the competitive purpose of its acquisition. Clearly, P&G's decision to sell over-the-counter

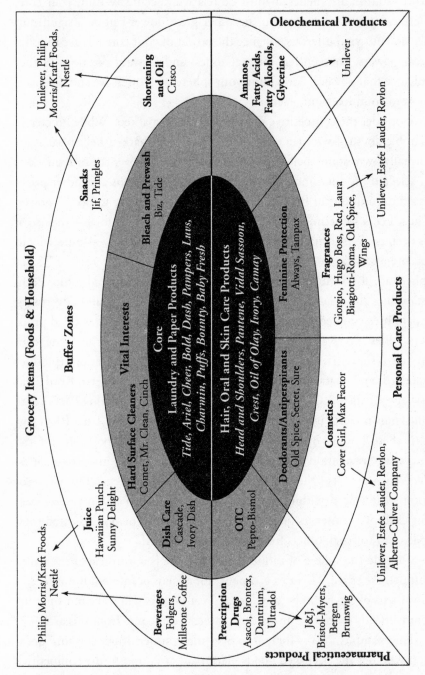

Exhibit 1-6: P&G's Sphere of Influence in North America in 1998

Oleochemical Products

Unilever, Philip Morris/Kraft Foods, Nestlé

Shortening and Oil
Crisco

Unilever

Aminos, Fatty Acids, Fatty Alcohols, Glycerine

Snacks
Jif, Pringles

Bleach and Prewash
Biz, Tide

Grocery Items (Foods & Household)

Buffer Zones

Vital Interests

Core
Laundry and Paper Products
Tide, Ariel, Cheer, Bold, Dash, Pampers, Luvs, Charmin, Puffs, Bounty, Baby Fresh

Hard Surface Cleaners
Comet, Mr. Clean, Cinch

Hair, Oral and Skin Care Products
Head and Shoulders, Pantene, Vidal Sassoon, Crest, Oil of Olay, Ivory, Camay

Feminine Protection
Always, Tampax

Fragrances
Giorgio, Hugo Boss, Red, Laura Biagiotti-Roma, Old Spice, Wings

Unilever, Estée Lauder, Revlon

Juice
Hawaiian Punch, Sunny Delight

Dish Care
Cascade, Ivory Dish

Deodorants/Antiperspirants
Old Spice, Secret, Sure

Cosmetics
Cover Girl, Max Factor

Personal Care Products

Philip Morris/Kraft Foods, Nestlé

OTC
Pepto-Bismol

Unilever, Estée Lauder, Revlon, Alberto-Culver Company

Beverages
Folgers, Millstone Coffee

Prescription Drugs
Asacol, Brontex, Dantrium, Ultradol

J&J, Bristol-Myers, Bergen Brunswig

Pharmaceutical Products

drugs in pharmacies and health stores as well as in supermarkets makes sense from a synergy-based perspective because it shares P&G's distribution and sales force resources. But the strongest, most cohesive spheres of influence are not always synergistic in the usual sense. They consider not only the benefits of synergies but the strategic intent—the competitive uses—for each new zone added to the sphere. If P&G's ownership of these pharmaceutical assets doesn't create more power over its rivals (for example, a deterrence effect on other pharmaceutical companies seeking access to supermarkets), then its overall sphere—and the pursuit of preeminence in the greater competitive space—is not served by this foray.

Because pharmaceutical companies are not big players in American supermarkets, P&G appears to have made this foray into over-the-counter drugs only because it thought it could leverage its distribution competencies from its core markets. But that focus is rather narrow compared to the larger sphere of influence perspective. This perspective asks the critical questions: How does the change in your geo-product portfolio defend your sphere against attacks? How does it create a launch pad for invasions or retaliations into the spheres of others? How does it give more credibility to your signals to rivals? Given those issues, P&G's synergistic perspective or rationale is sorely lacking. In fact, it makes a lot more sense for P&G to use its resources to enter new geo-product markets that offer both synergies and power over its rivals for supremacy in supermarkets.

While a sphere of influence rarely looks as haphazard as a conglomerate, it also may not always look as strictly focused as a set of businesses connected by a core competence. Great powers realize that their success depends not on a narrow focus but rather on a cohesive sphere of influence that allows the player to shape the playing field for itself and others. With only a few exceptions, P&G has used its product portfolio to establish a cohesive sphere of influence within supermarkets by positioning itself against several rival powers who could encroach on P&G's shelf space and by creating power over supermarkets, as shown earlier in Exhibit 1-6.

As a footnote to recent history, in early 2000, P&G's market value dropped significantly, perhaps because its preeminence declined as a result of the overall enlargement of the competitive space and the failure of its growth intiatives. In addition, its growth and margin problems were asso-

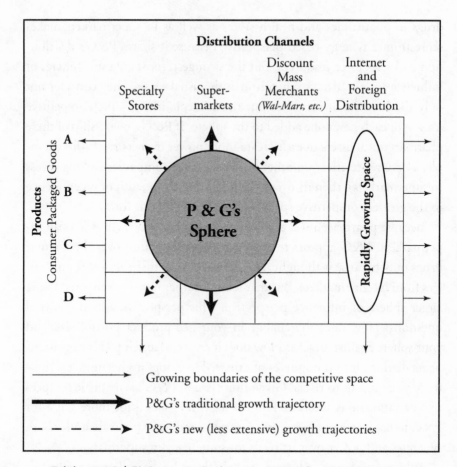

Exhibit 1-7: P&G's Supremacy Declines in an Expanding Competitive Space

ciated with the rise of the Internet, specialty stores, and discount mass merchandisers in the United States as well as the increasing importance of foreign markets where P&G was not strong. While P&G remains a global power, it no longer has as much supremacy in its competitive space as it did during its former glory days when the consumer packaged goods space was limited solely to supermarkets in the United States (see Exhibit 1-7).

THE BIG PICTURE: MAPPING YOUR SPHERE TO EVALUATE
YOUR STRENGTH, COHESIVENESS, AND FUTURE

To achieve strategic supremacy, your company needs both a unique position relative to your competition, and a sufficiently large and central position within the competitive space. Mapping your company in terms of its products and geographies can reveal whether your firm is indeed a sphere, and if that sphere is on target in terms of the kind of positioning necessary to achieve or sustain strategic supremacy.

Thus far, I have used business examples of the sphere of influence primarily based on positioning in product space. But product space is only one part of the picture, or map of the competitive space. More realistically, the map consists of longitude and latitude lines that represent both the product and geographic markets that are of interest to an industry leader. On this map are located the positions of the great powers within the space, and the strategic intent of each great power for the zones that interest them within the geo-product space.

Using this kind of mapping to reveal the coherence (or not) of your sphere of influence demands that you assign your intentions properly and arrange them in a logical way on the map. Creating a map that offers this kind of insight will likely require more than one attempt, and you may need to shuffle and reshuffle the columns and rows on your map, as illustrated in Exhibits 1-8A and 1-8B. The first test of whether you have any reasonable semblance of a sphere is whether you can reshuffle the rows and columns to construct a map with a core at the center, and vital interests, buffer zones, forward positions, and pivotal zones radiating outward from this core.

The second test of the strength of your sphere is whether you have organized the competitive space in some logical manner. For example, when looking at adjacent geographic columns on your map, are they physically near each other or do they share a practical commonality? Do the adjacent geographic columns share traits such as having geographic proximity and the same distribution system? Or are the customer needs and tastes similar in the two geographic regions? When looking at adjacent product rows on your map, the products—like the geographies—should share some defining characteristics, such as similar customer needs, technologies, or customer types.

Without some logic that fits products and geographies closely together, the sphere you have created may be spread too thin or it can contain too much "white space"—opportunities for others to enter—between the columns or between the rows. These tests will determine whether your sphere is focused and solid versus diffuse and full of holes.

As Exhibit 1-8B illustrates, a good map can also reveal strengths and weaknesses of your sphere. The hypothetical sphere in 1-8B reveals several important insights:

- A serious vulnerability in the sphere's southeastern quadrant
- A significant move (forward positions) against competitors in its western quadrant

Geographic Markets

		1	2	3	4	5	6
	A	Vital Interest		Buffer Zone		Forward Position	
	B	Forward Position					
Product Markets	C	Core	Pivotal Position	Vital Interest	Vital Interest	Forward Position	
	D	Forward Position	Pivotal Position		Pivotal Position		
	E	Buffer Zone	Pivotal Position	Buffer Zone	Vital Interest	Forward Position	
	F						

Exhibit 1-8A: Assigning Intentions to Geo-Product Zones

Geographic Markets

		5	3	1	4	2	6
	D	Power Vacuum	Power Vacuum	Forward Position	Pivotal Position	Pivotal Position	
	E	Forward Position	Buffer Zone	Buffer Zone	Vital Interest	Pivotal Position	
	C	Forward Position	Vital Interest	Core	Vital Interest	Pivotal Position	
	A	Forward Position	Buffer Zone	Vital Interest	Power Vacuum	Power Vacuum	
	B	Power Vacuum	Power Vacuum	Forward Position	Power Vacuum	Power Vacuum	
	F						

Product Markets (row label)

Exhibit 1-8B: Reshuffling the Grid to Find a Coherent Sphere of Influence

- A major bet on the future (pivotal positions) in the northeastern quadrant
- A midwestern core well supported and protected by vital interests and buffer zones, respectively

Exhibits 1-8A and 1-8B also illustrate that spheres are not built in a unidimensional competitive space based only on selected positioning among the products. Building a sphere involves staking out strongholds in geo-product space. Geography can be further divided into channels reaching into that geography. Products can be replaced with customer type or need. Thus, you can build a sphere in channel-product space, geo-customer space, etc. Geo-product space, however, best represents the competitive playing field most firms play on in today's global environment.

Cyberspace represents a particularly interesting challenge because geography isn't really a factor once the language issues are overcome by translating the site. In such cases, a reasonable representation of cyberspace may be based on services provided (e-tailing, securities trading, auctions, etc.) and distribution channels (prominent positions on MSN, AOL, Yahoo!, or other Web pages, and priority on their search engines). Because of the different ways to map your space, you may need to try several methods before you discover a coherent sphere that reveals how your competitors see the world, or before you clarify how all the components of your sphere fit together.

In practice, this geo-product analysis can be quite complex as more detail is added. Consider how General Motors and Toyota might represent their spheres of influence in the automotive industry (see Exhibits 1-9A and 1-9B, respectively). Toyota has built one transnational sphere—one core used as a worldwide base with a globally integrated administrative apparatus. GM has build two separate "multidomestic" spheres—one based on large cars in North America, another on smaller cars in Europe. Each sphere is administered separately and can be attacked separately. It is clear from Toyota's forward positions and targeted zones that GM's sphere of influence is far from preeminent. Toyota appears to have the better-defended core, while GM's core and vital interests are being undermined step-by-step.

By mapping your firm's sphere of influence and the spheres of influence of your competitors, it becomes very clear where (and how many) key points of conflict exist. It also becomes clear where your company should focus its resources and attention in building its strength, and where it should direct its defensive maneuvers in the face of a potential attack by another great power. Using this geo-product analysis, you can fine tune the strategic intentions of each of the zones to achieve a more cohesive and powerful sphere.

This process of building a coherent sphere of influence adds tremendous value to the enterprise, often improving profitability through the use of forward positions and buffer zones to create barriers to entry, less aggressive competitor behavior (such as mutual forbearance), and more indirect competition (such as focusing on growth in non-overlapping di-

Customer Need/Product Markets	Geographic Markets												
	Americas				Europe			Africa	HK	China	Asia		
	Canada	U.S.	Mexico	Brazil	West	East	Russia				Southeast	Korea	Japan
Basic transport													
Subcompact cars	PV	PV	PV	PV	B	B	PV				O	O	T/O
Compact & basic midsize sedans	B	B	C	F	CI	B	PV		PE	P/F	O	O	O
Family transport													
Large sedans	B	V	C	PV	B	B	PV	E		T			
Minivans	B	B	B		E	E	PV	E		PV			
Sport utility	B	B	B		E	E	PV	E		T			
Luxury													
Prestige cars	B	CI	B	PV	O		PV	E		T			O
Sport utility	B	B	B	PV	O		PV	E					O
Sporty/adventurous													
Race cars	B	TG	B	PV	O								
Light trucks	B	V	B	PV			PV			T			
Electric cars	NF	NF											

Exhibit 1-9A: Mapping General Motor's Strategic Interests in Passenger Vehicles—A Multi-Domestic Sphere of Influence

Customer Need/Product Markets	Geographic Markets												
	Americas				Europe			Africa	Asia				
	Canada	U.S.	Mexico	Brazil	West	East	Russia	'	HK	China	Southeast	Korea	Japan
Basic transport													
Subcompact cars	F	F/V	F	F	F	F	PV		PE	P/F	B	B	CI
Compact & basic midsize sedans	F	F/V	F	F	F	F	PV		PE	P/F	B	B	CI
Family transport													
Large sedans	O	O	O	F	F	F	PV	E			B	B	B
Minivans	T	T	E	F			E						
Sport utility	T	T	T					E					
Luxury													
Prestige cars	F	F/V	O		F			E			B	B	B
Sport utility	F/O	F/O	F/O					E					
Sporty/adventurous													
Race cars	O	O	O										
Light trucks	F	F	O										
Electric cars	E	E	E	E									

Exhibit 1-9B: Toyota's Strategic Interests in Passenger Vehicles—A Transnational Sphere of Influence

Key to exhibits 1–9A and 1–9B

(1) Basic Strategic Intentions:
CI = Center of interest/core
V = Vital interest
B = Buffer zone
P = Pivotal zone
F = Forward position
PV = Power vacuum (a zone without any major player but potentially of interest)

(2) Specific Types of Forward Positions:
PE = Point of entry into competitor's narket or a huge market
T = Targeted zone (designated to be taken away from a rival)

(3) Specific Types of Pivotal Zones:
TG = Testing ground for high-potential, next-generation products
NF = New frontiers/long-term experiments or options in the potentially critical markets of the future

(4) Specific Types of Vital Interests:
C = Colony (used as a part or low-cost labor supplier)
V = Vital customer markets providing economies of scale or scope

(5) Expendable Zones:
E = Expendable zones that will be abandoned or ignored (even if attacked)
N = Neutral zones (negotiated with a rival)
O = Occupied zone (which will not be attacked because it is too heavily defended)
Blanks = Undecided (too small to consider or not enough information to decide)

rections). Rigorous research has found strong evidence of such improved profitability and/or favorable influences on rival behaviors in highly competitive industries as diverse as banking,[8] cement,[9] mobile telephone service,[10] knitwear manufacturing,[11] petroleum,[12] and hotels[13] on both the global or local levels. In addition, a ten year study of over 2000 technology, product, and service firms by the prestigious strategy consulting firm, Bain & Company, found that having a strong and well protected core provides a solid growth platform and engine to fuel that growth.[14] Going well-beyond these studies, this chapter provides a deeper and more practical understanding of how to use and structure a sphere strategically, and it relates spheres of influence to diversification strategies more explicitly.

The first Roman Emperor, Augustus Caesar, understood how the diverse territories of Rome's sphere—along with the Roman ideology—contributed to a cohesive whole. This sphere of influence, and the offensive and defensive firepower inherent in such a strong and cohesive sphere, allowed Augustus to lay the foundation of history's greatest and most enduring empire and to create tremendous wealth in the process. Trade flourished. Infrastructure was built. Stability prevailed. In Augustus' own words, "I found Rome a city of bricks and left it a city of marble."

Chapter 2

Leading the Evolution

Circumventing Competitive Compression to Grow the Power of Your Sphere

OVERVIEW

From Rome to Redmond, Washington, great powers have built and sustained their spheres of influence through a process of constant evolution and growth. Growth generally increases the power of the sphere unless growing into a new market uses up more power than it gains. The key is to balance your strategy for growth against the forces of competitive compression *applied by your rivals. You first need to establish your* natural growth pattern—*a strategy for growing your sphere of influence—based on your competitive environment, capabilities, and aspirations. Are you better at being a developer, pioneer, discoverer, nomad, or opportunist? At the same time, competitors will try to hold or beat back your progress through four primary compression strategies:* managed containment, gradual constriction, sequential stripping, *or* toppling dominoes. *How do you anticipate, recognize, and thwart these strategies? How do you circumvent these forces of competitive compression so that your growth adds to the power of your sphere, rather than wasting its energy? As both the Roman Empire and Microsoft found, the evolution of their spheres was a process of accumulating power, selectively shifting their spherical growth strategies to circumvent the obstacles placed in their way by rival great powers.*

THE RISE AND FALL . . . AND RISE OF SPHERES

Rome's sphere of influence continued to evolve for centuries. From 133 B.C. to A.D. 200 the Roman Empire was riding high. Its sphere controlled most of the known world and it enjoyed a period of prosperity and peace—the Pax Romana. But after A.D. 200, the winds of change managed to permeate even Rome's cloak of invincibility. Rome's vast sphere of influence faced incessant pressure by Germanic tribes in the North and the Persian Empire in the East. As the besieged empire tried to defend itself on several fronts at once, Rome's resources became stretched to the breaking point. Overwhelmed by internal challenges and attacks from rival empires, Rome made a clutch move, splitting into Eastern and Western empires with separate cores and their own spheres of influence. Later, Constantine I (ruler of the Western Empire) reunited the entire empire. After victory, he moved the empire's capital to Constantinople, and became its one and only emperor. While Constantine's strategy eventually dealt the final death blow to the already weakened former capital of Rome (essentially handing it over to Germanic hands), it also enabled the Eastern part of the empire to endure with a new core. Ultimately the reconstituted Eastern Roman Empire with its new capital in Constantinople evolved into the Byzantine Empire, which built a strong sphere in the East and existed until its defeat by the Ottomans in the 1400s.

Microsoft, headquartered in Redmond, Washington, undertook a more meteoric rise to preeminence in the 1990s. Nevertheless, Microsoft's *spherical growth* provides a similar example of how an evolving sphere of influence plays a key role in achieving and sustaining strategic supremacy. Like Rome, Microsoft arose from a power vacuum created when IBM outsourced key software for its personal computer and failed to "lock up" exclusivity of that software. Microsoft seized the opportunity to establish a strong position in microcomputer operating systems with MS-DOS and Windows—a position that allowed the company to define the playing field not only for Microsoft, but also for its partners and competitors.

With the defeat of Apple and OS/2, Microsoft rapidly extended its sphere of influence outward, creating buffer zones to protect against the expansion of application providers in word processing, spreadsheets, presentations, and e-mail. One at a time, Microsoft took on its opponents by assimilating its own version of these applications into Microsoft Office. This offered users a form of temporary "citizenship" in the Microsoft world. Like Roman citizenship, Microsoft provided a common language, infrastructure, and other benefits to those who joined. Microsoft then extended its sphere of influence by marching its legions (or those of its client states) into diverse new regions that could be pivotal in the future, including news and entertainment, cable television, multimedia, video game hardware called the "X-box," and the Internet. Meanwhile, the company continued to widen its sphere to include vital interest in Windows CE and Windows NT while adding new features to its Office Suite.

In the late 1990s, Microsoft, like Rome, faced attacks on several fronts. Sun Microsystems, Netscape, and other apostles of the new computing ideology used Java, Web Browsers, and the Internet to challenge Microsoft's Windows standard. Instead of fighting this insurrection directly, Gates absorbed the rebellion into his sphere, "embracing and extending" the browser concept (much as the Emperor Constantine did in adopting the once "subversive" Christian religion). The Explorer browser moved from a forward position (in 1998) to Microsoft's core by 2001, becoming "integral" and "inseparable" from its operating system according to Microsoft.

Still, other sources of unrest remained untamed. Even though customers appeared to be satisfied with the benefits of belonging to Gates's empire, other powerful forces such as federal antitrust regulators succeeded in challenging Microsoft. As fallout from the antitrust suit continues to settle, Microsoft, like Rome, finds itself in a position where it may have to divide itself in two (as Rome did) and/or migrate its core significantly in order to survive. Or if the Bush Administration drops the suit, Microsoft may have to fight off the Internet-based barbarians and the PC-replacing PDA and consumer electronics manufacturers simultaneously. As Microsoft's story continues to play out, the company that had built a seemingly invincible sphere of influence may see its future following a remarkably similar evolution to that of Rome's.

As both Rome and Microsoft demonstrate, no great power, no matter how strong its sphere of influence, is immune to the forces that drive evolution and compress growth (see Exhibits 2-1 and 2-2, respectively). Even

Date: Stage:	Before 500 B.C. **Independence**	500 – 340 B.C. **Defensive Posture**	340 – 133 B.C. **Offensive Posture and Growth**
	Core	Core / Buffers	Pivotal Zones / Core / New Buffers / Forward Positions
Core interests:	Rome	Rome	Rome
Vital interests:			
Buffer zones:		Northern & Central Italian city-states	Other Italian city-states
Pivotal zones:		Northern & Southern Italian city-states	Spain (loss would shift the balance of power to Carthage in the early part of this period)
Forward positions:			Sicily (against Carthage and Macedonia in the early part of this period)

Exhibit 2-1: Evolution of the Roman Sphere of Influence

Date: Stage:	133 BC – AD 200 **Consolidation**	AD 200 – 450 **Defensive Response**	AD 450 – 600 **Sphere Migrated to the East**
Core interests:	Rome & Italian city-states	Rome & Constantinople	Constantinople
Vital interests:	Egypt, Spain, Sicily (food and manpower suppliers)	Italian Peninsula for the Western Empire; Turkey & Macedonia for the Eastern Empire	The Balkans, borders with Middle Eastern States
Buffer zones:	France, Northern Africa		East Turkey, Macedonia
Pivotal zones:	Alps (loss would shift balance of power to the Germanic tribes)		
Forward positions:	West Turkey, Northern France into Southern England	Outlying areas	

Exhibit 2-1 (Continued): *Evolution of the Roman Sphere of Influence*

	Pre-1979 **Pre-Independence**	1980 – 1983 **Independence from Language Licensors and Defensive Posture in IBM World**	1984 – 1989 **Offensive Posture Created and Growth Orientation Established by Forward Positions**
Date: Stage:	Core	New Buffers Core	New Buffers Forward Positions Core
Core interests:	Licensing mainframe programming language for adaptation to PCs	PC Languages and the MS-DOS operating system	MS-DOS & Windows for IBM
Vital interests:			
Buffer zones:		Applications — Word processing/spreadsheets for IBM Network software — Xenix	More applications added for IBM and Network communication programs for IBM's OS/2
Pivotal zones:			
Forward positions:			SQL servers (databases) Applications added for Mac platform reference materials (bookshelf)

Exhibit 2-2: Evolution of Microsoft's Sphere of Influence

Date: Stage:	1990 – 1996 Consolidation of the Center of Interest	1997 – 2000 Continued Expansion in Cyber-Space — Possible Split in Half: Applications and Operating Systems
		 Government Pressure to Split in Two
Core interests:	Consolidation of MS-DOS/Windows/applications into "Office"	Windows & "Office" including DOS
Vital interests:		• Windows CE (an operating system for consumer electronics and hand-held devices) • Windows NT (an operating system for office networks)
Buffer zones:	• Continued improvement and addition of new applications • Reference material (Encarta)	• Key applications for the workplace and hand-held devices • Reference materials • MSN
Pivotal zones:	• Digital content (games, money, etc.) • On-line services • MSN	• Many positions for potential future influence over content in the workplace, home, communications, hand-held devices, and multimedia • Microsoft.net
Forward positions:		• Explorer (against Netscape)

Exhibit 2-2 (Continued): *Evolution of Microsoft's Sphere of Influence*

these seemingly invincible empires discovered that monumental moments in the sun can be quickly followed by monumental moments under the gun.

Understanding and managing the evolutionary growth process is crucial to building and sustaining strategic supremacy. Growth can be costly or it can add to the power of your sphere. Even if your current sphere of influence is unsustainable under the pressure of invaders, strategic supremacy can be sustained by evolving the sphere to meet new challenges, respond to threats, and seize opportunities.

In Chapter 1, I offered a way to analyze and map your sphere of influence. This map is a snapshot of a sphere of influence, frozen at a particular point in time. This map can help to understand where the sphere is today and where it is headed. But in actuality, your sphere is constantly in motion. Its supremacy unfolds by building on its past successes and rethinking its parts as it moves forward, and as its competitors make their moves. In essence, for any great power, the waxing and waning of its sphere is the result of two countering pressures:

- Internal pressure to grow—manifested in your firm's strategy used to grow the sphere and to support the core with investments in vital interests, buffer zones, pivotal zones, and forward positions.

- External pressure to compress—manifested in a rival great power's strategy to contain, conquer, attack, or weaken the sphere.

Although the design of a sphere of influence (as discussed in Chapter 1) appears to be very logical and orderly on paper, it is not always so in practicality. Because of these two countering forces, a sphere will often grow in seemingly uncontrollable directions. Thus, the evolutionary path of a strong sphere of influence does not always progress by expanding outward through building concentric rings around a core.

To understand the structure and logic of a sphere's design, it is not only necessary to map your current position in geo-product space. You must also understand the past growth pattern of the sphere and adjust the sphere's design to reflect new realities, as well as anticipate and overcome the pattern of competitive compression applied against the sphere. The shifting struggle between the sphere's internal pressure to grow and the external pressure to compress its scope creates a complex evolutionary process.

This means that you will have to create a vision for the sphere you want to build using the mapping methods in Chapter 1. You will also have to choose a growth pattern that will get you there and recognize that, at any particular moment in time, your actual sphere will not look as logical as your vision, nor will it be what Wall Street might like. However, a well articulated logic for the sphere and a reason for the path you are taking will go a long way on The Street because the financial community is evaluating your vision for growth as much as it is looking at your current portfolio. Wall Street knows that the logic of the sphere is not created in an antiseptic lab, but typically by the rather messy give-and-take progress of history. As Oliver Wendell Holmes said, "Upon this point, a page of history is worth a volume of logic."[1]

FIVE NATURAL GROWTH PATTERNS: "THE DESPERATE DESIRE TO GROW"

A great power has an evolutionary imperative—to grow its sphere in a way that increases power and absorbs new wealth. As Milton Friedman, a winner of the Nobel Prize in economics, once said, "We don't have a desperate need to grow. We have a desperate desire to grow." Whether that "desire" is fulfilled or not depends in large part on your growth strategy—your guidelines for how and where you seek out new territories for your sphere. In general, companies follow one of five proven patterns of evolutionary growth—developers, pioneers, nomads, discoverers, and opportunists (see Exhibit 2-3).

Developers

These homebodies do not seek to extend their markets outside their borders. Instead, they find new space within their borders, either by "mining" their current markets, or serving as complements to other markets. The Japanese shoguns during the 1700s to the mid-1800s maintained dominance over all of Japan and sought little expansion beyond their shores.

	Exploitation of the Sphere's Current Markets	Exploration of Markets Nearby the Sphere	Exploration of Markets Distant from the Sphere
Keep the Sphere's Existing Core	Developer	Pioneers	Discoverers
Shift the Sphere's Core		Nomads	Opportunists

Exhibit 2-3: Natural Growth Patterns

Similarly, companies with preeminent brands or other strong barriers to entry may choose to stake out a territory and mine it extensively. Two examples are Mattel's preeminent position in dolls or Wm. Wrigley Jr. Company's preeminent position in chewing gum. Mattel's Barbie has undergone nearly constant evolution since her creation in 1959—from glamour model to high-tech "Talk With Me Barbie," that plugs into the owner's computer and can be programmed to speak customized dialogue with lips that move.[2] (By year 2000, Barbie was faltering a bit. While Barbie is only part of Mattel's business, it is a very significant part—so Mattel as a whole may not be pursuing a pure "developer" strategy. Nevertheless, Barbie illustrates that the developer approach can be sustained for forty years.) Wrigley has also moved to mine its approximately one-hundred-year-old bubble gum sphere of influence with Hubba Bubba and deeper penetration of its global markets.

Pioneers

These Daniel Boone types move into adjacent markets the way U.S. pioneers settled the West, or Rome extended the territory of its empire. Sporting-goods manufacturer Easton leveraged its competency in aluminum sporting goods by moving from arrows into baseball bats, ski poles, and hockey sticks. Another example is Hewlett-Packard, which moved from calculators to adjacent markets for personal computers and printers. Hologic represents a company that started as a developer and became a pioneer. Founded in 1986, Hologic was a leader in diagnostic equipment for osteoporosis. The company created the first X-ray bone densitometer and continued to extend its clinical diagnostics equipment with advances such as a whole-body scanner and densitometers that incorporated new technologies. A decade later, Hologic initiated a more pioneering strategy of moving into other types of imaging, beginning with its merger with FluoroScan, an imaging company for minimally invasive surgery. The move began to shift the company from developing only diagnostic equipment to meeting broader medical needs for imaging.

Nomads

These wanderers move from core market to core market, abandoning the old as they enter the new, in the way that Mongols swept through Asia into Europe. Rather than consolidate their sphere, nomads live off one temporary opportunity after another. Facing declining fortunes in its core industry, M.A. Hanna abandoned its mineral mining business to move into a new core business of specialty chemicals in just a few years. By 1986, it shed all but a few vestiges of its mining business, and engaged in a rapid spurt of acquisitions in specialty plastics and rubber, as well as global expansions that built the company sales from $197 million in 1986 to $1.1 billion in 1991. This revenue came almost entirely from its new businesses, as the company divested its last natural resource firm in 1991. Hanna has continued on a growth path ever since. Nokia (moving into cellular phones) and Morton Salt (moving into rocketry) have experienced similar successful shifts in their core, and have achieved rapid growth as a result.

Discoverers

These fearless folk go farther afield without abandoning their cores, discovering new lands like the explorers of colonial Spain and Britain. Discoverers take dramatic leaps into exotic places: undeveloped space in which there is no great power; undiscovered space created by a breakthrough in technology; or unprotected space vulnerable to attack by ill-prepared inhabitants. Discoverers find these spaces and then build colonies in them. They have a long-term base (core market) from which to operate and explore for new discoveries. During its early years, Sony built its position as a discoverer. It moved from transistor radios to the major new inventions such as Trinitron color television to the VCR to the Walkman.

Opportunists

These adventurers take bold leaps, but without holding onto their past businesses. They are like the Vikings who sailed from base ports to raid known territories as opportunities for plunder emerged. They then moved on to new targets. Thermo Electron has achieved rapid growth as a complete opportunist, building diverse technological capabilities in diverse areas, including X rays, radar, laser hair removal, and low-orbit communications satellites. Thermo Electron doesn't rely on a single core technology. Instead, the company explores these new technologies opportunistically and then spins off the successful companies. Its subsidiaries, such as ThermoTrex, then spin out their own subsidiaries in narrower areas.

What Comes Natural to Some Is Unnatural for Others

Developers, pioneers, nomads, discoverers, opportunists. Which growth pattern describes your firm's growth strategy? Most companies have a natural growth strategy that they follow instinctively. Consider your company's evolution thus far. Do you tend to search near or far for growth opportunities? Is every addition to your sphere directly related to the core or do you have a tendency to abandon your existing core as soon as something bigger and better comes along?

The choice of growth strategy is often engrained in the culture of the company, often based on the personality or skills of the founder. The growth process may also result from the expeditionary and invasionary capabilities of the firm, its capabilities for change, the marketing group's prowess at entering new markets, or the leapfrog research skill of R&D departments.

That said, it's important to remember a company's growth strategy isn't set in stone. Say your company is suddenly faced with a major threat to its core market (such as potential obsolescence or significant decline). Or a new territory suddenly blows open the competitive space, the way the discovery of the New World set off a frenzy of exploration in the Americas. Or the way the introduction of consumer packaged goods into mass merchandisers and e-commerce dramatically changed P&G's competitive space, as described in Chapter 1. When one sphere's natural growth pattern causes a significant shift in the playing field, such as these events did, it may compel other spheres to shift their growth strategy, stop the growth of the sphere that's causing the playing field to shift, or risk being left behind in the dust.

ADJUSTING YOUR NATURAL GROWTH STRATEGY: THERE'S NO PLACE LIKE HOME . . . OR IS THERE?

All of the strategies I just described are proven methods for uncovering opportunities for growth and for forging even widely diversified zones into a strong and cohesive sphere. But some of these strategies focus the growth process close to home—revealing opportunities for you to mine your core. Others illuminate possibilities for moving away from your core, or possibly replacing it altogether. With such a broad spectrum of alternatives, firms can likely relate to the warning by catcher-cum-philosopher Yogi Berra, "You've got to be very careful if you don't know where you're going, because you might not get there."

How do you determine which growth strategy is right for your firm? That answer greatly depends on four factors discussed below:

- How strong is your position in the core and how strong is your commitment to it?
- What is the pace of growth in your industry?
- Is your organization capable of moving to a new core or to distant places and markets?
- And how will the relationship between the new and old territory help or hinder the power of your sphere of influence?

Your Strength and Commitment to the Core

Take a long, hard look at your core business. Because more than one skilled management team has mis-assessed or undervalued a profitable core, and the results have been disastrous. Consider Bausch & Lomb, the seemingly immutable leader in the eye care industry through the mid-1980s. Then the company began diverting its resources and attention from its core lens and solutions business, investing in new markets related to dentists, dermatologists, and hearing specialists. But rather than adding value to the company, the move proved to be a drain and a distraction. Sales in the core flattened out. Worse yet, the diversification opened the door for a powerful new player in the contact lens business, Johnson & Johnson. While J&J was enjoying success with its new disposable lenses, B&L's market share was declining, eventually drifting below J&J's. Despite a history of 120 years in the eye care business, Bausch & Lomb didn't see the writing on the wall until it was too late. Eventually, a new management team came in and returned the company's focus to its core, but not before critical ground, time, and capital had been lost.

To avoid falling into the same trap as B&L, you need a clear assessment of the value of your core. If your core is rock solid, logic dictates you should grow with it. Coca-Cola has enjoyed decades of strong performance and market share leadership in its core business. So has USAA, which practically owns a customer niche among former military employees by earning their total loyalty and devotion.

But what if your core isn't secure, or suddenly faces a serious threat? Sigma-Aldrich provides an example of the latter. The company, which had remained preeminent in the market for specialized esoteric research chemicals for decades, now faces a new and successful Web-enabled challenger, Chemdex. If the rival has more power in cases like this, logic dictates you must evolve the sphere by adopting a search strategy that explores for more opportunities farther away from the besieged core, and that you create stronger forward and pivotal positions.

The Pace of Growth in Your Core

Beverages. Clothing. Tires. Supermarkets. The world is full of slow-growth industries. Companies that are experts at mining their core somehow manage to supersede the sluggish growth within their own industries. Nike's 27 percent growth over ten years was in sharp contrast to the 6 percent growth of the shoe market, its core business. Coke has managed to grow at more than twice the rate of its industry. For long periods, Mattel, Harley-Davidson, and Gap Inc. have also managed to transcend their industry growth rates. But these players are the exception, not the rule. And even more recently Nike, Mattel, and the Gap have experienced downturns or strong fluctuations in their cores.

Mining the core in a slow-growth market can often be the equivalent of trying to get blood out of a turnip. You may be better off switching your growth strategy to the broader world of opportunities, where you can build your forward positions and pivotal zones, and prepare for the future. This is especially critical if you're in a declining market, where the need to migrate your core is a foregone conclusion.

The Capabilities of Your Organization

Does your organization have the skills to move into a new growth market? The flexibility? Can you acquire the skills? When is the right time to make the switch—while the going is still good or when the jig is up? Or would it be better to stay put and serve as a cash cow? These are all value judgments without easy answers. This dilemma is faced by many of today's large insurance companies that have traditionally been stable cash generators. These companies tend to stick close to home. But in today's rapidly globalizing financial world, one insurance company, AIG, has built the capability to globalize and has become successfully focused on growth overseas. While those who have stayed at home have been successful today, what will their future look like if AIG becomes the global leader and they lack the power to counter AIG?

The Negative Synergies Created

When AT&T built Network Systems (now Lucent Technologies) it thought it was in synergy heaven. Network Systems manufactured equipment for AT&T and all its local subunits at first. After the 1983 breakup of AT&T, Network Systems manufactured equipment for the independent regional Bell operating companies as well as AT&T itself. AT&T anticipated having the latest networks and technologies at its disposal. AT&T also probably anticipated that control over Network Systems would mean control over the standards for all the baby Bells. But AT&T didn't anticipate the negative side of its synergy with Network Systems. In reality, the baby Bells were afraid to buy Network Systems' equipment for two very good reasons: They feared they'd be strengthening their rival's coffers; and they suspected that only AT&T would get access to Network Systems' cutting-edge technology. In the end, Network Systems, languishing in a bad marketing position and bad technological position, spun off from AT&T, renamed itself Lucent, and, up until recently, became a better value creator than its former parent.

COMPETITIVE COMPRESSION: FOR EVERY ACTION, THERE IS AN OPPOSITE AND EQUAL REACTION

You have a desperate desire to grow. Your rivals have an equally desperate desire to compress your growth. Newton's third law of motion—for every action, there is an equal and opposite reaction—has direct application to firms trying to lead the evolution of their spheres.

As you attempt to grow your sphere, your rivals react, resulting in a constant pressure on your perimeter. I call this external pressure on a sphere *competitive compression*. The concept of competitive compression can be illustrated through the analogy of a balloon as it inflates. Press the balloon more firmly on one side, and its expansion at that point is compressed, but the other side pops out more prominently. But of course no balloon can expand indefinitely. Since outside air pressure is always around its perimeter, trying to inflate the balloon too much in any direction can only result in its bursting.

Sometimes the competitive compression on a sphere is felt more acutely in one of its zones; other times it's more of a uniform squeeze. And sometimes the competitive compression felt by a sphere comes primarily from one rival, while other times it's the result of a gang of competitors intentionally or inadvertently working together. Regardless, this compression—as much as the sphere's own natural growth strategy—drives the sphere's evolution.

Four Patterns of Competitive Compression

Whether a sphere is on the receiving or giving end of competitive compression, the pressure typically manifests in one of four general patterns. Specifically, compression is put on a sphere to *contain* its growth, *gradually constrict* its boundaries, *strip* it of its vital interests or other critical zones, or *domino* through its buffer zones. The domino strategy involves toppling buffers one by one, and thus gaining the momentum and the capabilities necessary to make a strike at the core and the sphere's value leadership. I have termed these four patterns of competitive compression "managed containment," "gradual constriction," "sequential stripping," and "toppling dominoes." While competitive compression is hardly the only challenge to growth that firms must confront, one or more of these four patterns of external pressure almost always plays a role when the growth and supremacy of spheres decline.

When one of these patterns of competitive compression is used, it is usually determined by two factors: first the attackers' resources (relative to the target's sphere, of course); and second, the attackers' time horizon (bigger threats require faster action).

Managed Containment

This pattern of competitive compression is based on surrounding a rival sphere and restricting it to a narrow part of the competitive space (see Exhibit 2-4). It does not obliterate the integrity of the targeted sphere, but merely stunts its growth into new markets and limits its scope. This strategy or inadvertent pattern of pressure may even be conducted by several firms targeting the same sphere. Containment can take a long time because it does not provide a decisive victory. However, it can be less costly than the other more aggressive compression patterns, especially if the early containment policies work and the rival settles down into its own sphere and adopts a developer growth strategy.

In 1970, ABC invented one of the most successful formats for prime-time programming. Its *Monday Night Football* program dominated U.S. television sets at the start of the week through the 1970s and early 1980s. Mondays became the core of ABC's profit-making machine. Its prime competitors, NBC and CBS, were unable to develop a lineup of shows to compete.

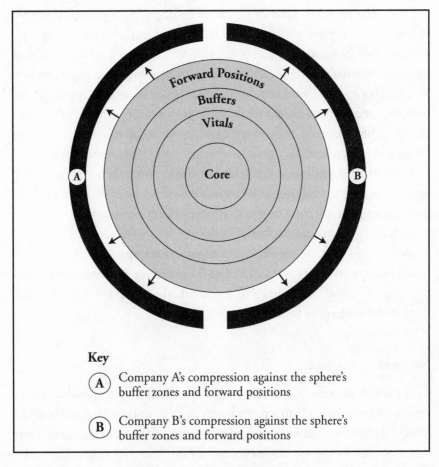

Key

(**A**) Company A's compression against the sphere's buffer zones and forward positions

(**B**) Company B's compression against the sphere's buffer zones and forward positions

Exhibit 2-4: Managed Containment

Realizing they didn't stand much of a chance of competing for the Monday night sports-oriented male audience, CBS and NBC conceded that audience to ABC. CBS focused instead on a highly effective strategy of putting together a package of sitcoms (the move was initially scoffed at by the other networks) that targeted women and non-sports viewers. The sitcoms were centered on women—*Designing Women* and *Murphy Brown*—and a nondomineering male, *Newhart*. The shows were well directed and produced, and *Designing Women* and *Murphy Brown* were considered among the best sitcoms on television. During the 1991–92 season, CBS replaced *Newhart* with *Northern Exposure*, a light-hearted drama series that explored the meaning of life. Again, this new show was targeted at the non-football viewer.

Meanwhile, NBC worked to contain ABC on a different front: Tuesday and Thursday night. Its "Must See TV" on Tuesday and Thursdays included top-notch sitcoms like *Taxi*, *Cheers*, and *Wings*, as well as award winning dramas like *Hill Street Blues*.

By targeting a completely different audience, CBS took advantage of the declining interest in Monday night sports, the increase in the number of televisions in the home, and the larger female viewing audience to expand viewership and obtain market share on Monday night. CBS captured a significant portion of the market that did not view *Monday Night Football*. Additionally, the sitcoms it aired on Mondays were strong enough to attract *Monday Night Football* viewers during the non-football season. NBC, meanwhile, targeted audiences on other nights and audiences seeking higher quality programming.

CBS moved past ABC to become the dominant network on Monday nights. On the first day of the 1991 television season, *Designing Women* beat *Monday Night Football* by five rating points.[3] ABC was placing its best sitcoms—*Growing Pains*, *Who's the Boss*, and *Moonlighting*—on Tuesday night, because it couldn't compete directly with CBS on Monday nights.[4] But these shows were countered by NBC's outstanding lineup (including *Cheers*), so ABC was caught in a vise and lost its leadership of the market. By the mid-1990s NBC's high-quality Thursday night lineup, including *Frasier* and *Friends*, helped it become the leading network at the time. Even though containment seems difficult, it can work for a period of decades.

Gradual Constriction

A second pattern of competitive compression begins by surrounding a competitor's sphere and then gradually encroaching on its current position (see Exhibit 2-5). This can either mean physically surrounding a geographic territory or surrounding a specific product or customer market. The aggressor or group of aggressors then slowly tightens the grip on the sphere through a series of thrusts. For this pattern of competitive compression to succeed, the challenger has to have deep pockets or strong allies, since gradual constriction requires simultaneous aggressive moves in many markets. The challenger also has to expect counterattacks, since it's pushing against the targeted sphere's crown jewel, its core.

Whether intended or not, the response by Chiyoda Co. to the entry of

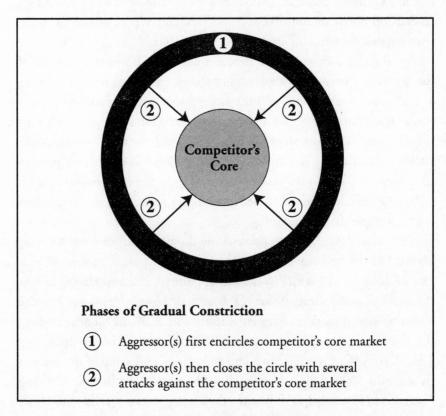

Phases of Gradual Constriction

①   Aggressor(s) first encircles competitor's core market

②   Aggressor(s) then closes the circle with several attacks against the competitor's core market

Exhibit 2-5: Gradual Constriction

Toys "R" Us into Japan resembles an example of geographic constriction. When Toys "R" Us built its first store in Tokyo in December 1991, it created its Japanese core and a base for its expansion in Japan. Its largest local competitor surrounded the new store with smaller stores. Chiyoda, a discount chain for toys, announced plans to build a cluster of 3,500-square-foot stores surrounding the 33,000-square-foot Toys "R" Us store. Before the opening of Toys "R" Us, Chiyoda built five stores in the surrounding area. Chiyoda then opened a sixth store—across the street from Toys "R" Us.

By this strategy of surrounding the large store with smaller stores, Chiyoda hoped to cut off Toys "R" Us from its customers by luring them into Chiyoda's stores before they reached its larger competitor. This strategy appears to be designed to constrict the competitor geographically and absorb Chiyoda's rival's customer base in its core market.[5]

Of course this strategy can be used with larger spheres that span multiple products and multiple geographies. It can even happen inadvertently from the uncoordinated actions of several rivals. So gradual constriction can be the equivalent of greater and greater water pressure on the hull of a submarine as it goes deeper in the ocean.

Another method of gradual constriction was alleged by Scott McNeally, CEO of Sun Microsystems. He complained that Microsoft was "buying pieces of all my customers!"[6] Microsoft paid $5 billion for a chunk of AT&T, $600 million for a stake in Nextel, and $212.5 million for part of the Roadrunner cable modem service. Microsoft also paid $200 million for a piece of Qwest, $1 billion for a portion of Comcast, and $400 million for a stake in Canada's Rogers Cable. Microsoft also made investments in several dozen other telecom and cable companies during 1998 and 1999. According to *Fortune*, McNeally sees this as a strategy to squeeze and perhaps kill his company because his biggest business is selling servers with Sun's Solaris UNIX operating systems to his biggest customer category, communications companies.

Sequential Stripping

This pattern of competitive compression is the sequential dismantling of a competitor's sphere, zone by zone (see Exhibit 2-6). Unlike gradual constriction, which chokes the competitor's core markets directly, stripping focuses on the competitor's vital and peripheral (buffer and pivotal zones, and forward positions) geo-product zones. It takes out each of these zones one at a time, ultimately leading to the destruction of the competitor's hold on its sphere. If the competitor survives, it usually manages to hold onto only its core, and precariously at that. Stripping can be done alone or, more frequently, in concert with a number of other firms seeking to reduce the supremacy of a market leader. This form of competitive compression requires a lengthier time frame than some of the other types, but the flip side is it may also draw the least response. In addition, if the stripping effort is focused, it may eat up fewer resources.

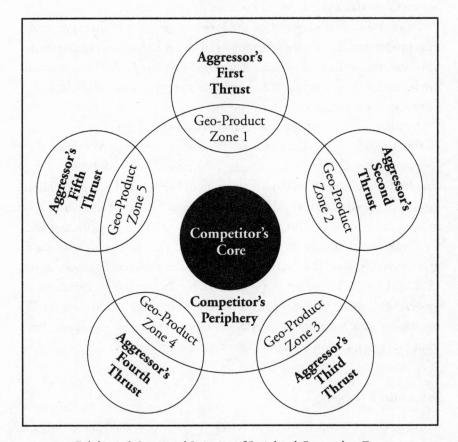

Exhibit 2-6: Sequential Stripping of Peripheral Geo-product Zones

Whether intentional or unintentional, the dismantling of Computervision offers an example of how sequential stripping takes place. Computervision began as the undisputed leader and industry pioneer in the CAD/CAM software industry. Its CADDS software package spanned the entire process of product development, including conceptual design, product design, drafting, analysis, and manufacturing. By 1990, the company had an installed base of more than 150,000 machines.

But by the end of the 1990s, its competitive position had significantly eroded. The broad coverage of its product, which had been an asset, now became a liability. It found itself picked apart bit by bit by a variety of other competitors. McDonnell Douglas introduced a Unigraphics package that was considered superior for manufacturing applications. SDRC's IDEAS was narrowly focused on product analysis. Intergraph developed a product to meet the needs of the architecture, engineering, and construction segment. Cadence, Valid, and Mentor went after the electronics market. Autodesk specialized in PC-based design and drafting, offering functionality that satisfied well over half of CAD/CAM users at a fraction of the cost of a CADDS seat.

Computervision reacted to this competitive threat by introducing a new version of its software. But because of its large installed base, any changes had to be incremental to avoid alienating existing customers. This position, once considered a strength, seriously limited its flexibility. In the words of Parametric Technology Corporation's head of research, Computervision was "like an aircraft carrier; Parametric is like a torpedo boat."[7]

These "torpedo boats" caused Computervision to retreat. By 1991, Computervision had slipped to third place in the industry, with only 13.3 percent of the market, compared with more than 30 percent for IBM and more than 16 percent for Intergraph.

Computervision's sphere has apparently been dismantled one piece at a time by numerous competitors who were probably acting independently. This stripping left Computervision with a technically superior program in only one small area, drafting. But even this section of the industry is increasingly under assault by competitors. Thus Computervision has little room to compete even in the last zone of the sphere it once held.

Competitive compression through stripping can have a potentially devastating effect on a dominant player in the industry. The leader is fig-uratively killed by a thousand bee stings. By concentrating on a small seg-ment of the sphere, each rival can more fully satisfy that part of the market. Meanwhile the target is spread too thin because it is trying to sat-isfy a wider range of customer needs. Although in this example a group of firms appeared to strip zones from the dominant player—apparently with-out collusion—sequential stripping can be just as effective if one large ri-val goes against individual zones of a company's sphere one at a time.

Toppling Dominoes

This pattern of competitive compression uses toppling dominoes to move into the core of a competitor's sphere of influence (see Exhibit 2-7). One domino at a time, the attacker takes a position, builds a stronghold, accu-mulates the skills needed to enter another more vital zone, and leverages its position to enter that more vital zone. Attackers use their forward positions to enter a buffer zone, move to a vital interest, and then attack the core of a rival's sphere as their strengths and capabilities build with each move. Like gradual constriction, toppling dominoes requires deep pockets, because this form of competitive compression eventually requires the aggressor to fight it out in the core of the targeted sphere. In addition, the targeted sphere is bound to come back strong with a counterattack in the aggressor's core.

Lomas & Nettleton seemingly used a toppling dominoes strategy to become the leading independent mortgage banking firm (before its later

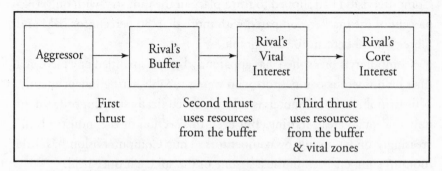

Exhibit 2-7: The Toppling Dominoes Strategy

fall from grace due to a sudden decline in the Texas real estate market). Lomas initially competed in loan origination and gained critical economies of scale, growing during a period of intense competition. It then focused its resources on a nearby target market, the servicing of loans. By 1989, Lomas dropped out of the market for originating loans and concentrated only on servicing loans.

It had built a loan portfolio of over $24 billion, placing it squarely in the core of the largest traditional banking rival in the region. This step-by-step process brought Lomas to a place it never could have attempted at the beginning of its journey. It's too bad the core it went after collapsed a few years later. Unfortunately Lomas & Nettleton failed to build its own sphere of influence and capture some pivotal and vital interests that could have supported the core during troubled times and reduced the risks of relying on the Texas real estate market.

The toppling domino strategy can also be done by groups of firms, typically in alliances that exchange competencies. Each exchange adds another domino in the lineup toward the core of the targeted sphere.

CIRCUMVENTING AND COUNTERING COMPETITIVE COMPRESSION

In Chapter 1, I described the primary strategic intents for each zone of a sphere of influence. Now I'd like to revisit this issue in light of competitive compression.

- Your core and vital interests are your crown jewels. These zones serve your critical customer and geographic segments. In these markets you "own" the customer's relationship or loyalty. Your core and vital interests are the zones where you don't want to feel *any* competitive compression.

- The buffer zones in your sphere block competitive entry of your core and vital interests. Buffers are the zones that *respond* to a competitive attack, and deal with the competitive compression put on your sphere.

- Pivotal zones are a bet on the future—for example, a potentially high-growth market. Pivotal zones are also used to pursue power vacuums, those untapped markets where no player has established a stronghold . . . yet. Pivotal zones are the facilitators that allow you to sidestep the stranglehold of competitive compression. If a rival or gang of rivals is squeezing you tight, your pivotal zones give you the means to extract yourself from the vise you're in.

- Forward positions are your footholds in a rival's sphere. These zones serve to deter or dampen the intensity of competitive compression. They can also be used to launch counterattacks. You use your forward positions aggressively (rather than defensively like buffers) to invade a rival's sphere of influence with the intent of capturing it, or applying a dose of competitive compression of your own.

In combination, when the five zones of the sphere of influence are individually achieving their unique strategic purposes, the collective result is a cohesive sphere of powerful proportions. And this power is multifaceted:

- *Competitiveness.* For starters, a cohesive sphere gives you the power of competitiveness. The source of your competitiveness comes from the combined force strength of your core and vital interests. Vital interests allow you to capture (1) economies of scale, scope, and integration with the core; (2) supremacy in these key marketplaces; and (3) the ability to bundle products and services to add more value. In combination, your core and vital interests allow you to achieve lower costs, better service, increased quality, greater innovation, and more choices, all for the benefit of your customers.

- *Reputation.* A cohesive sphere also gives you the power of reputation. The use of your forward positions, buffers, and pivotal zones creates a reputation for fierceness, risk propensity, boldness, and aggressiveness that can keep rivals away from your sphere.

- *Barriers to entry.* The sphere also creates power through barriers to entry. This is a byproduct of the first two facets of power—your ability to be more competitive and your reputation for fierceness. In combination, your competitiveness and your fierce reputation make you a lean, mean contender.

- *Resources.* In addition, a cohesive sphere creates power through its resources—deep pockets, political clout, and a deep bench of talented managers. The sphere works as a launch pad for growth efforts that can increase the power and scope of the sphere while also increasing the amount of resources available for the firm (so you don't get spread too thin).

All four of these sources of your sphere's power—its competitiveness, reputation, barriers to entry, and resources—are inextricably related to which evolutionary growth pattern you are following. Which, in turn, is inextricably related to the kind of competitive compression that your sphere is experiencing. The pattern of competitive compression on your sphere plays a major role in whether you use these four sources of power in the periphery (i.e. in certain buffer and/or pivotal zones, or forward positions) or in the core and vital interests of your sphere. You might, for example, use your power to erect barriers to entry in the periphery of your sphere, or you might use the power of your resources throughout your sphere to counter selective parts of the compression you are experiencing.

In the face of competitive compression, some great powers (like Rome) must dramatically alter their spheres. For example, they migrate their cores or even maintain multiple cores when the pressure gets too intense. Can two cores be better than one in offsetting competitive compression? The jury is still out on that one. Some companies are able to create a sphere of influence with multiple cores. This works if the firm establishes two or three separate and solid spheres—sometimes with overlap but other times as relatively independent entities. Each individual sphere of the overall firm establishes (or fails to establish) supremacy in its own areas.

General Electric built its supremacy around the related centers of electrical products and consumer finance (see Exhibit 2-8). Later GE successfully added two more centers, plastics and broadcasting, making the company highly diversified. Tyco International has built a fast-growing business around a triple core of disposable medical products, fire protection systems and services, and flow control products like valves and electrical components. In each of these three spheres, Tyco has tried—and essentially succeeded—in achieving great power status. From 1992 to 1997, the company achieved goals of a 15 to 20 percent annual increase in earnings growth, and stock price increases of 30 percent per year. Yet, Tyco chief executive Dennis Kozlowski does not like to refer to his firm as a "conglomerate."[8] Tyco is three separate spheres built around three separate cores, but tied together by the company's overall expertise at creating and leading the evolution of powerful spheres.

Despite GE's and Tyco's success stories, it is fairly rare to find a com-

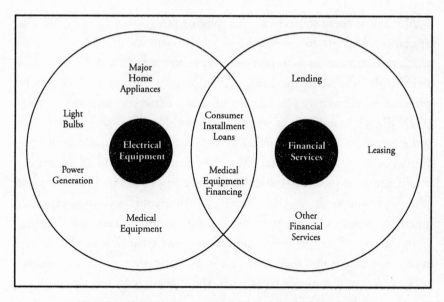

Exhibit 2-8: GE's Traditional Dual Cores and Overlapping Spheres

pany with the financial resources, discipline, and management breadth to build strategic supremacy across multiple spheres simultaneously. Typically, the situation of a company with multiple cores is a temporary one, reflecting the firm's transition from one center of interest or core to another. The challenge in managing a global enterprise with multiple cores is the extreme potential for conflict across the diverse parts of the business or empire. The Roman Empire's dual cores (in Rome and Constantinople) led to serious overstretch of Rome's resources. Only by eventually abandoning the capital city of Rome and migrating the core to Constantinople did the Romans manage to extend the life of the empire.

Similarly, in the business world PepsiCo found it difficult to hold onto its dual core in soft drinks and fast foods. AT&T found it extremely difficult to hold onto its multiple cores in long-distance service, computers, and telecom equipment manufacturing, despite the alleged synergies between the three cores. (In 2001, AT&T was again splitting itself into four pieces for similar reasons.) PepsiCo and AT&T eventually had to divest themselves of their secondary and tertiary cores because they lacked the financial and management resources to achieve strategic supremacy in more than one sphere at a time.

Particularly for rising powers (including the once fledgling great empires of Rome and Microsoft) the fastest route to strategic supremacy is to build a sphere piece by piece around a single core. The core has the greatest chance of surviving by avoiding contact with major rivals until it is secured by capturing value leadership. Only then does it make sense for a rising star to shift priorities, first adding buffer zones, then later filling in vital interests, forward positions, and pivotal zones. Thereafter the pattern of a sphere's evolution depends on the pressure on its core. The choice of growth strategy is directly related to the degree of pressure on the sphere (see Exhibits 2-9A and 2-9B). You won't always be able to follow the priorities as I have outlined them above because your best moves may have been preempted or your firm may lack the capabilities to pursue the right moves at the right time. Nevertheless, patient movement toward your vision for a cohesive sphere is possible.

Step by step you can create a strong sphere and achieve (and sustain) strategic supremacy if you are continuously aware of two factors:

1. How to adjust your pattern of growth in response to the containment and conquest pressure exerted on the sphere

2. How to use your sphere to compress the spheres of rival ascendant and great powers

Before the advent of the Internet, specialty retailers, and mass discount merchandisers, Procter & Gamble provided a good example of how to circumvent and counter the competitive pressure it was experiencing. A company's number one priority should be to gain preeminence in one core market by establishing value leadership there. In the 1950s and 1960s P&G consolidated and extended a strong core in phases (see Exhibit 2-10). During the 1970s and 1980s, its growth pattern switched from the pioneer strategy (tightly moving around its core) to a discoverer approach (see Exhibit 2-11). This switch was necessitated by the competitive compression created by the growing presence within American supermarkets of foreign corporations such as Nestlé, Unilever, and others. The need to add buffer zones to protect against these European companies pushed

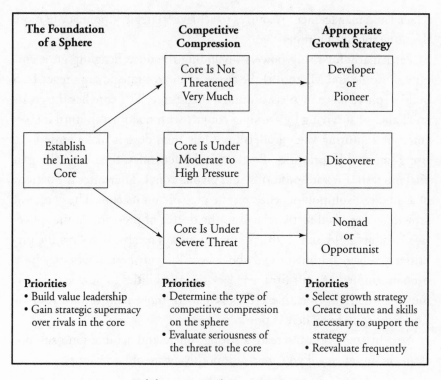

Exhibit 2-9A: Evolutionary Priorities

P&G to move into product lines that were not as tightly related to its core in household laundry and paper products and personal core products. P&G also made a foray into the pharmaceutical markets, giving it a buffer against the large pharmaceutical houses that were starting to enter the nonprescription market, and diversifying into cosmetics. (The threat from this quarter has subsided as pharmaceutical companies have consolidated and refocused on blockbuster prescription drugs. P&G has since divested the prescription drug portion of this buffer zone and focused only on the over-the-counter medicine market.)

In a third phase of its growth, P&G has taken forward positions in the core European markets of Unilever, Nestlé, and others. Plus it has added some pivotal zones in the potentially high-growth markets of the future, such as Asia and Latin America (see Exhibit 2-12). These moves were not made merely to take advantage of P&G's distribution synergies. P&G

Competitive Compression	1st Steps	2nd Steps	3rd Steps	Typical Sequential Goals
Core is not threatened very much	Add buffers*	Add forward positions**	Add vital* and pivotal** zones	*Step* 1. Protect the core 2. Position to counterattack rivals who might invade the core 3. Enhance the profitability of the present and prepare for the future
Core is under moderate to high pressure	Add forward positions** and vital zones*	Add pivotal zones**	Add buffers***	*Step* 1. Protect and support the present core to hold on to it 2. Search for and discover new zones that can be safe havens outside the focus of the current competitive compression or be a new core if the compression gets worse 3. Protect the future of the initial core or a successful pivotal zone
Core is under severe threat	Add pivotal zones**	Add forward positions**	• Drop old core • Build buffers* and forward positions** around the new core	*Step* 1. Prepare for migration of the core using funds from the initial core 2. Buy time to migrate by positioning against rivals who might attack the initial core 3. Secure the future around the new core

Key:
* Near (or related) to the initial core
** Potentially unrelated to the initial core
*** Both * and **

Exhibit 2-9B: Circumventing Competitive Compression—Setting Growth Priorities

could have moved in many directions within the grocery world. It could have focused on just the lucrative U.S. market, or on the potentially vast Asian market, avoiding the European strongholds of Unilever, Nestlé, and the like. Instead, the company's moves were made to enhance its arsenal in its offensive battle for strategic supremacy over supermarket shelf space, and to combat the forces of competitive compression working to thwart its growth. P&G adjusted its growth pattern in relation to the ebbs and flows of competitive compression from other great powers outside its sphere. By leading the evolution of its sphere in this way, P&G created both solid defensive and offensive positions relative to Nestlé, Unilever, Kraft, and others competing in the grocery space.

Procter & Gamble's story of evolutionary progress versus competitive compression has continued into the twenty-first century. In 1999, P&G completed its largest acquisition ever by shelling out $2.3 billion for Iams, a leader in premium pet nutrition sold through specialty pet stores and vets. The move was a means of leveraging P&G's core competency—its power over supermarket shelf space. Because Iams pet food is being intro-

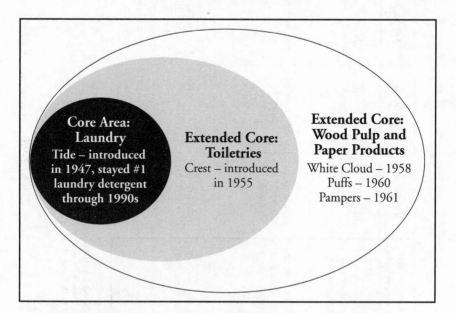

Exhibit 2-10: Stage 1—P&G Builds Its U.S. Base (1950s and 1960s)

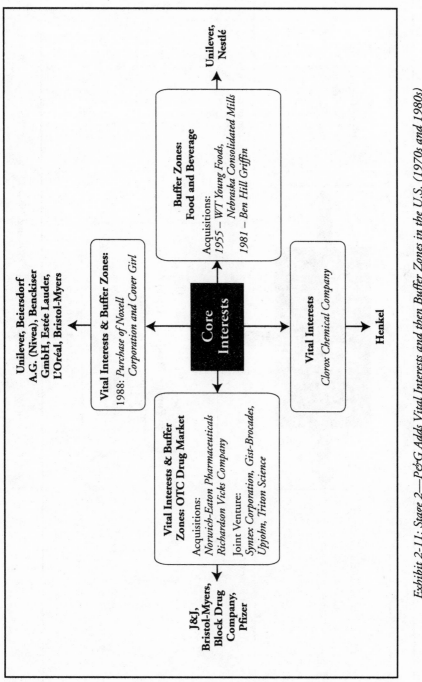

Exhibit 2-11: Stage 2—P&G Adds Vital Interests and then Buffer Zones in the U.S. (1970s and 1980s)

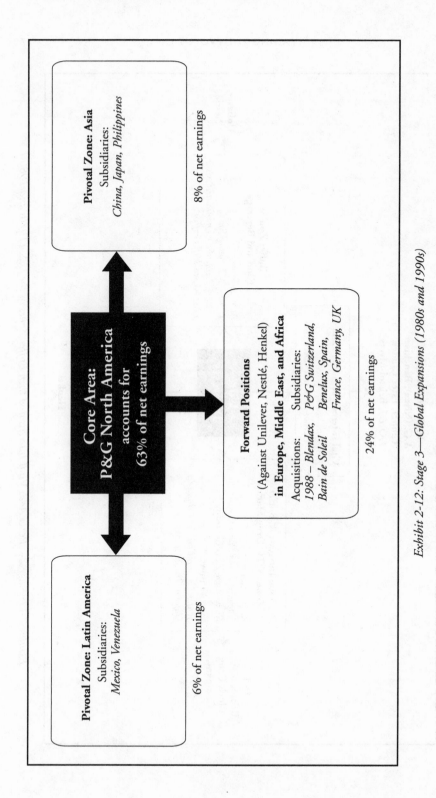

Exhibit 2-12: Stage 3—Global Expansions (1980s and 1990s)

duced to supermarket shelves, this acquisition applies some competitive compression on rival Nestlé, which owns Carnation and its pet food products. Even though Nestlé has a position in pet foods, P&G's purchase of Iams does not seriously threaten Nestlé because Nestlé derives only a tiny percentage of its revenues from pet food. Its core markets lie elsewhere. Therefore, P&G's acquisition of Iams was a move that attacked Nestlé in a place where it was unlikely to respond aggressively, especially while Iams does not have a large share of supermarket sales.

Yet despite P&G's success in introducing Iams in supermarkets, the acquisition may have been seriously shortsighted. For one thing, P&G is provoking channel conflicts with vets and specialty pet stores. What's more, its Iams acquisition will undoubtedly provoke players known for their aggressiveness in defending their core businesses. Ralston Purina, for example, was not a big rival of P&G previously, but it sure is now. And nobody—not even a giant like Procter & Gamble—gets this kind of formidable rival mad at them, if they can avoid it. In the past, Ralston has doggedly fought price wars and even used brand confusion tactics. For example, Ralston introduced the Graaavy brand against a rival's Gravy Train brand to defend its core market in dry pet food.

With its purchase of Iam's, P&G provides a useful lesson for those who want to lead the evolution of their own spheres. When growing or adding to your sphere of influence, consider more than leveraging your core competency. Consider also the new opponents you gain. The sphere of influence approach provides an additional guide for your firm's acquisition and diversification strategies, because it focuses attention on the overall impact of an evolutionary move versus the competitive compression working against your sphere and the compression that you bring on yourself.

The relative power of a sphere and those who wish to compress it determines whether that sphere will gain or keep its supremacy. For example, U.S. Cellular has not become preeminent in the wireless telecom market (despite its successful growth strategy). It lost valuable time building its wireless sphere and faced the pressure of powerhouses like AT&T Wireless and Bell Atlantic Wireless (now Verizon). U.S. Cellular started in rural telephone systems, adding adjacent regions to expand its reach. In 1982, it moved into cable television and a year later began purchasing cellular operating licenses. The cellular business became the core of a rapidly growing empire that expanded into nearly two hundred markets and became one of the largest cellular telephone companies in the United States. U.S. Cellular provides a great example of a firm that has achieved great power status but does not have strategic supremacy in the marketplace. AT&T Wireless captured a firm lead over the market with its 1999 One Rate Plan (reducing both the cost and complexity of rates for heavy users), its wider national coverage, and its ability to bundle traditional long distance service with cellular service. By 2001, the ensuing price war is draining all wireless competitors, forcing them to seek greater economies of scale. U.S. Cellular's future as an independent wireless company may be threatened by consolidation of the market, especially as wireless prices continue to decline further, making economies of scale and connectivity even more important.

The cleverness and determination with which each great power uses its sphere to garner more power is very important. The balance of power shifts to:

- Those who can mobilize the maximum power from their existing spheres to counter competitive compression whenever it is crucial
- Those who are best at executing the four competitive compression strategies against a targeted rival
- Those who select the correct pattern of growth (even if some individual growth efforts fail) to circumvent the pattern of competitive compression they face, and who do so without bringing new sources of compression upon themselves

THE SIBYLLINE BOOKS: THE CHALLENGE OF EVOLVING WITH IMPERFECT VISION

According to legend, Tarquinius Superbus (the last king of Rome during the period before Rome became an empire) was offered a set of nine books of wisdom by the sibyl of Cumae. These Sibylline Books, as they were called, laid out the entire destiny of Rome, but proud Tarquinius haggled over the price and the angry sibyl ultimately burned six of the nine volumes. The remaining three books were kept in the Temple of Jupiter to be consulted in times of extreme emergency. Unfortunately for Rome, this partial set of books offered only an incomplete vision of where the empire was headed.

Many of the most successful of today's firms would consider themselves lucky if they could know in advance three-ninths of what the future held for them or their industry. With 2,000 years of history behind us, we can now see the inevitability of the decline of the Roman Empire that its own leaders failed to recognize until it was too late. The marvel is not that Rome fell, but that it endured for so long—far longer than any great power in business. Rome endured through selecting growth strategies that took into account the type of competitive compression it was facing at the time. After defeating Carthage and Macedonia, Rome extended its supremacy for centuries by following its natural growth pattern: pioneering. This allowed the empire to grow along the path of least resistance for centuries, and to adjust to the competitive compression it felt from rival empires in the East. Later, Rome switched to a nomad growth strategy when the Germanic barbarians applied too much competitive compression on the western part of Rome's sphere, forcing it to migrate its core to the east.

Like the leaders of Rome, you too can push forward the evolution of your sphere of influence by adding or dropping zones to suit your natural growth patterns and to circumvent or counter competitive compression when necessary. While even the greatest empires ultimately fall, those that skillfully evolve can grow their power without exhausting their power to do so. And they can sustain their strategic supremacy even in the face of discontinuous change and competitive attacks. We might paraphrase Heraclitus and say, "nothing endures but great powers that change."

Chapter 3

Paradigms for Power

Routing Your Resources to Unleash
the Potential of Your Sphere

OVERVIEW

What gives your sphere of influence its power? Even some of the most successful companies in the world fail to recognize how spheres—including their own—follow certain paradigms for power. Depending on which paradigm you choose, your company may operate as a walled, fluid, colonial, or advanced sphere of influence. Each of these distinct types embodies a dramatically different pattern of resource routing—how you move your financial, human, and other assets around your sphere of influence in ways that strengthen your company and create advantages over local, lesser, and nearby great powers. By understanding your sphere's paradigm for power—and the far-reaching implications of its resource routing pattern—you then gain a more insightful picture of how you can apply what *you have to* where *it will do the most good. You will unleash the power of your sphere . . . and you will achieve and maintain strategic supremacy.*

SUPERCHARGED AND POWER-PACKED

Throughout history, great political empires have supercharged and power-packed their spheres of influence by using one of four major paradigms for power necessary to achieve strategic supremacy. The ancient Chinese Han

Dynasty, for example, established a powerful "walled" sphere of influence. The dynasty used its resources to build the Great Wall to clearly define its borders from the uncivilized world and block attacks by its enemies. By using its resources in this way, the Han Dynasty, as well as successive Chinese dynasties, was able to accumulate centuries of wealth without being plundered by the West. To this day, the Great Wall of China is still the only man-made construction that can be seen from outer space.

Yet another paradigm for power is the "fluid" sphere of influence, as exemplified by Alexander the Great's empire. Alexander marched his troops across Turkey and into Persia and India without ever stopping to define and solidify his empire's borders, hence its "fluid" nature. By routing his human resources in this way, Alexander was able to capture and absorb the wealth of these invaded territories.

A third paradigm for power is the "colonial" sphere of influence. The British built one of the most important colonial spheres the world has ever known. At its peak, one quarter of the world's citizens lived under British rule. When it controlled the American colonies, Britain followed a mercantile system, importing raw materials from its distanced holding to feed its growing manufacturing base, and the rising demand of its citizens for manufactured goods. Later, the Industrial Revolution enhanced the wealth of Britain greatly, so the British evolved into what Lenin (the infamous Russian revolutionary) called an imperialistic system. An imperialistic system (according to Lenin) routes its excess resources (military, technological, and investment funds money) from the core and invests those resources into its colonies. By moving to an imperialistic system, the British Empire was able to strengthen some of its colonies so that they were better able to buy more manufactured goods from the British. Following a colonial paradigm, Britain's sphere of influence was able to achieve long-term economic and military preeminence relative to its European rivals, and relative to the colonies.

Finally, the fourth and most complex paradigm for power is the "advanced" sphere of influence, as exemplified by the United States post–World War II. Some have argued that America's sphere resembles the British colonial imperialistic sphere, but there are significant differences. The United States routes its resources to empower not only its own sphere, but the spheres of *other* players who are part of a larger American sphere. This is done, through the use of foreign aid (e.g., the Marshall Plan) and the extension of American military protection over others, including through NATO and the nuclear strategic umbrella that covers Canada and Japan. In addition, the use of alliances and free trade has allowed the different pieces of America's loosely knit sphere to strengthen each other, without having to route all resource transfers through the United States. Members within the sphere are allowed to trade among themselves, and even on occasion with America's opponents. America's advanced sphere of influence demonstrates the seeming irony, that a sphere with a looser hold on its constituents can prove to be even more powerful than an empire that maintains an iron grip over its sphere. With its advanced sphere paradigm, America has been able to increase its global influence and economic power from post–World War II through today. This is evidenced by its strategic supremacy over the Soviets, who collapsed despite having created their own colonial sphere in Eastern Europe and parts of the Third World.

Walled spheres. Fluid spheres. Colonial spheres. Advanced spheres. The historical paradigms described above are as applicable to great powers in business as they are to powerful political empires. Indeed, a business's chosen paradigm for power directly affects a company's ability to achieve strategic supremacy in the geo-product markets that matter most to it. Like the Han Dynasty, Standard Oil created a walled sphere of influence that gave J.D. Rockefeller supremacy in the oil business. Rockefeller erected a significant entry barrier in the oil industry by acquiring and consolidating most oil refineries. Drillers who wanted to reach the market had to pay a fee to pass through Rockefeller's "wall." In addition, Rockefeller used his heavy-handed influence with distributors (pushing them to carry only Standard Oil's products) to prohibit other refiners from succeeding in the industry.

Comparing Alexander the Great's empire to Rubbermaid may seem far-fetched, even laughable, but in its heyday Rubbermaid created a fluid sphere of influence with ever-changing boundaries. Acting like marauders, the company constantly entered new territories beyond food containers and kitchen items, making its mark from toys to toolsheds by surprising the traditional leaders with a high-quality plastic version of wood and metal products while these traditional leaders continued to believe that plastic wasn't good enough. Thanks to its "conquest" of numerous new markets, Rubbermaid succeeded in becoming even more powerful than the industry's previous leader, Tupperware. No one ever expected Alexander to reach India; nor did anyone ever expect Rubbermaid to become the manufacturer of the best-selling car in the world—the plastic Flintstones-like kiddie car that actually sold more units per year than any real car sold in America. In 1999, Rubbermaid became part of Newell Rubbermaid, an even more aggressive firm with a fluid sphere, gobbling up not only plastic products but also endless varieties of nonplastic products that complement Rubbermaid's product line

Like the British Empire, Motorola's supremacy in the cellular phone and pager markets during the 1980s and early '90s was based on a colonial sphere of influence. The key to Motorola's power was its ability to route its technology and engineering resources from its peripheral microprocessing chip business and two-way radio business to set the American standard for consumer wireless telecommunications and infrastructure. Motorola's pioneering efforts to create the wireless industry peaked with the introduction of its Startak phone. Later Motorola began leveraging its core in wireless communications into new markets, such as satellites and systems for cars like OnStar. Thanks to the look and feel of its *Star Trek*–like communicator, the company made it clear to the world that the future had arrived two centuries earlier than even *Star Trek*'s creator Gene Roddenberry had envisioned.

And though Bill Gates and the federal government have had their differences recently, Microsoft rose to supremacy in the software market by creating an advanced sphere of influence with Intel, not unlike the United States' advanced sphere of influence. Microsoft's alliances with Intel, NBC, and numerous others benefited several players, while creating power for Microsoft in its early struggle for supremacy over IBM and beyond. Microsoft's complex interactions (not all centrally controlled like the other sphere designs) allowed the company to pool and route superior resources for setting the standard in PC operating systems, graphical user interfaces, and software applications like Microsoft Word and Excel.

Today, as much of the thrust of competition extends to the cyberworld, these historical paradigms continue to play out among the most successful Internet companies. Yahoo's fluid sphere is using a marauder strategy (now known as content aggregation) to constantly move into newer content areas. Cisco Systems has created a colonial sphere of influence with routers (the equivalent of the switchboards of the old telecom systems) as its core and its colonies in other equipment peripheral to that core. Cisco is working to gain preeminence in the peripheral devices that go from the Internet into the router, thus protecting its core by preventing anyone else from gaining a position that could be used to invade its core router market. And some would argue that Microsoft's advanced sphere of influence actually evolved into a walled empire, with the company using its barriers to entry created by owning the graphical user interface residing on most desktops in the world. In fact, Gates's walled sphere successfully (but perhaps not legally) used its walls to block Netscape's access to PC manufacturers who might put Netscape on their equipment.

Why is it helpful to understand these paradigms for power? Why does it matter whether your company thinks of itself as a walled, fluid, colonial, or advanced sphere of influence? Because by thinking of your sphere of influence as operating within one of these paradigms—even for a limited period of time—you gain a logic and vision for how you unleash your sphere's full power. As I emphasized in Chapter 2, companies leading the evolution of their spheres often have to grow in seemingly haphazard manners, depending on factors ranging from competitive compression to unforeseen growth opportunities. Since you can't rely on "logical" spherical growth, the logic of the paradigm becomes even more critical in helping you maintain a framework or focus for creating power. Each paradigm creates a distinct type of sphere. Each accumulates wealth differently. Each projects its power differently. And each establishes a different norm of behavior in the greater competitive environment. By understanding these paradigms and recognizing which one best meets the needs of your company, you can then use this framework for routing your resources to the zones in your sphere that will maximize your power and help you achieve and sustain strategic supremacy.

THE POWER OF RESOURCE ROUTING:
KNOWING WHERE AND WHEN TO MOVE YOUR ASSETS

The heart of a large company's power rests with the firm's ability to move financial and human resources around the sphere of influence in ways that strengthen the sphere and create advantages over local, lesser, and nearby great powers. For example, depending on your priorities and ambitions, you can route resources to key forward positions for offensive purposes, buffer zones for defensive purposes, or pivotal zones for growth purposes. Resource routing systems can be coordinated, but they are more often than not institutionalized—that is, turned into routines and standard operating procedures that are followed instinctively. If your resource routing pattern is correct, you have the ability to project your power onto lesser powers, both inside and outside your sphere. In turn, by projecting your power successfully, you establish the norms of your relationships with other great powers within the larger competitive space.

Each paradigm for power—walled, fluid, colonial, and advanced—embodies an extremely different resource routing pattern. Each sets the direction of resource flows, and hence where you project your power. As a consequence, they regulate the degree or nature of conflict within the competitive space. Thus, by understanding the pattern of resource routing of your sphere's paradigm, you gain a more insightful picture of how you can apply *what* you have to *where* it will do the most good in helping you achieve and maintain strategic supremacy.

Here, I want to make some important distinctions. When I refer to resource routing, I'm not talking about intraorganizational trade or resource allocation. Intraorganizational trade refers to trading goods and services between subunits in an equitable exchange. One unit sells something. The other unit pays for it. And both subunits benefit from the transaction. In contrast, resource routing is about taking the resources out of one geo-product zone (not necessarily corresponding to a subunit's market scope) and using those resources in another zone of the sphere. It is a calculated transfer of financial, human, and other resources determined by your priorities, as well as by where your company faces internal unrest and external threats.

Resource routing is more than resource allocation. Resource allocation is a formal activity undertaken by headquarters, such as the budgeting of funds for operations and capital investments. The process is routinized; however, the direction of the movement of the resources is not explicitly inherent in the type of budgeting system that has been adopted. The direction that resources flow in a resource allocation system can change from year to year, or even from project to project, if investment opportunities are reviewed using financial evaluation tools such as hurdle rates and internal rate of return calculations. Such methods can inadvertently undermine the strength of the sphere if people don't understand the larger purpose of the sphere.

Resource routing is more than process. It's the strategy that underlies the movement of all types of resources toward a bigger goal. Over the long run, patterns of resource routing can be designed to achieve different goals, including improving the sphere's ability to defend itself, strengthen its core, create growth opportunities in the periphery (or core), or fend off a pattern of competitive compression that has been going on for years. Because resources are limited, firms must prioritize or choose among these goals, necessitating a choice of a particular pattern of resource flows.

The real power of the sphere comes from defining the goals for your resource routing, and then maintaining a long-term pattern of resource routing to support those goals. Many firms grow into new product and geographic markets because they hope to capture the benefits of resource sharing (synergies) and resource efficiency through global economies of scale that spread fixed costs over more volume. But while resource sharing and efficiency may be some of the goals underlying resource routing, resource routing can achieve power in and of itself by concentrating resources on a given geo-product market. Your firm can drop sustained mega-tonnage on any geo-product zone. This becomes a source of power that can be used to keep order in your sphere or to project your sphere's power into the spheres of rivals.

In addition, the power of resource routing, per se, can be much more effective than either resource sharing or efficiency. For example, many companies can attest that capturing cross-product and cross-border synergies can be difficult, if not impossible. Organizational structures, such as the matrix organization, were designed to help capture synergies, yet matrix structure has brought its own set of headaches. Administering the complexity of a matrix system can result in continual conflict between country managers and product managers, slowing decision making and adding lots of overhead costs. In the case of hopelessly complex matrix structures, the cure can actually be worse than the disease.

Similarly, global economies of scale can be equally difficult to capture. Large firms try to spread R&D, branding, overhead, and centralized plant and equipment costs over global sales. But economies of scale are not universally available. In fact, as a recent Harvard Business School study of twenty global industries found, "the problem with these levers (economies of scale) is that they are harder to manipulate than they are to identify."[1] Even in heavy industries like aluminum, where economies of scale are expected to be prevalent, this study reported that the Alcoa-Reynolds merger resulted in a cost reduction of only about one percent of combined sales. Moreover, the authors found that cross-country differences in costs, prices, and profitability, as well as exchange rate fluctuations, may make economies of scale difficult to realize.[2]

Despite the fact that resource routing is the most realizable source of a large company's power, most firms have a limited vision as to how they can route their resources, often relying on a single model, while overlooking other options. In addition, firms often don't understand the nature of the power they've created with their resource routing. Traditionally, product portfolios are managed by allocating resources to the high-margin zones or the growth zones without a larger vision of the type of world they wish to create. For example, many managers may not realize that aggressive and constant routing of resources to growth markets typically forces others to join the "land grab," causing a world full of marauders and possibly stimulating markets to converge. In contrast, routing all resources to high-margin markets can create a world where others are easily able to surround and compress a sphere by occupying less desirable, but nevertheless large, markets from which to contain, constrict, strip, or domino into the sphere.

The sphere of influence model provides four paradigms that suggest logical patterns for routing your resources in ways that direct the power of the sphere toward three larger purposes:

1. Accumulating and creating wealth

2. Creating mechanisms to project your power over the rising players operating inside your sphere of influence

3. Establishing the norms of behavior in your relationship with nearby great powers

Each of these four paradigms is based on a different kind of sphere distinguished by the clarity of the sphere's borders and the degree of complexity underlying the transfer of resources among the different parts of the sphere (see Exhibit 3-1).

For the sake of clarity, I describe the four paradigms for power as "pure types," yet it is clear that these are simplifications. Spheres can be embedded in more than one paradigm at a time. For example, the British Empire's sphere in 1917 could be seen as a colonial sphere from a global perspective, but it was also an advanced sphere from the perspective of its relationships on the European continent. As mentioned earlier, Microsoft can be seen as walled (around DOS/Windows/Office Suite) or advanced (with its alliances with Intel and NBC) depending upon when and how you look at it. At any given time, a successful sphere of influence may even reflect a hybrid of the four paradigms, based on its needs at the time.

Nevertheless, understanding these paradigms for power makes it easier to identify benchmarks against which to compare your sphere, and to cre-

Borders of the Sphere

		Clearly Defined	Ill-Defined
Complexity of the Sphere's Resource Routing	**Simple**	Walled spheres	Fluid spheres
	Complex	Colonial spheres	Advanced spheres

Exhibit 3-1: Four Type of Spheres

ate a common language for people selecting a vision for their firm's resource routing strategy. Without a resource routing strategy, the power that results from your sphere may be unplanned or uncontrolled, at best. At worst, your sphere's power may be nonexistent or even destructive because the purpose of the sphere and its vision are unclear or misdirected. The four paradigms for power serve to remind us of what Adlai Stevenson once said: "Power corrupts, but *lack* of power corrupts absolutely."

THE WALLED SPHERE:
GOOD FENCES MAKE GOOD BUSINESS

Walled spheres have clearly defined borders and contiguous controlled territory. By erecting entry barriers around the sphere's vital interests (inner walls) or buffer zones (outer walls), the walled sphere limits the threats of attack from outside firms and the defection of customers from within. A walled sphere is firmly committed to the core. Because its priorities are to strengthen the core and vital interests, the sphere employs a straightforward pattern for resource routing. All resources are focused on keeping the walls strong (i.e., building high barriers to entry), concentrating on markets inside the wall, damping unrest (upstart competitors), and maximizing the profits derived from the customers inside the walls. Resources are also used to accommodate a developer growth strategy within the walls. This concentration of resources, as well as the sphere's walled impenetrability, combines to create the sphere's power. The point of the paradigm—the sphere's larger purpose—is to protect the existing sphere. Of all the four paradigms of power, the walled sphere of influence is the one that most easily can be carried too far and result in an abuse of power that could trigger antitrust problems.

In modern business, DeBeers provides one of the best examples of a walled sphere, with its walls encircling the diamond market in the United States, Europe, Latin America, Australia, Africa, and, more recently, Japan. Within its walled sphere, the company holds three-quarters of the world's uncut diamond supply, giving it the power to restrict world supply and influence prices. DeBeers's "wall" is based on barriers to entry created by its leadership over diamond producers, distribution, cutting, and access to jewelry manufacturers. In addition, the company's strong ideology, as embodied in its phenomenal marketing campaign, "a diamond is forever," has enabled DeBeers to capture the hearts and minds of customers. As a result, the company is able to build customer demand and keep prices high. This combination of barriers and ideology (a reporter once commented that meeting with DeBeers managers is like a visit to a "religious sect"[3]) has allowed DeBeers to sustain the the diamond empire established by Cecil Rhodes in 1888.

Wealth Accumulation through Feudal Power

Like a medieval king, a powerful walled sphere extracts monopoly profits from captive customers. Potential invaders are helpless to attack the monopoly prices within the walls, enabling the king and his nobles to hoard their abnormally high profits. This method of creating profits reflects a business strategy described in Michael Porter's Five Forces model (a model that suggests you build barriers to entry and then within those barriers you use your monopoly power over customers to charge them extra). DeBeers apparently exemplifies this model for wealth creation in its ability to produce monopoly prices through its feudal power over the diamond industry. When DeBeers extended its walls around the Japanese market, as is the company's pattern, it absorbed this new market completely into its sphere. The extension of its walls appears to have paid off nicely for the company, as evidenced by an increase in the percentage of Japanese brides receiving diamond engagement rings from 5 percent to 70 percent between 1960 and 1997.[4] (Note that while Japan is a noncontiguous geographic market, it represents a contiguous product market.)

The "Walled" School of Power Projection

A great power with a walled sphere of influence doesn't go looking for a fight, but if a rival even thinks about invading its turf, the company has one thing to say: "Go ahead. Make my day." Walled spheres keep the competition outside their borders through a tough reputation for swift, severe punishment. An extreme historical example of this form of power projection is Vlad "the Impaler" Tepes, the fifteenth-century Romanian dictator who discouraged the Turks through his penchant for displaying impaled bodies on his border. (Some historians speculate that Vlad served as the basis for Bram Stoker's Dracula.)

A much less extreme, yet equally effective example from the business realm is DeBeers's tough enforcement policies for "suppressing" uprisings within its sphere, as well as repelling invasion attempts by great powers outside its sphere. For example, in 1996 several lesser powers, the Australian producers, were members of DeBeers's sphere of influence. But these Australian producers became unhappy with DeBeers's restrictions over the market and tried to defect. Quickly, they found they couldn't go it alone under the pressure of DeBeers's mighty competitive advantages. DeBeers also managed to undermine an external invasion by a great power outside its sphere, the Russians. Despite the fact that Siberian mines account for one quarter of the world's gem-quality diamonds,[5] the Russian producers were eventually made to join DeBeers's sphere in order to gain access to worldwide distribution, quality diamond cutting, and jewelry production. Given the strength of DeBeers's barriers, even against the formidable foe of Russia, it seems that the DeBeers walled sphere, like its diamonds, may indeed be forever—or at least until the fiercely protected cartel meets a match capable of making it succumb to free market forces.

Norms of Behavior Based on Isolationism

The walled sphere practices a policy of isolationism, attempting to avoid conflict by creating clear and defensible walls around non-overlapping spheres of influence. In other words, a walled sphere stakes out its turf and stays there—unless another sphere gains so much power it poses a threat with its ability to overcome the walls. DeBeers has isolated itself on a mound of diamonds, far from the producers of other gemprecious stones and precious metals.

Inherent Challenges: When the Walls Come Tumbling Down

For spheres shaped by the walled paradigm, there are two inherent challenges in maintaining strategic supremacy. First, the walled sphere can become very inward looking and susceptible to being surrounded and contained by a rival building a much larger sphere around it in preparation for a later attack. Walled spheres may also be vulnerable to competitive compression strategies such as gradual constriction, sequential stripping, and toppling dominoes, particularly if the protective "walls" turn out to be more permeable than expected.

For example, eBay created a walled sphere by concentrating all of its resources into building a brand name in the United States as the premier on-line auction site. But while doing so, the company failed to anticipate or deal with rising rivals in Europe. As a result, eBay's site has so far been unable to establish the same preeminence in Europe as it has in America. What's more, it remains questionable whether the company will be able to wall off the United States from these European-based sites, or other sites such as Amazon.com. In cyberspace, walled spheres may suffer from much more permeable barriers than spheres based in the bricks-and-mortar world.

A second inherent challenge is that a sphere's walls can come crashing down due to revolution. If the sphere captures monopoly profits from power over its customers and suppliers, eventually the customers and suppliers are likely to get together and revolt. For example, when P&G's Pampers brand of disposable diapers became too dominant, supermarkets and paper companies combined to challenge Pampers with private labels. These private labels eventually drove profits out of the diaper business.

THE FLUID SPHERE: MARAUDERS, GUERRILLAS, AND SHIFTING BOUNDARIES

Fluid spheres have blurry, indistinct, and ever-changing borders. Resources are constantly being routed into uncaptured zones within or near the sphere. A company with a fluid sphere routes its resources to grow through any or all of the five growth strategies—developer, pioneer, discoverer, nomad, or opportunist. Fluid spheres are created by firms acting "hypercompetitively," using continuous disruption to seize new zones and then move on. Companies with fluid spheres purposely create chaos by shifting the basis of competition to new critical success factors. In this way, they make it easier to seize new zones because competitors are no

longer able to respond or defend themselves effectively. The use of se-
quences of disruptive and temporary advantages to create wealth is most
successful in geo-product markets that are changing rapidly.

Some companies with fluid spheres act like "guerrillas," moving their
resources from the easy-to-capture (outlying) zones to the more difficult-
to-capture (mainstream) zones. Sam Walton's Wal-Mart started like this,
first capturing rural areas (much like Mao's position in China before he
took control of the cities away from Chiang Kai-shek), then moving into
the suburbs, and later the cities. The larger purpose of this guerrilla pattern of resource routing is to consolidate the sphere by moving from
niches and smaller positions into the geo-product zones that someday
might comprise a stronger core. For Walton, this strategy has contributed
to Wal-Mart's rapid rise from a single store in Rogers, Arkansas, in 1962,
to America's largest business (based on number of employees) in 2000.
Wal-Mart now has a reach so broad that it is transforming whole industries, from consumer manufacturing to retailing and food processing and
sales. Indeed, Wal-Mart is lending extra momentum to important elements of the new economy, including the globalization of manufacturing
and the use of technology to achieve productivity gains.[6]

Other companies with fluid spheres act like "marauders," routing their
resources to the edge of the sphere to be used for invasion of nearby zones.
For marauders, the larger purpose is to achieve critical mass and then absorb the wealth of nearby critical zones, the way Enron has been expanding its geographic scope in the energy industry and its product scope in
trading other commodities.

Within the fluid sphere paradigm, it can often be difficult to distin-
guish between guerrillas and marauders. Rubbermaid in its heyday provides an example. Fueled by its goal of plasticizing the world, Rubbermaid
relied on both guerrilla strategies to create new niches within existing markets, and marauder strategies to enter new markets.

Wealth Accumulation through Temporary Advantages

It takes a lot of energy to succeed as a marauder or guerrilla, since you
need to constantly create new advantages, new products, and new value

for customers. Yet the reason marauders and guerrillas make money is because their slower moving opponents have to spend even more energy catching up and reacting. In essence, the fluid sphere of influence creates wealth by constantly improving itself, and by doing so more quickly and inexpensively than rivals. The wealth comes from entering and absorbing "value bubbles," untapped markets that offer temporary profits, lasting only until others follow, next-generation products appear, or customer preferences change. A value bubble also has potential to expand into a lasting market or to become a platform for growth into another value bubble market. The fluid sphere with the greatest ability to see, capture, and move on to new value bubbles becomes the odds-on favorite in the race for power vacuums. And this can be especially powerful wherever customer tastes and product characteristics are constantly changing.

The "Fluid" School of Power Projection

The fluid sphere projects its power by exhausting or outmaneuvering rivals through an ongoing series of surprise tactics and preemptive strikes. Marauders and guerrillas both seek to strike first, strike hard, and move on without need for an extended (and costly) defense of their gains. Typically marauders expand through the use of pioneer and discoverer growth strategies, and less frequently nomad and opportunist growth strategies. Guerrillas, on the other hand, typically use a developer strategy, and less frequently nomad and opportunist growth strategies. By the time the rivals catch on, the new boundaries of the sphere of influence are a *fait accompli*. To avoid the potential for exhaustion in this type of power projection, marauders and guerrillas know how to conserve energy and resources through preemptive strikes, or leveraging the weaknesses of rivals.

- *Marauders project their power by exploiting markets with high pre-emption potential.* The aggressive marauder targets markets with high preemptive potential—that is, large markets controlled by a small number of customers (see Exhibit 3-2). The marauder can enter quickly at a reasonable cost, hold on to customers more easily when followers arrive, and gain economies of scale that can be used to secure the rest of the market. This small number of large customers allows the marauder to preempt other great powers by rapidly scooping up key accounts. If the marauder secures these accounts, it may preempt a countermove by a rival empire because the market no longer holds enough potential to make a fight worth the risk. Similar strategies can be used with respect to pre-

---

Supply Systems

(1) Secure access to raw materials or components
(2) Preempt production equipment
(3) Dominate supply logistics

Product

(1) Introduce new product lines
(2) Develop dominant design
(3) Position
(4) Secure accelerated approval from agencies
(5) Secure product development and delivery skills
(6) Expand scope of the product

Production Systems

(1) Proprietary processes
(2) Aggressive capacity expansion
(3) Vertical integration with key suppliers
(4) Secure scarce and critical production skills

Customers

(1) Segmentation
(2) Build early brand awareness
(3) Train customers in usage skills
(4) Capture key accounts

Distribution and Service Systems

(1) Occupation of prime locations
(2) Preferential access to key distributors
(3) Dominance of distribution logistics
(4) Access to superior service capabilities
(5) Development of distributor skills

Source: Ian MacMillan, "Preemptive Strategies," *Journal of Business Strategy*, 1983.

Exhibit 3-2: Sources of Preemptive Opportunities

empting distribution channels, market segments, customer types, geographic locations, technologies, and other strategic factors.

- *Guerrillas project their power by exploiting the inflexibilities or response barriers of competitors.* Guerrillas also gain the advantage over competitors by hitting them where it hurts—right in their inflexibilities. By developing a mental model of a competitor's strengths and inherent inflexibilities, guerrillas are able to perform what Peter Drucker calls "entrepreneurial judo"[7]—the art of throwing the competition's own weight and inflexibilities against itself. The guerrilla's rival is also foiled by exit barriers that inhibit it from moving out of positions it already occupies, as well as inertia barriers that slow its responses to the guerrilla's actions (see Exhibit 3-3).

In the 1960s, acting as both a marauder and a guerrilla, Sony took advantage of AT&T's regulatory inflexibilities by recognizing the full potential of the transistor invented by AT&T's Bell Labs. Sony bought rights to use the transistor for a mere $25,000 and preempted the transistor radio industry.

Norms of Behavior Based on Militarism and Expansionism

Great powers with fluid spheres of influence live—and sometimes die—by the sword. Their credo: survival of the fittest. Fluid spheres meet every new power outside their sphere of influence with an attack, causing competitors and customers to react to their moves. This militarism works as long as the sphere has superiority over its targets, and as long as it can keep moving forward without needing to civilize and govern the territory it conquers. The marauder Enron stormed into the Philadelphia market just as the walled sphere of PECO Energy Co. was putting the finishing touches on a plan worked out with regulators and consumer groups. PECO hoped this plan would sustain its walled monopoly for a few more years during a transition to a more open market. Enron arrived with a blitz of advertising and lobbying for an alternative plan to open the market more quickly. The marauder was at the gate, using the aggressive tactics that had built Enron into an empire of over $65 billion in assets.

Enron's sphere has evolved from its focus as a gas-pipeline business to a global power merchant to a trader of many things. Enron became the

- **Economies of scale:** High investment is needed to be cost competitive.
- **Differentiated product:** Customers identify and are loyal to a specific product or brand.
- **Capital requirements:** Large amounts of capital are required to provide credit, lease equipment, build image by advertising.
- **Switching costs:** Customers would have to pay a lot to switch brands.
- **Distribution channels:** Access to channels is blocked.
- **Components and raw materials:** Access to supplies is blocked.
- **Prime locations occupied**
- **Preferential treatment from governments**
- **Experience benefits:** Know-how and experience benefits are kept from competition.
- **High expected retaliation:** Competitor may retaliate violently.
- **Price cutting**
- **Lack of opportunities to share costs** (among many other products and markets)
- **Specialized skills:** Access to critical skills is blocked.
- **Interest groups:** Threat of, or actual, government, union, etc., objections to move by competitors.
- **Patents**

2. Exit Barriers That Slow Movement Out of Current Markets (*Porter [1980], Harrigan [1980], and others*)
   - **Effect of large investment write-offs**
   - **Damage to prestige/image of company**
   - **Damage to ego of management**
   - **Government prescription:** Government prevents exit.
   - **Large clean-up costs:** To leave sites in original condition.
   - **Union agreements:** Prevent exit.
   - **Shared costs:** Which would have to be borne by other products/markets.
   - **Suppliers, customers, distributors:** Prevent exit.

3. Inertia Barriers That Delay All Types of Responses (*Identified by MacMillan and McCafferty [1982]*)
   - **Strategic choice:** To control the move would be counterstrategic.
   - **Strategic challenge:** Move is regarded as nonthreatening.
   - **Distraction:** Competitor is distracted by major problems or opportunities.
   - **Visibility:** Move is not visible to competitor.
   - **Portfolio position:** Division affected has low priority in company.
   - **Structural:** No specific division is responsible, or motivated to respond.
   - **Procedures:** Correct response calls for major policy revisions or costly revisions of procedures.
   - **Bureaucratic politics:** Response creates jurisdictional disputes and bureaucratic disruptions.

* Each competitor will have a unique set of response barriers. In fact the creative challenge of guerrillas and marauders lies in identification of the barriers unique to their competitors.

Source: Ian MacMillan, "Seizing Competitive Initiative," in *Competitive Strategic Management,* edited by Robert B. Lamb, Englewood Cliffs, NJ: Prentice Hall, 1984, p. 274.

*Exhibit 3-3: Some Common Response Barriers**

dominant gas and electric power trader in the United States. It then moved on to be the largest gas and power trader in Europe. By 2001, its total worldwide volume reached a whopping 74 trillion BTUs of energy per day. Recently, it has opened innovative trading operations in paper, coal, plastic, and even Internet bandwidth. The company also has started selling broadband capacity on fiber-optics networks. And, since inception in late 1999, Enron's eCommerce transaction platform for all these products surpassed one million transactions, with over $685 billion in total gross value (as of July 12, 2001.) With the exception of broadband and India, almost all of this growth was highly profitable. It is also targeting expansion to the ossified power industries in Japan and India where it can take advantage of other slow, sleepy utilities. Enron, a marauder from the natural gas market, has moved into market after market in the United States and abroad with great success. Since December 1999, Enron's number of products has grown by over 2700% and its delivery locations by over 375% (as of July 2001.) Enron wasn't waiting for the walls to fall; it was determined to drive them down.[8]

Inherent Challenges: Running Out of Steam . . . and Room

For spheres shaped by the fluid paradigm, the challenge is twofold. These firms may exhaust themselves and be tempted to settle down, but lack the capabilities for ruling a more stable sphere. Or they may run out of room to expand, forcing them to stop their progress unless they can radically reinvent their capabilities.

Fluid spheres, whether constructed through marauder or guerrilla tactics, are the most impermanent, frequently shifting to other paradigms for power. Maintaining strategic supremacy as a hypercompetitor demands a level of flexibility and creativity that few organizations can sustain for more than a few decades. Nevertheless firms such as Wal-Mart, 3M, and Hewlett-Packard have been able to sustain fluid spheres for decades with great success.

THE COLONIAL SPHERE:
WHAT GOES AROUND COMES AROUND

A colonial sphere consists of a core and peripheral geo-product zones, which are not necessarily near or similar to the core. This type of sphere tends to expand through a discoverer growth strategy, looking afield for new space to colonize but never abandoning its core. Because the sphere owns these peripheral holdings outright and is committed to keeping them, the borders of this type of sphere are clearly defined. Contrast this to fluid spheres with borders that ebb and flow across different geo-product markets, leaving the exact perimeter of the sphere less defined.

Given the wide differences that can exist between a colonial sphere's core and its more peripheral markets, the sphere has a more complex pattern for routing resources than walled or fluid spheres. One type of colonial sphere, the mercantile model, routes resources from the periphery directly to the core. The larger purpose is to strengthen the core so that it has the ability to suppress internal uprisings within the core and fend off external attacks against the core from other great powers. Another type of colonial sphere, the imperialistic model, routes resources from the core to the peripheral zones. The larger purpose is to create growth opportunities that will benefit the core.

Colonial spheres are necessary when walls no longer protect your firm against overpowering marauders or when there is incessant guerrilla activity inside the walls. Colonial spheres allow you to accumulate even greater wealth from outside your original walled core so you can fend off these attacks and preserve your sphere. The colonial sphere, therefore, can be used to change the balance of power.

By the year 2000, Sony (which had a fluid sphere in the 1960s) had grown to a much larger, highly diverse global colonial sphere, utilizing both imperialistic and mercantile tactics. Using the imperialistic model, the company routes resources from its core geo-product markets (competencies in electronic miniaturization and brand name) to compete in several markets, including televisions, VCRs, LCDs, some computer chips, and peripheral devices such as CD-ROM drives and monitors. It uses its branding to move into new digital electronic markets, including personal computers, video games, and more powerful digital consumer electronics. Sony's moves into movie making and cinemas completed its shift from a pioneer growth strategy to a discoverer strategy. The company originally thought of these moves as a mercantile strategy, arguing that its core market in hardware was commoditizing and needed help. They thought only content, bundled with hardware, would create competitive advantages in their core in the future. As it turns out, the bundling of content and hardware was difficult because consumers would not buy movies and records that played only on Sony hardware. Instead, Sony's moves actually turned out to be an imperialistic strategy. The underlying basis of Sony's strength in its core—a brand name that means quality and innovation, excellent marketing, and wide distribution—became the resource that was routed from the core and into these new territories.[9]

Wealth Accumulation through Cross-Subsidization

Colonial spheres route knowledge and resources from the core to the periphery and vice versa. Either the core subsidizes the periphery, or the periphery subsidizes the core. Instead of erecting a wall, this type of sphere makes money by having a valuable resource that many customers want to use outside the walls of a narrowly defined geo-product market. The company, in essence, uses its core's competencies to colonize the world, or it uses the assets of its colonies to strengthen the core.

The "Colonial" School of Power Projection

Colonial spheres project their power on local rivals and lesser powers through the rapid deployment of superior resources. Zone by zone, the firm maintains control of its colonial sphere by routing resources to hot spots as they arise. At the same time, the colonial sphere helps the local rivals and lesser powers operating within its sphere by providing protection from other great powers that could enter and grab the niches of these smaller players. These local rivals and lesser powers find that they live under a strategic umbrella that no great power dares to penetrate for fear of retaliation, especially if these local and lesser powers are located in the great power's core or vital markets. Thus, the local and lesser powers are safe to live in their niches and hold onto their smaller positions, as long as they don't threaten their colonial "big brother."

The ability to protect and intervene in multiple geo-product markets, often at the same time, requires the colonial sphere to have a centrally co-ordinated but flexible resource routing system. The British relied on a superior navy and control over key ports and waterways throughout the world (Hong Kong, Suez, Singapore, Cape of Good Hope, etc.) to allow for rapid deployment of resources to and from its colonies. In business, a company with a colonial sphere also needs rapid deployment capabilities and other methods to maintain and protect its peripheral markets. But at the same time, it must also be conscientious of conserving its human and financial resources, because it is impossible to protect its position and to douse disruption in every geo-product market at once.

- *Rapid deployment.* Trouble brews quickly. That's why the colonial sphere has to have a flexible resource routing mechanism, capable of moving financial and human resources quickly and catching potential dissidents off guard. In business this translates to surprising competitors in diverse markets. To do so, colonial spheres create flexible cost structures (for example, low-fixed-cost, non–capital-intensive manufacturing systems that can be expanded or contracted as needed, rather than large-investment fixed plants). And they use flexible manufacturing equipment (which has a high fixed cost but even more applications). This kind of flexibility enables the company to rapidly enter markets, swiftly switch gears, and "keep the locals guessing" about its next moves. Baxter Health Care is one extreme example of this flexibility. The company has used "rapid prototyping" and "mobile factories" to set up in new markets within a mere twenty-four hours after receiving specifications. Imagine the surprise of a local competitor who wakes up to find such a company setting up shop in its own backyard. Canon too has used the flexibility of its competencies in precision mechanics, fine optics, and microelectronics to move quickly from cameras to industries as diverse as copiers, semiconductor lithographic equipment, and laser imaging and cell analyzers.[10]

- *Buffering the buffers and vital interests.* Buffers protect the sphere's core. But what buffers the buffers and vital interests? The British Empire used Burma and Nepal as a buffer against Chinese aggression in its vital interest, India. Similarly, colonial spheres in business can also protect their vital interests through a loosely linked portfolio of products, some of which are related to products associated with the core, but not directly useful to it. For example, big audit firms such as Ernst & Young have diversified from audit to tax to actuarial and financial advisory services to MIS systems to strategic advisory services and human-resource-related consulting. Each new addition is intended to support previously developed services by allowing bundling of multiple services. Of course, the concept of buffering vital interests can go on ad infinitum, making the sphere a fluid one or spreading the company too thin. In colonial spheres, buffers on buffers are carefully chosen, limited in scope, and relatively stable over time. Otherwise there are probably less resource-intense alternatives to defending the sphere's vital interests from attack. Ernst & Young, finding it had gone too far, sold some of its consulting services to Cap Gemini because of rising potential conflicts of interest with its core auditing business, as well as insufficient presence in the divested services.

Norms of Behavior Based on Mercantilism and Imperialism

Colonial powers enhance their power by gaining colonial territories. The purpose is to establish peripheral geo-product zones that strengthen and complement the core. In the event of a clash over the cores of two colonial powers, the peripheral zones can be used to support each power's fight to preserve its core. If skirmishes with other colonial powers occur, the players prefer to focus on the periphery, rather than on each other's core. But colonial powers escalate the conflict closer to, or inside, their cores when they run out of power vacuums—existing open territories or undiscovered territories—to compete over. In this way, colonial spheres change their power relative to other colonial spheres and develop resources that are beyond the reach of rival great powers. Britain discovered that its success in colonizing Africa, Australia, Canada, and India and other parts of Asia helped it survive World War I and World War II by using colonial resources to defend its interests in Europe.

A good example of the behavioral norms among colonial powers is the global struggle between AOL and Yahoo! Each player has been fighting to lock up local Internet service providers and content providers in its effort to gain global preeminence. During the struggle for these international markets, each colonial power has routed its resources from its core to its periphery. But as the battle between AOL and Yahoo! in their core American market continues to intensify, these colonial powers may find that their new international markets have become cash generators or content suppliers needed to win in the U.S. marketplace. Thus, the strength of each colonial system determines the relative power of the players in both the global struggle over colonies and in the defense of their cores.

Inherent Challenges: Trading Off between the Core and Periphery

For spheres shaped by the colonial paradigm, the challenge is to maintain a colonial style resource routing system with norms of behavior that do not take on a life of their own. As Britain learned with its colonies in America and India, when members of the colonial empire feel they are not getting their fair share, they will attempt to defect, and the cost of holding these colonies can escalate. In business, Arthur Andersen experienced this situation with its partners at Andersen Consulting, who demanded that AC be divested or that more of "their" profits be used for AC's growth and partner compensation, rather than being routed back to the partners at Arthur Andersen. Ultimately AC was spun off and became Accenture.

For marauders, the inherent challenge of the colonial sphere is that once the open territories have been captured, the great powers collide more aggressively, trying to sap each other's strengths by attacking each other's newly acquired colonies or using the colonies as a base to attack each other's cores. The players are therefore required to shift resources to the colonies or the core to defend their spheres from attack. This is the case with McDonald's and Burger King's geographic markets in the United States, where the streets are practically made out of hamburgers, but the hamburgers are no longer paving those streets with gold. Thus, these systems of mercantilism and imperialism help to determine the balance of power, or mutual destruction of the great powers.

THE ADVANCED SPHERE: ALL FOR ONE AND ONE FOR ALL

Like the other three paradigms, an advanced sphere is a collection of geo-product zones. However, this type of sphere is managed in a very different manner. The borders of advanced spheres are more elastic than walled and colonial spheres, with differing degrees of commitment to various zones on the periphery. Unlike the previous three paradigms in which the spheres occupy their geo-product zones primarily through controlling and owning their organizational subunits, the advanced sphere makes more use of alliances, fifty-fifty joint ventures, and minority investments to occupy some, but not all, of its zones. It is difficult to define the borders of the advanced sphere because the alliance partners may operate in many geo-product zones, with only some of these zones being within the sphere of influence of the central player.

Routing of resources within an advanced sphere occurs not only from the core to the periphery and vice versa, but also directly from one peripheral zone to another. In this way, the advanced sphere avoids the trade-offs and struggle over resources that can occur between core and peripheral markets in colonial spheres. With the advanced sphere's use of its more complex, spiderweb-like pattern of resource routing, it can often take advantage of opportunities that would never surface in a more centralized colonial sphere. Advanced spheres can become so sophisticated that multiple subsystems can evolve in different parts of the sphere, each with a different decentralized resource-routing pattern. Hence the advanced sphere may grow using any or all of the five evolutionary growth patterns. In addition, advanced spheres make extensive use of other people's money through alliances and creative financing mechanisms, such as limited partnerships for financing research and development, or shared plant, property, and equipment investment.

The larger purpose of the advanced sphere is to create an energized system in which the sphere's power is enhanced by simultaneously strengthening the company's core and peripheral zones, and its alliance partners.

The zones aid each other in an all-for-one and one-for-all pattern, depending on who needs help when.

Corning, Inc., the leader in the glass industry, provides one example of a company with an advanced sphere. The company built a series of joint ventures and alliances, including Dow Corning and Owens Corning, designed to combine its glass technologies with the manufacturing and distribution resources of other companies. Corning has built a system which takes core glass technology resources and deploys them to several peripheral businesses, including medical equipment, fiber optics, optoelectronics, and automotive substrates. Rather than controlling everything centrally, Corning's resource routing pattern among its internal resources and alliance partners allows the company to capture more opportunities than it could afford if it used only its internal resources. Corning also fosters human and technological transfers directly between its different geo-product zones in order to energize further its advanced sphere.

Corning also demonstrates the extreme flexibility of the borders of an advanced sphere. The company recently divested Corning Consumer Products, which once served as its core business. Once-core brand names, including Corelle, Pyrex, and CorningWare, were sold with the consumer products division because the company was migrating its core to specialty and high-tech glass. Corning has also continually experimented with its borders. For example, the company acquired a clinical lab company to buffer its glass-based medical equipment products because Corning considered its medical equipment division a vital interest for its core specialty glass business. But when Corning found it was transferring too much money away from its core specialty glass business to finance the clinical lab business, it divested the lab to free up resources. Some of these resources were transferred to a wider variety of glass-based medical equipment businesses to serve as buffers and vital interests to its original medical equipment business.

Wealth Accumulation through Reassembling the Pieces

Advanced spheres accumulate wealth by assembling lots of flexible subunits and alliances that can then be quickly and relatively inexpensively reassembled or discarded in the event of a revolutionary shift in the market-place. Oracle was a database management and data warehousing software company devoted to mainframe computers, work stations, and micro-computers. With the Internet revolution, the firm had to switch over to operating in a different world. To create its Oracle e-business Suite, the company needed to build business intelligence into the use of its software for electronic supply chain and customer processing management. Using its advanced sphere—including its internal resources, alliances, and li-censes—Oracle quickly pulled together applications, tools, and technol-ogy to provide enterprise business intelligence for e-businesses using the information from Web-enabled supply chain, operations, and customer management processes. Today Oracle has a competitive product posi-tioned against all the major e-business software firms (see Exhibit 3-4). What's more, the company offers one-stop shopping. This feat could not have been achieved so quickly or efficiently if Oracle had operated as a walled or colonial sphere. (But Oracle must also beware of its vulnerabil-ity to simultaneous attacks from competitors in Exhibit 3-4. Such an at-tack could result in the constriction or stripping of Oracle.)

Another benefit of the advanced sphere is its ability to pool the efforts of its peripheral geo-product zones and those of alliance partners to create new geo-product markets and business models that no single firm or cen-trally controlled firm could achieve by itself. NATO, for example, with its integrated technologies and fighting force, did more than the United States could do alone in its efforts to gain the upper hand during the Cold War. In business, a great example of an advanced sphere is Dell Com-puter's virtual organization. With its ability to pool together the numerous geo-product markets of suppliers and logistics firms, Dell revolutionized the business model in its core geo-product zone, manufacturing and mar-keting PCs. Similarly, Toyota's *keiretsu* redefined the business model for manufacturing cars. With their flexibility and adaptability, the advanced spheres of Dell and Toyota accumulate wealth in three ways. These are: leveraging other people's money, using alliances to create the right combi-nation of geo-product zones at the right moment, and reducing the costs associated with change when they need to reassemble new combinations of geo-product zones to seize a new opportunity.

Software Products/Services Offered by Oracle	Major Competitor
Database	Microsoft
Marketing	E.piphany
Sales	Siebel
Webstore	IBM
Procurement	Commerce One
Manufacturing	SAP
Supply chain management	i2
Financials	SAP
Human resources	PeopleSoft
Support	Clarify

Exhibit 3-4: Oracle's E-Business Suite

With their flexible resource routing patterns and their ability to pool resources from a variety of geo-product zones, advanced spheres are better able to "quilt" their spheres together, covering the exposed white space between their existing geo-product zones. For example, HP uses its ability to transfer resources such as teams with technical expertise or business innovation skills and to combine them with other teams from different divisions. HP creates an advanced sphere where people are temporarily assigned to one zone and often reassigned with the purpose of creating new businesses that did not exist before. The company has combined teams from a new networked laser-jet printer business unit (based on an emerging technology for peripheral computer equipment) with teams from an older, cash-cow business unit focused on printing. This resulted in several new products for traditional printers. HP reroutes teams with market knowledge, technological expertise, or business innovation skills, as well as cash, quilting them together to create new markets before anyone else does, and to capture the wealth associated with these new markets.

The "Advanced" School of Power Projection

The three previously discussed paradigms sometimes rely on discipline to project their power and hold themselves together. For example, walled spheres use strong barriers to entry, fluid spheres use militaristic market expansion, and colonial spheres use resource transfers to contain uprisings in peripheral zones. In contrast, the advanced sphere projects its power through the use of diplomacy as well as occasional disciplinary actions. This type of sphere allows a larger number of players to share in the victory, which in turn encourages more alliances within the great power and more cooperative behavior from the other great powers outside the sphere.

When success depends on the cooperation of other great powers—and those powers are too equally matched for an advanced sphere to be the global policeman—the firm must find another way to project its power. Typically, it opts for a mixture of discipline and diplomacy—weighted toward diplomacy—to create a "negotiated consensus" among the great powers. They explicitly agree on how resources will be transferred among themselves and tacitly agree among themselves about two primary issues: the borders of each player's sphere and the limits of each player's ability to gain greater preeminence within the competitive space. Without these tacit constraints among them, the great powers would not be able to trust each other with the resources they are routing among themselves. The advanced sphere uses several methods for projecting its power, including building alliances and signaling the new order.

- *Building alliances:* Alliances, either implicit or explicit, are one of the primary ways companies use diplomatic facilitation to create order in the competitive space. The Netscape–Sun Microsystems alliance in the late 1990s, centered around Java and the Internet, was created as an informal advanced sphere to challenge the preeminence of Microsoft's sphere of influence, based on the Wintel standard.

- *Signaling the new order:* In geopolitics, diplomacy often is handled through direct negotiation among the great powers. In business, competitors often use a combination of public announcements and aggressive forward positioning in selected zones to signal their desired borders and to discipline uncooperative rivals.

Illustrating these two points, the major airlines (such as American and Delta) have helped to create order in what was once a chaotic, hypercompetitive environment. Each of the majors has staked out hubs and enforced its turf by price retaliation and scheduling changes targeted at transgressors. Lesser powers have learned to act as feeders to some of the majors, to use the secondary (inconvenient) airport in major hubs, or center on out-of-the-way and smaller city airports. Unlike the early postderegulation days when we saw the rapid growth of airlines such as People Express, Texas Air, and numerous others, we are not seeing the rise of as many new players today. This is because the great powers learned to tacitly coordinate their efforts dealing with these upstarts. Each took on People Express, for example, in different hubs with price wars. People Express ended up fighting everywhere, while each major carrier was fighting in only selected markets.

Norms of Behavior Based on Pragmatism

Because its reach usually extends only as far as others are willing to cooperate, the advanced sphere shapes a world order based on pragmatism. In its relationships with other great powers or even parts of its own sphere, the advanced sphere is neither hawk nor dove. Instead, it chooses discipline or diplomacy, depending on the situation. It prefers the lower-cost alternative of diplomacy, but the aggressive use of deep pockets, price wars, and other forceful actions are always looming as options. As pragmatists, advanced spheres acknowledge that they can't run the world by themselves. Their goal is often to create a stable, peaceful world with a little help from their friends. Ideally, these great powers protect their spheres of influence with lesser investments by using other people as surrogates and using diplomacy (including alliances) more than costly force.

Inherent Challenges: Crossing the Line of Acceptable Behavior

In the world of international affairs, it's perfectly acceptable for advanced spheres to project their power to create a negotiated consensus. A consensus may be about which members of the sphere should occupy what parts of the sphere, or the consensus may determine which rival spheres "own" what parts of the larger competitive space. But in the business world, the line between cooperation and collusion is blurry, so it is easy to slip into illegal antitrust activity. Outside the United States, the tolerance for cooperative and even collusive corporate behavior is often much greater. Legal constraints must be reviewed country by country and situation by situation.

Like fluid and colonial spheres, advanced spheres have more options than walled spheres in how they use and deal with competitive compression. Because of its inherent flexibility, an advanced sphere can undertake a containment, constriction, sequential stripping, or toppling domino strategy to surround a walled sphere. But these activities can destabilize the existing order, affect third party great powers, and provoke those other great powers to defend the status quo. In addition, an advanced sphere may use quilting and alliances to facilitate aggressive product launches and withdrawals, or it may use diplomatic signals to communicate its dissatisfaction with the current consensus among the sphere's members. These actions can trigger disintegration of the sphere rather than a cooperative readjustment.

While the advanced sphere paradigm has the potential to unleash the most power from a sphere, it is also the hardest to execute because of the cost and difficulty of simultaneously managing a spiderweb of many loose linkages, complex alliance networks, and multiple subsystems with different, decentralized resource routing patterns. The scope of the advanced sphere is widely dispersed, ill defined, and always has the potential to evolve in unexpected ways that lead to diffusion of the sphere's power. Thus, for some great powers, the advanced sphere paradigm is not an option.

REAPING THE REWARDS OF YOUR RESOURCE ROUTING
PATTERN . . . WITHOUT SOWING THE SEEDS OF DESTRUCTION

Walled spheres and fluid spheres have relatively simple patterns for resource routing. Colonial spheres and advanced spheres follow much more complex routing patterns (see Exhibit 3-5). These patterns are a reflection of different visions or goals for the sphere. Because the different resource routing patterns create different types of power projection, they also signal that you want very different competitive norms and relationships with other great powers (see Exhibit 3-6).

Just as importantly, the different resource routing patterns result in very distinct methods of wealth accumulation. It is interesting to note that each paradigm's distinct method for wealth accumulation parallels a method represented by today's leading business thinking. For example, walled spheres use the monopoly-like power described by Michael Porter in his Five Forces model, which focuses on getting power over buyers and suppliers and on building barriers to entry.[11]

In contrast, fluid spheres gather wealth by preemption or constant, creative disruption of markets. This perspective was addressed in my 1994 book, *Hypercompetition: Managing the Dynamics of Strategic Maneuvering*,[12] and in Shona Brown and Kathleen Eisenhardt's *Competing on the Edge: Strategy as Structural Chaos* (1998). This same issue was also addressed by Tom Peters in *Thriving on Chaos* (1987), in which he described strategies based on fad and fashion. Peters suggested that many markets are becoming like the fashion industry because product life cycles are getting shorter at an accelerating rate, forcing many firms to adopt marauder and guerrilla strategies.

Colonial spheres create wealth by transferring resources in and out of the core. This view is reflected in "The Core Competence of the Corporation" in *Harvard Business Review* (1990) by C. K. Prahalad and Gary Hamel. Prahalad and Hamel suggested an imperialistic-like model in which resources are routed or leveraged from the core to the periphery. Later, in a 1998 *HBR* article, "The End of Corporate Imperialism," Prahalad and Kenneth Lieberthal described a mercantile model, which advo-

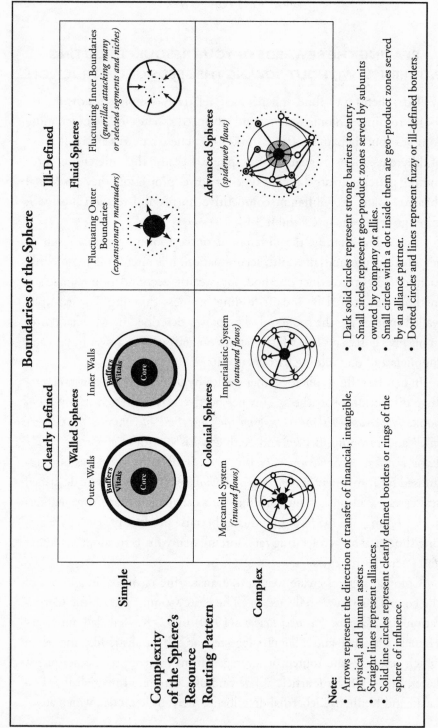

Exhibit 3-5: Resource Routing and Four Types of Spheres

Type of sphere	Subtypes	Resource Routing Strategy	Goals of the Use of Power	Power Projection Strategy	Signaled Norms Among the Great Powers	Wealth Accumulation Strategy
Walled spheres	Inner walls	• Resources are used to build barriers to entry to keep others out of the core and vital interests • Resources are concentrated on clearly defined core and vital interests to "own" them	Defend and dominate the existing sphere	• Defend borders with barriers • Teach others to respect the boundaries • Retaliatory strikes to discipline invaders	Isolationism	Porter's Five Forces Model of power over buyers and suppliers (1980)
Fluid spheres	Guerrillas	• Resources are moved to easily captured zones • Resources are first used to seize critical zones within the sphere and fill in holes in the spheres piecemeal	Consolidate a sphere		Militarism and expansionism	D'Aveni's *Hypercompetition* Model of Creative Disruption (1994)
	Marauders	• Resources are moved to the edge of the sphere • Resources are continually used to invade nearby zones, even if core markets are left behind	Achieve critical mass and absorb new wealth	• Constant or large-scale disruption or invasion • Deplete or absorb rivals		

Exhibit 3-6: Spheres, Resource Routing Strategies and Their Implications (continued on next page)

Type of sphere	Subtypes	Resource Routing Strategy	Goals of the Use of Power	Power Projection Strategy	Signaled Norms Among the Great Powers	Wealth Accumulation Strategy
Colonial spheres	Mercantile systems	• Resources are moved to the core • Resources are used to create growth in the core and power over lesser powers in the core	Strengthen the core	• Build strong core using the periphery or vice versa • Rapid deployment to and from the core and periphery • Build layers of buffers and forward positions on the periphery	Mercantile and imperialistic colonial competition	Prahalad & Hamel "The Core Competence of the Corporation" (1990)
	Imperialistic systems	• Resources are moved to the peripheral zones of the core • Resources are used to improve the periphery, which, in turn, strengthens the core	Create growth opportunities for the core in the periphery			Prahalad and Lieberthal "The End of Corporate Imperialism" (1998)
Advanced spheres	Spiderwebs	• Resources flow in many directions, not always routed through the core or controlled by headquarters • Resources are routed to strengthen the weak links as well as to support the strong links	All for one and one for all improvement	• Negotiation of common standards and pursuit of common goals • Talk softly but carry a big stick (just over the horizon)	Pragmatism	James F. Moore *The Death of Competition: The Death of Leadership and Strategy in the Age of Business EcoSystems* (1997)

Exhibit 3-6 (Continued): Spheres, Resource Routing Strategies and Their Implications

cated that global firms should look to the peripheral geographic parts of their portfolios for ideas and resources to bring back to their core markets.

Finally, advanced spheres create and accumulate wealth by cooperating with competitors and forming symbiotic ecosystems. This view was described by James F. Moore in his book, *The Death of Competition: Leadership and Strategy in the Age of Business Ecosystems* (1997).

Are any of the four paradigms for power superior to the others? No. Each of these paradigms is better suited to a certain type of competitive environment, depending on the frequency of change or disruption, and the nature of those disruptions within that environment. (I address this subject in much greater detail in the following chapter, "Dousing Disruption.") In addition, there is no typical progression from one paradigm to the other. For example, reaching "advanced sphere" status is neither inevitable nor universally desirable.

While all four paradigms have inherent benefits, they also have inherent short-term challenges. Too often, management *mis*manages these challenges by changing the paradigm itself. Then, as soon as managers are confronted by the inherent challenges in the new paradigm, they abandon that paradigm as well, and so on and so on. Thus, the company never gets to take advantage of any paradigm's long-term potential for unleashing the sphere's power. In this way, a skittish management team, by not understanding the larger purpose of a sphere's paradigm, can actually sow the seeds of a sphere's own destruction.

Consider the disguised, real-company case illustrated in Exhibit 3-7. Here, management's reflex reactions to pressing, short-term challenges interrupted the momentum of having a consistent paradigm for power. The company started with a fluid sphere of influence. The sphere's excessive growth resulted in a lack of consolidation of the sphere. But management—rather than controlling growth in order to consolidate its new territories—overreacted by putting up walls around the unconsolidated sphere to protect it. Thus, they cut off the growth potential of their fluid sphere, even though there was a lot of growth potential left in the marketplace. Hence, the company experienced its first unnecessary and power-reducing paradigm shift.

Then, while implementing the walled sphere, the management team blundered again by using their company's monopoly power to overcharge its customers within the walls. Eventually, these customers revolted. Rather than raising quality to fit their higher prices, or eliminating their monopolistic pricing policy, management looked for new sources of profitability outside the core that could be used to control the deteriorating situation by feeding cash back to the company's walled core. Hence, the creation of a colonial sphere with mercantile resource routing approach occurred almost inadvertently.

As management struggled to implement the colonial (mercantile) sphere, it overdid its mercantile system of resource routing and drained its peripheral markets. The company then switched its colonial sphere to an imperialistic model, routing its resources back to the periphery. Strengthened by this infusion of resources, the sphere's peripheral markets began to enjoy greater importance and power, until eventually the company's colonial paradigm gave way. Hence the transition to an advanced sphere of influence.

Then, as the periphery demanded even more autonomy, the company's advanced sphere experienced looser and looser linkages between its subunits, until each was acting independently (as tubs floating on their own bottom) and often without adequate resources. Rather than prune the sphere's scope in recognition of its overstretched sphere and inadequate resources to serve all its markets, management allowed the company's advanced sphere to disintegrate. Hence the company drifted into a conglomerate lacking the value of any of the four paradigms for power.

This case illustrates how easy it is for management to reactively change its company's paradigm for power. But even without this type of reactive response to short-term problems, one paradigm can drift into another. This can happen when management doesn't fully understand the company's paradigm for power and its resource routing pattern. For example, when faced with new growth opportunities, management might adjust the resources being routed. This may seem like nothing more than a shift in emphasis when in fact the move could inadvertently result in a change in the very paradigm that has made the company successful or that is needed to protect the company's present position.

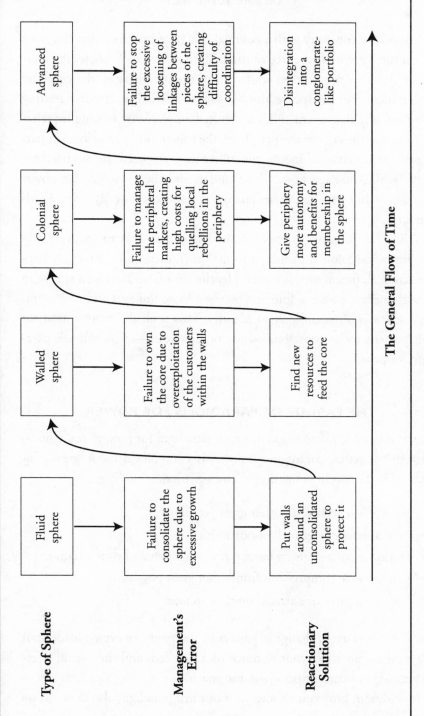

Exhibit 3-7: Reactionary Transitions in a Sphere of Influence

Consider a company with a colonial sphere of influence that follows a mercantile pattern of resource routing. With this type of sphere, the mercantile flows (with resources routed from the periphery to the core) are predominant, but the sphere also has some imperialistic resource routing going on. If management suddenly shifted emphasis by routing more resources from the core to the periphery, the sphere could actually shift paradigms, from a colonial mercantile sphere to an imperialistic model. And, all the while, managers who don't understand the paradigm for power concept might construe the net change in resources flows as a simple adjustment.

While the previous example showed how easy it is to inadvertently shift from one colonial paradigm to the other, these shifts can easily happen across all paradigms. For example, the shift from advanced sphere to a conglomerate crosses a fine line between loose linkages and disintegration, which is often difficult to identify. This is all the more reason for management to be conscious—and conscientious—of its sphere's paradigm for power.

THE PARADE OF PARADIGMS FOR POWER

Does it ever make sense to change your paradigm for power? Yes. Choosing your company's paradigm for power is a complex decision greatly influenced by factors in your competitive situation, including:

- Your power relative to other great powers
- New sustainable growth opportunities
- Insurrections and rising lesser powers that demand your attention
- Competitive compression from other great powers
- Your own proactive attacks on rival spheres

If any of these factors change in your core, periphery, or even outside your sphere, they can affect your resource routing needs and the overall effectiveness of your current paradigm for power.

In addition, how you choose your optimal paradigm also depends on whether other great powers are offering a world of isolationism, militarism, colonialism, or pragmatism, as well as your own ambitions and desire to accept the norms of behavior they are offering. For example, you may want to be an isolationist but face a lot of marauders, or you might want to create a colonial sphere but face a lot of walls. Because of all these factors, the sphere of influence may need to adapt by changing its paradigm for power to one more suited to the new competitive environment.

It may even make sense at times for a sphere to follow a hybrid paradigm for power, if the sphere is confronted by two conflicting competitive conditions. Consider the walled-in advanced sphere in Exhibit 3-8. A walled sphere is useful when a firm needs very strong buffers to protect its core and vital interests from the competitive compression it is experiencing. However, if the rapidity of change within the firm's core and vital interests requires the firm to also operate as an advanced sphere within these zones, a hybrid sphere becomes necessary.

Rather than a sign of failure, a *calculated* transition to a new paradigm, or even straddling two paradigms, can be a natural, indeed necessary part of a great power's efforts at sustained supremacy. The important thing is to be deliberate about your choice and understand what you gain and lose from the switch.

The British Empire's long period of strategic supremacy—from the Elizabethan period to World War I—was due in great part to its ability to tranform its sphere of influence from one paradigm of power to another as new opportunities and threats emerged. During the reign of Elizabeth I, Britain demonstrated the strength of its naval forces by defeating the Spanish Armada. Its strong navy enabled the empire to use the Atlantic Ocean as a wall between Britain and the rest of the world. In the 1700s, the empire shifted to a colonial/mercantile paradigm, transferring great wealth from its American colonies to the core . . . until the American Revolution forced the empire to rethink its system of colonialism. In the 1800s, the British Empire shifted to a more sophisticated colonial/imperialistic paradigm, using the excess resources created by the Industrial Revolution in its core to invest in its peripheral holdings in order to create and control new markets in India, China, and Africa. For a time, the empire shifted back and forth between

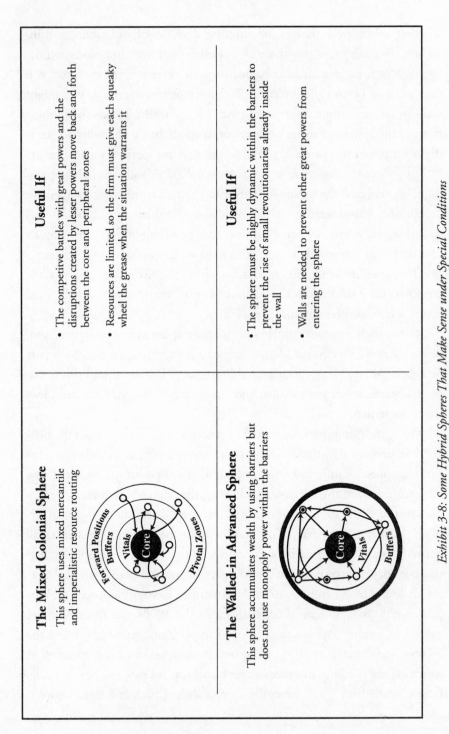

The Mixed Colonial Sphere

This sphere uses mixed mercantile and imperialistic resource routing

Useful If

- The competitve battles with great powers and the disruptions created by lesser powers move back and forth between the core and peripheral zones

- Resources are limited so the firm must give each squeaky wheel the grease when the situation warrants it

The Walled-in Advanced Sphere

This sphere accumulates wealth by using barriers but does not use monopoly power within the barriers

Useful If

- The sphere must be highly dynamic within the barriers to prevent the rise of small revolutionaries already inside the wall

- Walls are needed to prevent other great powers from entering the sphere

Exhibit 3-8: Some Hybrid Spheres That Make Sense under Special Conditions

The Walled Colonial Sphere

This sphere uses mixed mercantile and imperialistic resource routing

Useful If

- The cost of maintaining the barriers to entry to the core is very high

- There is high growth potential in the core that requires funding

The Marauding Walled Sphere

The walled core is funding marauder behavior in the periphery

Useful If

- The core is a cash cow with no place to reinvest its profits

- The safety of the core allows it to experiment opportunistically with parts of the periphery, which will eventually be pulled together into a larger sphere with clear borders and broader barriers to entry

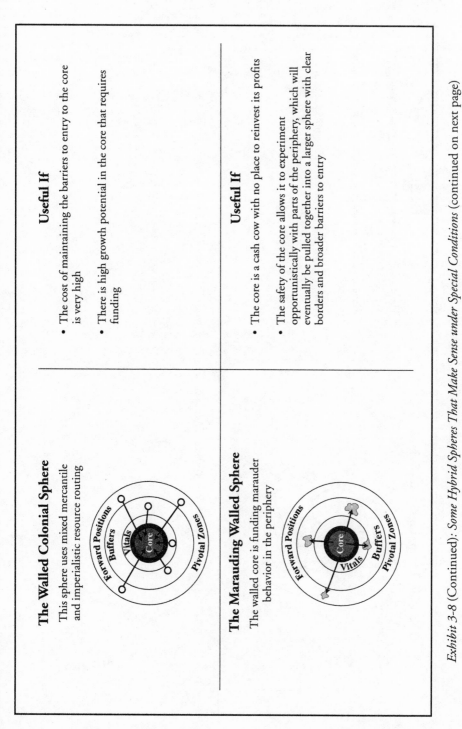

Exhibit 3-8 (Continued): *Some Hybrid Spheres That Make Sense under Special Conditions* (continued on next page)

The Walled Stepping-Stones Sphere

This sphere builds a lot of little fortresses with barriers, eventually accumulating a large collection of profitable zones

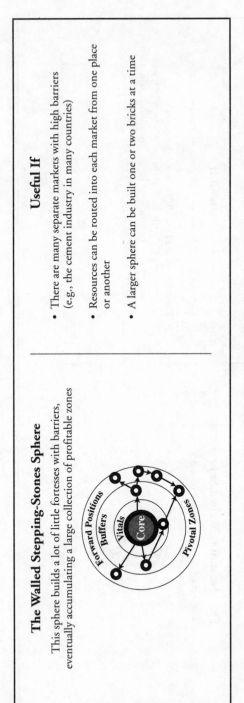

Useful If

- There are many separate markets with high barriers (e.g., the cement industry in many countries)

- Resources can be routed into each market from one place or another

- A larger sphere can be built one or two bricks at a time

Exhibit 3-8 (Continued): Some Hybrid Spheres That Make Sense under Special Conditions

the two models of mercantilism and imperialism, depending on the degree of unrest in the colonies and the empire's needs to defend its core. (For example, during World War I and World War II, Britain took resources out of its colonies to support the defense of its core in the European theaters.) After World War II, Britain's colonial empire disintegrated because the war placed extreme resource demands on the colonies, in part causing the colonists to seek independence. Thereafter, Britain joined America's advanced sphere of influence by participating in the NATO alliance. Britain has also decolonialized, without completely shedding its relationships with its former colonies. The formation of the British Commonwealth of Nations (as well as Britain's membership in NATO) has simultaneously placed Britain in two overlapping advanced spheres of influence. However, as time went on, the Commonwealth's purpose and cohesiveness evaporated, while the U.S. sphere became preeminent.

Like the British Empire, IBM has also adapted to changing competitive situations and shifting power balances by adjusting its paradigm for power (see Exhibit 3-9). The company built its power in the 1960s through the use of a fluid sphere. It maintained its supremacy in the '70s through its walled-in core of mainframe computers, and evolved into an advanced sphere in the '80s in order to adjust to a new wave of powerful players (Microsoft and Intel). By the 1990s IBM was shifting to a colonial sphere, using a series of acquisitions and expansions to leverage or support its revitalized mainframe and server core product market. IBM's new colonies were designed to help the company to compete with a new set of great powers (Dell, Sun Microsystems, Palm, and Cisco) operating in the new network-centric computing environment.

Thanks to IBM's ability to transition from one paradigm to another, the company has managed to weather (at least partially) a seemingly relentless storm of new players, new technologies, and other significant shifts in the competitive environment. No, IBM has not emerged from the storm unbattered. The company lost its uncontested supremacy over the computing world. This demotion, if you will, was due to a number of factors. The company failed to stop Apple by "absorbing" personal computers into its product line quickly enough. It failed to "dampen" the rising stars of the then lesser players Microsoft and Intel. And it failed to

Time Period	Type of Sphere Used by IBM	Method Used to Enhance its Strategic Supremacy	Competitive Situation
1960s	Fluid Sphere (marauder)	Massive expansion via disruption and preemption using a full line of compatible third-generation computers with interchangeable peripherals as memory units.	Left the second-generation computer producers, mechanical business machines, and typewriter manufacturers in a cloud of dust
1970s	Walled Sphere	Barriers to entry (e.g., a closed proprietary system architecture) supported by policing activities (price leadership, strong retaliation, etc.)	• Kept strong control over the "Seven Dwarfs" within its walls • Kept DEC and Wang outside the walls
1980s	Advanced Sphere	Diplomatic negotiation (to set open standards) using alliances	• Coped with the rise of new powers (Intel and Microsoft) by alliances with them and others • Defeated Apple in desktop personal computing
Mid-1990s	Colonial Sphere with outposts supporting network-centric systems in: • groupware (Lotus Notes) • systems integration • Internet software • e-commerce Web site development • massive parallel processing • large-scale user applications • higher value-added hardware • hand-held devices and software	Colonial expansion via acquisition and opening new product markets/services	• Responded to the distributed computing movement by building strengths in markets that would bolster network-centric computing power and hand-held devices • Outmaneuvered the advantages of Intel and Microsoft using high value-added software, systems integration and consulting, and other services • Positioned against Dell, Palm, Sun, and Cisco in the Internet world with strong e-commerce consulting

Exhibit 3-9: IBM—Adjusting to New Eras of Competitive Compression

"hedge" its bets by better preparing for the development of new hardware for the Internet, wireless, and hand-held spaces before Sun Microsystems, Cisco, and Palm grew too large. (The next chapter discusses in depth how great powers, with strategic supremacy, can cope with disruptive lesser powers and revolutionaries that threaten to upset the "Apple" cart.)

Nevertheless, despite IBM's failure to vanquish Apple, then Microsoft and Intel, then Compaq and Dell, and then Sun, Cisco, and Palm, the company has still remained a great power. IBM is still the largest computer-based business in the world in revenues and employees. It also has the largest non-PC based software business in the world. And before the overall decline in tech stocks in 2000, Wall Street handsomely rewarded IBM as the largest player in the e-commerce consulting and software space. IBM's current strong position gives the company the power to help shape the future of the industry. But it now shares that power with Dell, Microsoft, Intel, Sun Microsystems, Cisco, Oracle, Palm, and a few others. (See the sidebar "IBM's Parade of Paradigms for Power.")

IBM'S PARADE OF PARADIGMS FOR POWER

Fluid Sphere: To build its power in the 1960s, IBM created a fluid sphere of influence that evolved from business machines (typewriters and mechanical calculators) and transistor-based computers to computer chip and mainframe manufacturing, operating system software, and numerous new computer peripherals. Its "bet-the-firm" launch of its 360-series mainframes was a marauder-like preemptive strike that allowed it to establish the preeminent sphere of influence in computing. This "$5 billion gamble" (in 1963 dollars!) was more than twice as expensive as the Manhattan Project during World War II. It rendered existing computers obsolete and challenged the marketing structure of the industry. IBM disrupted its competitors with third-generation, chip-based business computers—and placed itself in a preeminent position in this sphere with a full line of six mainframe computers and numerous compatible peripherals. Other companies in the old computing world (transistor-based machines) now found themselves competing in IBM's chip-based business machine sphere, and IBM was on the attack to expand its sphere.

Walled Sphere: By the early 1970s, IBM had established strong leadership over the chip-based mainframe world with its 360 series. IBM built strong barriers to entry around its mainframe business and was head and shoulders above the smaller "Seven Dwarfs," such as GE, Honeywell, Prime, and others who followed IBM's lead and lived in its shadow. IBM single-handedly set the standards and prices in the business mainframe market and others followed or avoided IBM's path. Only companies like DEC and Wang found a way to survive by identifying niches in minicomputers and word processing that were outside IBM's walled-in sphere built around mainframe computers.

Advanced Sphere: In the 1980s, technology increased the complexity of the computing space, adding personal computers to the mix. New, powerful players appeared (including Apple, Intel, and Microsoft), forcing IBM to turn to a strategy of diplomacy to shape its sphere of influence. IBM's barriers to entry had collapsed and retaliation against the entrants was either too dangerous (because a powerful player such as Intel could respond with deadly force) or ineffective (because impudent new powers such as Apple would not listen to IBM's authority). With less relative power over rivals, the IBM empire turned to working for a negotiated consensus about the definition of standards and its sphere of influence. IBM worked hard to get competitors to agree on IBM's open standard for PC architecture and used implicit or explicit alliances to create an extensive advanced sphere of influence, which ultimately defeated Apple.

IBM's open architecture helped build consensus among hardware and software makers who shaped smaller portions of the industry. Eventually, IBM defined what the personal computer was made of and who would lead in many pieces of the market. However, as personal computers grew to become an increasingly important part of the market, IBM found its former "partners"—Microsoft and Intel—had become great powers in their own right. The danger of diplomatic facilitation is that cooperation can backfire if alliance partners become strong rivals.

Colonial Sphere: Building a colonial sphere seemed to be the goal of IBM in the 1990s. IBM went through a series of incremental moves—including its acquisition of Lotus's Notes groupware, expansion of IBM consulting to compete with Andersen Consulting, expansion of IBM's software development activity to become one of the largest applications developers for business, investment to help develop new Internet software and electronic commerce, big investments in massive parallel processing, and efforts to move to higher value-added hardware and hand-held devices. All of these are contributing to the creation of incredibly powerful networks, services, and supercomputers from non-state-of-the-art chips (which can serve as central nodes in the Internet world). Over time, IBM built a "network-centric" view of the world that is overthrowing the world of DOS-based, CISC-chip–based PCs created by Microsoft and Intel. During Lou Gerstner's early tenure, IBM's moves may have appeared unrelated, but they added up to a colonial paradigm. All the moves were based on leveraging or supporting IBM's core product market and core competencies in mainframe computing and servers for networked business applications.

The story of IBM is a story of a company that gained exclusive strategic supremacy, lost it, but still remains a player in shaping the future of the industry. By understanding the four paradigms for power and how each shapes your resource routing patterns, your organization, like IBM and like so many of the great empires throughout history, you can unleash the full potential of your sphere today . . . and tomorrow. While all firms are concerned about the future, great powers use their sphere's paradigm to do something about it. After all, as management guru Peter Drucker once said, "the only way to predict the future is to have the power to shape it."

Chapter 4

Dousing Disruption

Using Counterrevolutionary Tactics, Weatherproofing Strategies, and Competitive Cooperatives to Manage Insurrection

OVERVIEW

For many firms, even seemingly small insurrections can spell big trouble. Worse yet, firms face hundreds, perhaps thousands, of disruptions all over the globe, so they cannot react to all of them. That's why great powers need to know what to do when ambitious lesser powers and revolutionaries try to disrupt the status quo. Depending on the nature of the disruption, a variety of counterrevolutionary tactics *can be applied—preempting, shaping, absorbing, dampening, or hedging. Some of these tactics allow you to wait and see which revolutions boil to the top before acting. Depending on the pattern of disruption, you can also* weatherproof *your sphere by shifting your paradigm for power. You can also* form competitive cooperatives *with other major players equally vested in maintaining the existing* hierarchy of power. These competitive cooperatives include concerts of power, polarized blocs, and collective security arrangements. Whether you go it alone or join forces, one thing remains constant: Dousing disruption is all about winning the "little" wars that can play a big role in achieving and sustaining strategic supremacy.*

SURVIVING THE REVOLUTION

By the time Diocletian became ruler over the Roman Empire in A.D. 284, the vast empire had been in a state of chaos and instability for decades. Its borders were beleaguered by external invaders, its military was plagued by internal rebellion, and its citizens showed symptoms of mass anxiety and dissension.

In order to restore order, Diocletian instituted major economic, military, and religious reforms. He named his friend Maximian as co-emperor and placed the western part of the empire under his rule, while he himself continued to govern the Eastern Empire from the capital of Nicomedia. In 293, the co-emperors named two additional regents to co-rule and serve as their successors. The initial success of this tetrarchy, as well as Diocletian's other reforms—from reorganizing the army to revamping the tax system—had many citizens proclaiming the emperor as savior of the Roman world. But one threat to the traditional Roman way remained, this one not in the form of armies, but a disruptive ideology. To keep the support of the people, Diocletian believed he had to do something about the Christians.

From its humble origins in an obscure Roman village, Christianity had grown to become a mainstream religion, attracting large numbers to its fold with its comforting messages of love, humility, and an afterlife. In Diocletian's own government, many Christians occupied important positions. Indeed the emperor's own wife and daughter were believed to be followers of the faith. Nevertheless, many Romans believed Christianity spurned the gods who had protected and had brought greatness to Rome. Many also thought Christianity undermined the very values that were the basis of Roman society, which made the religion a lightning rod for persecution. Already, the third century had seen two periods of brutal, albeit fairly short-lived, government-sanctioned persecution of Christians under emperors Decius and Valerian. Now, it was up to Diocletian to try to appease those citizens who made their Christian neighbors scapegoats for the many troubles besieging the empire—trouble attributed to the Christians' refusal to participate in sacrifices to the Roman pagan gods that assured everything from victory in battle to good crops.

To keep the peace, Diocletian renewed the anti-Christian campaign, calling for the destruction of all Christian places of worship and written material, as well as mass executions. The brutal persecution began in his court, and quickly extended to the army, to the leaders of the Christian congregations, and ultimately to the general public, as Roman officials searched out Christians by checking the tax rolls. When the aging Diocletian abdicated in 305 (with the hope of peacefully growing cabbages at his villa) the persecution continued, albeit unevenly. The co-rulers in the Eastern Empire remained rabid persecutors, while the leaders of the Western Empire often ignored Diocletian's anti-Christian directives. This inconsistency was but one sign of the disintegration of the tetrarchy thanks to infighting among the various palaces after Diocletian's abdication.

Finally, the Roman people had had enough. After a decade of torture and terror, the government's anti-Christian campaign had not only failed to eradicate Christianity, but may have actually served to grow the Christian community and strengthen its faith. What's more, the dislike most pagan Romans felt for Christians had been far overshadowed by their dislike of the atrocities of their tyrannical government.

In 312, Constantine I defeated Maxentius at the Battle of the Milvian Bridge and became sole emperor of the Western Empire. He attributed his victory to a vision he had seen in the sky, showing him the sign of Christ and assuring him that "In this sign shalt thou conquer." A year later, after winning three more great battles against his rival in the Eastern Empire (thanks in part to local Christian support), he reunited the entire Roman Empire, moved its capital to Constantinople, and became its one and only emperor. That same year, he issued the Edict of Milan, pronouncing tolerance towards the Christians and taking the first official step toward converting the empire from paganism to Christianity. Even before the century was out, Emperor Theodosius I proclaimed Christianity the empire's official religion.

Constantine's Christianization of the empire marks one of the boldest phenomena in Roman history. And while the history books characterize Constantine as a profoundly religious man, it is more than likely that his actions in elevating the church were as motivated by his political convictions as they were by faith. Clearly, Constantine recognized that Christianity could not be squelched; in fact this once minor sect had become a widespread and fairly organized church, showing enormous potential for unifying the various conflicting people and classes that threatened the stability of the empire. While Dioclecian tried to stamp out Christianity, Constantine found a better way to deal with this revolution.

As the story of Christianity's impact on the Roman Empire demonstrates, even the most successful empires can be vulnerable to challenges from seemingly "minor" insurrectionists. In business, as in politics, great powers must weigh carefully their responses when facing a disruptive ideology. Do you ignore the ideology or try to dampen it, or do you absorb it and convert the empire, as Constantine did in his efforts to sustain Rome's strategic supremacy? CEOs of modern global businesses may chuckle at the thought of comparing threats to their own ideological leadership with Christianity's impact on the Roman Empire, but much is to be learned in how the Romans failed and succeeded in addressing this "disruptive" ideological challenge. And the Roman strategy of first battling and then absorbing this disruption may be much more relevant than you think.

ANHEUSER-BUSCH: A REVOLUTION WAS BREWING

Anheuser-Busch, the world's largest brewer and manufacturer of brands including Budweiser, Bud Light, Michelob, and Busch, is just one example of a great power in business that faced an ideological revolution which threatened to turn the beer industry on its head. In 1994, the big three U.S. beer makers (Anheuser, Miller, and Coors) were experiencing a market as flat as a two-day-old draft. But one new segment of the beer biz was taking off—microbrews. While this specialty category made up less than 5 percent of the total beer market at the time, its 40 to 50 percent rise in sales threatened a trend that didn't bode well for mainstream American brews.

Unlike the Roman Empire's delayed response to the rise of Christianity, Anheuser-Busch addressed the disruption caused by the microbreweries much more quickly. Its motivation was clear. The Mammoth Missourian held the largest market share by far of the big three brewers, but it was already experiencing a slide in Bud's sales, and it had the most to lose if the revolution truly marked the end of the old brands, as many were predicting. Faced with this prophecy of doom for mainstream beers, Anheuser's first move was to hedge its bets by tapping into the market. Anheuser became the first of the megabrands to invest in a prestige microbrew, Seattle's Redhook Ale. This play put the microbrewers on alert. In the October 1994 issue of *Inc.*, Jim Koch, founder of the Boston Beer Co. and brewer of Sam Adams, declared Anheuser's move "a declaration of war." Indeed, Anheuser made its intentions clear—its goal was to capture half of the $400-million microbrewery market within five years.

To that end, Anheuser converted a fifteen-barrel test brewery in St. Louis to its specialty beer business. This was its answer to the obvious question: How does a multibillion-dollar company produce a large number of small-volume specialty products that are perceived as unique enough to compete against the little guys—and simultaneously protect its economies of scale in manufacturing and its big established brands? As literally hundreds of microbrews and specialty beers entered the market, Anheuser joined in the fray. A-B introduced concoctions ranging from its nationally distributed American Originals line, which showcased the company's heritage, to its micro-targeted craft beers such as ZiegenBock distributed only in Texas, and Pacific Ridge Pale Ale distributed only in California. And while most big brewers tried to eliminate any associations between their corporate identity and their specialty lines, Anheuser didn't hide the fact it was the maestro behind the micros. In fact, Anheuser publicly lobbied against the tactics of the manufacturers of Samuel Adams, Pete's Wicked Ale, and Plank Road (brewed by Miller), all brands that purposely projected an image of small, folksy microbrews, when in fact, they were contract-manufactured by large producers at large facilities.

According to the Institute for Brewing Studies, from 1990 to 1999 the total of brewpubs, microbreweries, and craft-beer makers nationwide increased from 211 to 1,447. Yet by mid-decade the craft beer environment had changed dramatically. Once a welcoming industry for gifted amateurs, the overcrowded market had become a tough, even brutal business. Nationwide, hundreds of brewpubs and breweries had gone belly up, and the writing was on the wall for others. The shift to this tougher environment was due in no small part to Anheuser's deep pockets and aggressive actions.

It's interesting to note that the "King of Beers" never absorbed the new microbrew ideology in the way the Romans absorbed Christianity. Anheuser stayed true to its core-products strategy, never making a move to abandon its core traditional beers or convert all its big breweries to look like the microbreweries. In fact in 1996 Anheuser's Specialty Brewing Group only accounted for 1 percent of Anheuser's total shipments. But that fraction of involvement—reflecting a relatively minor but aggressive new product strategy that embraced the new microbrew ideology—enabled the titan to hedge its bets against the microbrewery threat and to reshape the microbrewery ideology to its own advantage.

Anheuser's tactics and timing for dealing with the microbrew revolution demonstrate just some of the options great powers have when it comes to dousing disruption. But while Anheuser was proactive in dealing with industry insurrection, many great powers ignore the danger when a new ideology or approach to value leadership appears on the horizon of the competitive space. Yet even "micro" insurrectionists can shake up the position of the great powers and turn stability into chaos in an amazingly short time period. Given that reality, great powers—even as they concentrate on the high-stakes game of competition with other great powers—must keep a wary eye on the revolutionaries and ambitious lesser powers that threaten their value leadership. As Leonardo DaVinci once said, "It is easier to resist at the beginning than at the end."

THE NATURE OF DISRUPTIVE IDEOLOGIES

When it comes to ideological challenges, not all disruptions are created equal. Disruptions can come from two types of insurrectionists: revolutionary upstarts competing within your sphere (new or small firms with revolutionary ideas); or ambitious lesser powers inside or outside your sphere (firms that have been around for years but previously had avoided the leader's sphere or remained niche players). Disruption can be controllable or uncontrollable, depending on its origin. Disruption can mean serious trouble for your value leadership and the value creation process supporting that leadership. Or it can actually serve to strengthen your value leadership, if you can co-opt, shape, or absorb the disruption to your advantage.

How vulnerable is a great power to disruptive ideologies from insurrectionists? That depends. Great powers typically have value leadership, size, reputation, and numerous other resources on their side. But creative insurrectionists have their own resources, particularly where they can harness the power of changing technologies and markets. U.S. auto makers, intent on relatively oligopolistic competition among the Big Four, were shaken by the arrival of then lesser powers Honda, Toyota, Nissan, and VW, all companies that didn't play by their rules. Major booksellers such as Barnes & Noble and Borders were rudely awakened by tiny upstart Amazon.com. Amazon threatened to turn their strength in real estate and geographic presence into a liability, especially for the non-impulse segment of "planned purchase" books, which included business books, do-it-yourself books, and books for professionals in medicine, law, and the like.

Obviously, no great power has the resources to dampen or absorb every new ideology that comes down the pike. So how do you know which challenge to your value leadership is worth dampening or absorbing? The answer to that question depends, in part, on the nature of the disruption and its competence-destroying or competence-enhancing activities.

Competence-Destroying Disruptions

Some disruptions can destroy a great power's value leadership by undermining the competencies required to deliver on that value leadership proposition, or by making obsolete the value proposition itself (see Exhibit 4-1). Old competencies may become irrelevant or obsolete due to shifts in customers' tastes and needs, technological substitution, imitation, widespread licensing or diffusion of a competence, or a competitor's active attempts to destroy, neutralize, or cripple the great power's ability to fund or improve its competencies. The competence of a great power can also be destroyed by shifts in customer demographics, deregulation and globalization, or a new larger scale, aggressive great power born of mergers or alliances.

Disruptions can also destroy a great power's value leadership by altering the definition of value and quality, creating a vastly superior value proposition that the great power does not and cannot deliver. In addition, insurrectionists can drive radical disruptions by clever innovation, or by significantly escalating the intensity of rivalry by raising more resources or acquiring and combining resources from alliance partners.

Competence-Enhancing Disruptions

While many disruptions serve to undermine the ideological leadership of the great powers, some actually can make a great power's core competencies and physical resources even more valuable (see Exhibit 4-2). These types of competence-enhancing disruptions can help support the continued value leadership of the great power and the reigning ideology in the marketplace. For example, Intel has experienced (or driven) a series of competence-enhancing disruptions with the arrival of new technologies that served to speed up CISC chips (e.g., MMX), improve yields in CISC chip manufacturing, and make it easier to design next-generation CISC chips. (This differs from a shift in technology from CISC to VLWI chips or to neural network chips. Such a shift would be competence-destroying for Intel because of the possibility of technological substitution.)

The determination of whether a disruption is competence-enhancing or not depends as much on the firm as the disruption itself. Consider the invention of lightweight, Internet-connected, easy to see, high-resolution screens (equivalent to the resolution of desktop monitors) for cell phones. This disruption would be competence-destroying for desktop computer manufacturers, creating a substitute for their product. However, for the leading manufacturers of cell phones (and maybe even personal digital assistants), such a disruption could enhance their existing competencies—but only if the existing cell phone leaders absorb the disruption and develop it in a timely fashion. If the leading cell phone manufacturers wait too long, ambitious challengers may be able to preempt their ability to use the new technology. These challengers could lock up patents or key providers, gain advantage by moving down the experience curve faster, or become the household brand name that consumers think of first when they think of the new product.

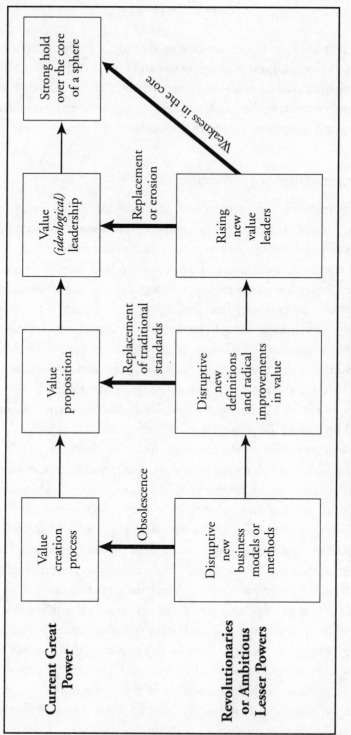

Exhibit 4-1: How Insurrection Diminishes a Great Power's Status

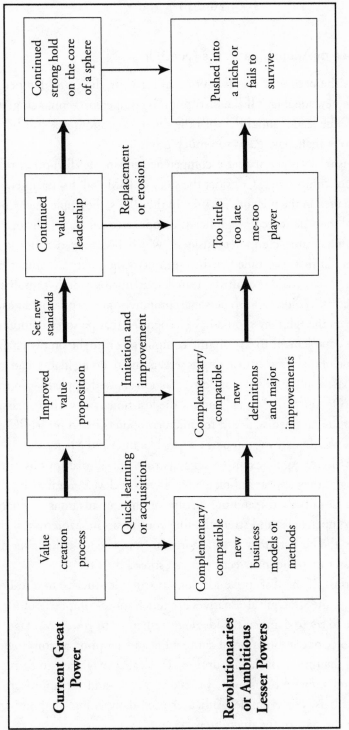

Exhibits 4-2: Reinforcement of Existing Value Leadership and Great Power Status

To Dampen or Adopt? That Is the Question

How does the nature of the disruption affect your choice to dampen or absorb the new ideology? If the disruption is competence-enhancing, it is clear the value leader should absorb the disruption and develop it before an ambitious challenger gains too much ground.

But it isn't always clear that a competence-enhancing disruption really will enhance competence. Consider the story of IBM's fall from supremacy that I presented in the previous chapter. In the 1980s, the Apple microcomputer revolution presented a significant competence-enhancing disruption to IBM's mainframe computer business, which necessitated a quick response. But, at first, Big Blue failed to see microcomputers as competence enhancing. Many IBM executives feared that micros would cannibalize mainframes. IBM didn't absorb personal computers into its product line fast enough, even though they should have recognized that personal computers are a great complement to mainframe computers, or might simply change the function of mainframes to acting as servers and to doing higher-end and large database applications. Their delayed action allowed Apple to gain momentum. (Of course, IBM made up for the lost time later with its massive effort to create an open standard for microcomputers based on its PC design, but it was too late to stop new powers like Intel and Microsoft.)

The IBM and Apple example suggests that not all disruptions are as threatening as they appear at first glance. If you're clever, you may be able to convert an initially threatening disruption into an advantage, enhancing your competencies and strengthening your position. Moreover, if this is the case, the best strategy is to absorb the competency-enhancing disruption faster than the insurrectionist can spread the fire.

In contrast, if the disruptive ideology is truly destructive to a leader's competence, the strategic alternatives are much more complex. Your best bet may be to try to dampen the ideology, reshape it to your advantage, or use a sequence or combination of dampening and adoption actions to better control the timing of the disruption. The leader may want to be more prudent and move more slowly, by taking a wait-and-see approach or hedging its bets. For example, Anheuser used dampening, shaping, and hedging at the start of the microbrew craze.

FIVE COUNTERREVOLUTIONARY TACTICS TO NEUTRALIZE
COMPETENCE-DESTROYING DISRUPTIONS

When it comes to countering truly threatening insurrections, great powers have two overarching goals: to prevent the insurrectionists from gaining power and to capture any opportunities those insurrectionists have created, if it makes sense. To achieve these goals, great powers can use five counter-revolutionary tactics—preempting, shaping, absorbing, dampening, and hedging—to deal effectively with new ideologies that threaten their status (see Exhibit 4-3). The first alternative, preemption, requires the great power to anticipate the market and move the most quickly, a difficult feat in highly ambiguous situations, especially for "slow-moving giants" who lack flexibility. The other four tactics—shaping, absorbing, dampening, and hedging—reflect more of a "wait and see" approach. The great powers watch how the disruption develops. If, after time, the insurrection merits a response, then they choose their methods for dousing that disruption.

Preempting

When facing a disruptive competence-destroying ideology, the earliest and most proactive response is to disrupt and destroy your own strengths and ideology before the competition does it for you. Preemption is a way to strike before the iron is hot—to adopt the new ideology quickly before anyone else lays claim to it. Anticipating the revolution enables you to be first to market. Preemption lets you gain first-mover advantages such as moving down the experience curve, and locking out the upstarts before they can get off the ground.

Fluid spheres do preemption all the time. But even great powers with nonfluid spheres can take advantage of this alternative successfully, if they use it only periodically, and build the capabilities to carry it off. Consider the Gillette example I offered in the introduction from another perspective. Gillette was being walled into a declining sphere by rival BIC. With its disposable razors, BIC was gradually constricting Gillette's sphere in cartridge razors by converting many users away from Gillette products. Gillette escaped this competitive compression by creating a series of pre-

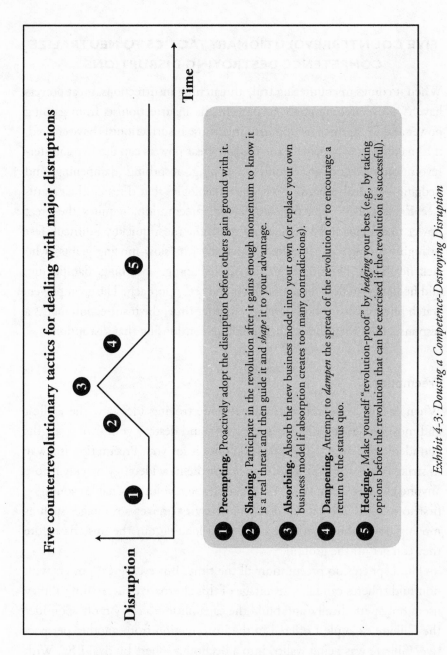

Five counterrevolutionary tactics for dealing with major disruptions

1 **Preempting.** Proactively adopt the disruption before others gain ground with it.

2 **Shaping.** Participate in the revolution after it gains enough momentum to know it is a real threat and then guide it and *shape* it to your advantage.

3 **Absorbing.** Absorb the new business model into your own (or replace your own business model if absorption creates too many contradictions).

4 **Dampening.** Attempt to *dampen* the spread of the revolution or to encourage a return to the status quo.

5 **Hedging.** Make yourself "revolution-proof" by *hedging* your bets (e.g., by taking options before the revolution that can be exercised if the revolution is successful).

Exhibit 4-3: Dousing a Competence-Destroying Disruption

emptive disruptions in shaving ideology based on radical improvements in the closeness of a shave. It did this through its massive global launches of the high-margin, very high quality Sensor and Sensor Excel. Gillette's rivals, BIC and Schick, were unable to anticipate or counter Gillette in a timely fashion. Gillette then kept its lead by preempting itself with the higher priced and even higher quality Mach3 razor. Today, Gillette's reinvigorated marauder-type sphere has effectively broken out of its walls and has regained its lost market share and then some. The company founded by King Gillette once again reigns as the king of shaving.

Given Gillette's success, shouldn't all great powers use preemption? For the "slow-moving giants" who lack the flexibility to anticipate the market and move quickly, preemption is an unlikely, perhaps even stupid, alternative. Even if a great power has the flexibility to use preemption, this counterrevolutionary tactic can be a risky business. You may act too quickly, cannibalizing your own strengths unnecessarily. You may waste your resources preempting disruptions that never materialize or take off in the market, especially if many potential revolutions are possible. You may choose the wrong direction, as did Sony with BetaMax (a VCR technology that was replaced by VHS), and Polaroid with PolarVision (an instant movie camera that was quickly replaced by the video camera).

At the early stages of a revolution there are often many competing business models, all vying to define the rules of competition. As can be seen in competition over the Internet and in telecommunications, it is anyone's guess who will be the big winners and what the dominant technologies may ultimately be. And finally, the stock market may brand you a lunatic or heretic if the existing ideology is already firmly institutionalized as "the truth." For example, IBM's "new" operating system, OS/2, and the "new" PowerPC with the Alpha (RISC) Chip inside were supposed to be the Microsoft DOS and Intel CISC chip killers. Despite the fact that both these attempts to preempt the future were decidedly better, they failed to displace the Microsoft and Wintel standards because these standards were so strongly entrenched. The OS/2 and Alpha challenges were the equivalent of heresy, and no one dared to adopt anything contrary to the one "true" way of Microsoft and Intel.

Shaping

This counterrevolutionary alternative allows you to shape the disruptive value proposition/process to your advantage, after the ambitious smaller firms have already begun to promote the new ideology. This has the advantage of avoiding the risks of being the first mover. You let the ambitious smaller firms rise up (slightly), and allow them to take the hard knocks that go with creating and promoting a new value proposition. Then you pick the strategic moment to hijack the new ideology and make it your own. Anheuser-Busch provides a good example. The giant brewer reshaped the perception of the microbrewery value proposition by producing one of the top-selling specialty beers, proving consumers will accept a small beer with a big brewer's name on the label. This undermined one of the core tenets of the microbrew ideology—microbrews have to be made in small breweries by obscure artist-like brewers. In other words, A-B reshaped the "microbrew" ideology into the "specialty" beer ideology—good specialty beers can be made in mass production plants.

The shaping strategy has become the most popular option among some of the most powerful high-tech players, who often use alliances in their efforts to shape the creation of technological and software standards. There are numerous possible wait-and-see responses to new norms or ideologies, several of which allow you to compromise or shape the new ideology to your advantage[1] (see Exhibit 4-4).

The challenge with this wait-and-see approach, of course, is that by the time you make your move the train may be moving too fast for you to jump on board and commandeer the engine. The longer you wait to shape the new ideology, the harder your task, and the greater the chance you'll be marginalized.

Absorbing

A great power can absorb the revolutionary concept by acquisition in order to gain control of the use of the new ideology. A variation of absorption is to adopt the revolutionary ideology, claiming it as your own, and acting as if it were always your own. True absorption requires the great power to convert the ideology inside its core. Constantine converted the Roman Empire to Christianity, just as Motorola replaced its old analog-based cellular phone strategy with a digital Web-enabled strategy that was successfully promoted by its most significant challenger in twenty years, Nokia.

Strategies	Tactics	Examples
Enhance and extend the new ideology	Habit	Following invisible, taken-for-granted norms of the new value proposition or process and adding improvements
	Imitate	Mimicking the new value proposition or process and adding improvements
	Comply	Obeying rules and accepting norms of the new value proposition or process but adding improvements
Compromise or shape the new ideology	Balance	Balancing the expectations of multiple constituents to modify the new value proposition or process
	Pacify	Placating and accommodating users of the new value proposition and process
	Bargain	Negotiating with stakeholders/owners of the new value proposition or process

Adapted from Christine Oliver, "Strategic Responses to Institutional Processes," *Academy of Management Review* 16.1 (1991): 152.

Exhibit 4-4: Shaping Rising Ideologies

Timing is everything with absorption. You need to move before the revolutionaries have become too powerful to stop, or you must be able to bring the revolutionary into your fold at a reasonable cost. In the case of Motorola, the company's timing wasn't so great. It adopted the digital revolution too late to prevent Nokia from becoming a great power in Motorola's core market. Despite the serious trouble Motorola experienced in the late 1990s, by 2000 the company was enjoying a major comeback against Nokia and regaining its value leadership position, thanks in large part to the ideology Nokia introduced to the market.

The main danger in absorbing a new ideology is that it may prove fatal, if your current organization is resistant. In some organizations, the true believers of the old ideology can become like white blood cells in your immune system, attacking the transplanted ideology as if it were a foreign object. Even when the body needs the transplant, it may reject it. In this case, the only solution may be to reduce the white blood cell count causing the problem.

Dampening

Another way to cope with competence-destroying disruptions is to enact various dampening tactics intended to prevent, slow, prohibit, or undermine the adoption of the new ideology by others. These tactics can range from passively resisting and avoiding the new ideology to defying and refusing to accept that ideology, to using manipulation to eliminate or reduce the threat of the new ideology (see Exhibit 4-5).

Dampening tactics can be a good way to buy time, as you wait and see which absorbing and shaping alternatives make the most sense. In the consumer product marketplace, influence over distribution channels has been used to dampen an insurrectionist's access to the market by flooding the channel with discounted product. In the high-tech industry, vaporware is frequently announced before it is ready in order to demotivate rivals from spending money to develop the same product.

Dampening is also used to "set an example." In this way, great powers discourage other insurrectionists who have yet to come out of the woodwork. A note of caution: Some dampening tactics can be considered anticompetitive or illegal under some conditions. In addition, dampening tactics are rarely effective if customers want the new value offered by the ideology. You can't kill the idea even if you bankrupt the company that first introduced it.

Hedging

This response to competence-destroying disruptions can help great powers with deep pockets make their companies more "insurrection-proof." You hedge your bets by creating "options," right at the very beginning of the revolution. But this is still a wait-and-see alternative because you don't exercise that option until after it becomes clear the revolution is already successful or is going to be successful. By exercising your "options" you are in a better po-

Strategies	Tactics	Examples
Passively resist and avoid the new ideology	Conceal	Disguising nonconformity with the new value proposition or value creation process
	Buffer	Loosening ties and attachments to users of the new value proposition or process
	Escape	Changing goals, activities, or domains to avoid using the new value proposition or process
Defy and refuse to accept the new ideology	Dismiss	Ignoring explicit norms and values of the new value proposition or process
	Challenge	Contesting rules, requirements, and assumptions underlying the new value proposition or process
	Attack	Assaulting the sources of pressure to adopt the new value proposition or process
Strive to eliminate/reduce the threat of the new ideology	Co-opt	Converting influential constituents so they abandon the new value proposition or process
	Influence	Promoting values and criteria that will change the new value proposition or process
	Command	Disciplining users, constituents, and practices to closely supervise the new value proposition or process

Adapted from Christine Oliver, "Strategic Responses to Institutional Processes," *Academy of Management Review* 16.1 (1991): 152.

Exhibit 4-5: Dampening a Disruptive Ideology

sition to quickly catch up to, and overtake, the insurrectionists. In addition, you avoid the risk associated with being a revolutionary, reduce your costs of being the original developer, and gain knowledge that allows you to improve on the original idea. Hedging can be particularly effective as a relatively low-cost way to deal with a large number of disruptions.

What types of options allow you to become more "insurrection-proof?" They might include buying licenses to use, or options to acquire, a new technology or new equipment related to the disruption. Options may also take the form of minority investments in the adherents of a new ideology to monitor their progress or capture their knowledge (recall that Anheuser's first move when faced with the microbrewery threat was to hedge its bets by its early investment in Seattle's Redhook Ale).

Like the other wait-and-see options, hedging can be risky if ill-timed. If you exercise your option too early, you could be wasting your money. If you wait too long, insurrectionists may capture first-mover advantages that are difficult to overcome.

Counterrevolutionary Combinations

Preempting. Shaping. Absorbing. Dampening. Hedging. Great powers often use more than one counterrevolutionary tactic, just as Rome ultimately shifted from dampening to total absorption in its efforts to deal with the challenge of Christianity. In addition, while these tactics are presented in Exhibit 4-3 in a linear fashion, they don't necessarily occur in this order. For example, great powers (at least the ones who want to remain great) don't always wait for the ideological revolution to peak before they resort to absorption or dampening methods. Also, a great power may create hedging options when the revolution is in its embryonic stage, but may exercise those options at any time before or after the disruptive ideology has reached its peak.

When using a combination of counterrevolutionary tactics, it's important to be quick to recognize a change in the degree of threat a disruptive ideology presents to your firm because this may necessitate a switch in tactics. Equally important, once it becomes clear which disruptive ideology is the most likely to be accepted by customers, you need to act quickly, even in the face of strong internal resistance to change. In almost all cases, it is better to accelerate the timing of the five counterrevolutionary tactics, rather than risk the consequences of doing too little too late . . . and watching the revolution pass you by.

"WEATHERPROOFING" YOUR SPHERE: SHIFTING PARADIGMS TO ACCLIMATE TO PATTERNS OF DISRUPTION

Insurrection is rarely a one-shot deal. Because most companies experience many disruptions over time, much is to be gained by looking at the pattern of these disruptions to determine whether your company needs to take more dramatic action than simply employing preemption, shaping, absorbing, dampening, or hedging counterrevolutionary tactics. To determine the pattern of disruption in your competitive environment, you need to ask two questions: How frequent are the disruptions in your competitive space? And what types of disruptions are they—competence-destroying or competence-enhancing? Taken in combination, these two factors can reveal a predominant pattern of disruption. This pattern reveals the type of competitive environment you're working in, which, in turn, suggests strategies for "weatherproofing" your sphere so you can acclimate to that particular environment.

The varying patterns of disruption can be boiled down to four radically different environments, which I've described as equilibrium, fluctuating equilibrium, punctuated equilibrium, and disequilibrium (see Exhibit 4-6). For example, a company experiencing little or no disruption enjoys life in a calm environment of equilibrium. Contrast this situation with the potentially wretched firm existing in disequilibrium, marked by a pattern of constant, competence-destroying disruptions. A firm that experiences frequent disruptions that are not very threatening to its competencies exists in an environment of fluctuating equilibrium. And firms that experience periods of stability marked by infrequent violent disruptions are living in a punctuated equilibrium environment.

Why is it important to understand your competitive environment in terms of its patterns of disruption? These four environments have a direct impact on the effectiveness of your paradigm for power, be it walled, fluid, colonial, or advanced. Whether you will be able to unleash the full power of your sphere depends in large part on whether your sphere's paradigm—with its inherent resource routing pattern—is most conducive to the type of environment you're experiencing.

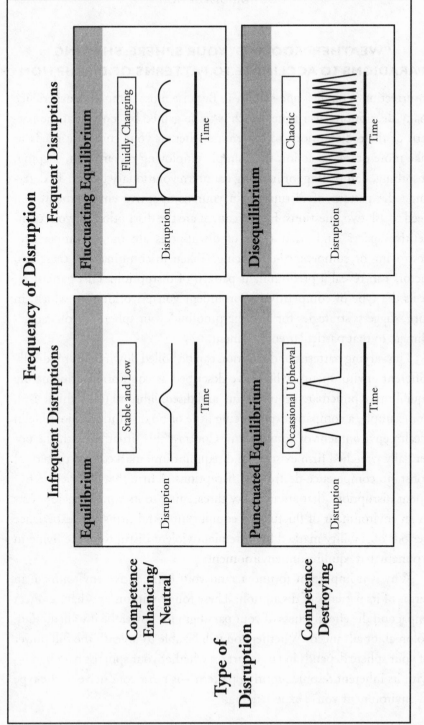

Exhibits 4-6: Four Patterns of Varying Disruption

It is not only essential to have a clear perspective of the general pattern of disruption in your space, it is also important to consider the location of the pattern of disruption in your sphere. Typically the most critical pattern is the one that is in your core and vital interests. Multiple disruptions in your buffer zones may have much less of an impact on your sphere than even a single major disruption in your core or vital interests. However, particularly severe conditions in your periphery may demand more attention than your core, if the situation in the core is relatively calm.

What's more, a great power's own geo-product market position and competencies play a big role in determining the environment. For example, if two great powers in the same industry have different core geo-product zones or competencies, one might see competence-destroying disruptions, while the other might experience the same disruptions as competence enhancing. Even within your own sphere you may have one area where there is competency-enhancing activity, and another area where the disruptions destroy your competency.

While I've described four distinct environments to represent the varying patterns of disruption by insurrectionists, it's important to note that there are no clear lines of demarcation between the environments. For example, a company in a punctuated equilibrium environment may experience increasing disruptions that nudge it into a disequilibrium environment.

Identifying the exact line between one environment and another is not the issue. The point is to understand the impact of disruption on your sphere's ability to deal with the insurrectionists driving these patterns of disruption. What follows is a more in-depth discussion of each type of environment, and its effect on your paradigm for power.

The Equilibrium Environment

The equilibrium environment is characterized by long periods of little or no competence-destroying disruption. This relatively stable type of environment is often created by strong barriers to entry or regulations that control change and competition. Banking, airlines, utilities, and telecommunications before deregulation supported and strengthened great powers such as Citibank, Eastern Airlines, PECO, and AT&T.

The height of the barriers and the stability of equilibrium environments may result from factors other than regulation. For example, the pharmaceutical industry in the 1980s created barriers to entry through the use of patents and proprietary technologies. These barriers gave the pharmaceutical companies profitable spheres built around blockbuster drugs. But by the late 1990s, technology became more advanced, and the same high barriers to entry no longer protected patented drugs. Pressure from the government, large health care providers, and insurance companies forced price competition. Alternative biotechnologies and new medical methods allowed unpatented, unforeseen substitutes to topple the walls of patents. This forced the pharmaceuticals to make significant changes, creating new barriers to entry by adding services and distribution to their spheres, including ownership of distribution channels and pharmaceutical benefit management.

In an equilibrium environment, great powers profit by shutting out invading great powers, by using power over buyers and suppliers to dampen insurrectionists, and by extracting monopoly profits from customers. Therefore, great powers in equilibrium environments frequently build walled spheres in which the citizens within the walls are made to pay higher prices, and the barriers to entry are used to prevent invaders and insurrectionists from driving down monopolistic prices.

The Fluctuating Equilibrium Environment

The fluctuating equilibrium environment is characterized by rapid disruption. Because the fluctuations don't destroy competencies, this environment allows the great power holding the key geo-product zones and competencies to sustain its leadership. By adding the disruptive new products and competencies on top of the old ones, leaders can stay ahead of the fray. The stability of its core competencies allows a great power to export these competencies into new colonies (geo-product markets) which send back the resulting income.

The consumer wireless telephone world in the 1980s experienced a period of fluctuating equilibrium, based on constant improvement and changes in cellular phones and cellular phone systems based on analog technology. This environment of fluctuating equilibrium allowed Motorola, for example, to leverage its core products and competencies into diverse product markets, such as pagers, two-way radios, and cellular phones and infrastructure. (As the Motorola-Nokia example I offered earlier showed, Motorola later faced the competence-destroying change of digital technology. This shift in environment forced the company to redefine its sphere and strategy to focus on fashionable, digital, Web-enabled wireless phones.)

In environments of fluctuating equilibrium, great powers like Motorola in the 1980s often build colonial spheres that leverage competencies from their core to profit in new markets, and use colonies (such as peripheral markets) to support or defend the core against insurrection. They also continually absorb competence-enhancing disruptions into their core. In addition, they stop the insurrectionists by keeping them from grabbing peripheral markets first. By picking up a variety of peripheral markets first, a great power can absorb numerous new disruptive ideologies that can be combined to create superiority over insurrectionists in a core market.

The Punctuated Equilibrium Environment

Punctuated equilibrium is characterized by brief, dynamic periods of discontinuous change. This environment alternates between a competence-destroying revolution and longer periods of convergence and greater stability (in which the market reorganizes around a common standard).[2]

Punctuated equilibrium environments are often seen in competitive spaces where there are periodic tectonic shifts in customers, deregulation, or technology. In this environment, many radical technological changes are followed by the emergence of a dominant design. The dominant design creates a period of stability until the next technological revolution, and the cycle repeats itself. These patterns have been identified in the cement, glass, and minicomputer industries.[3] In the flat glass industry, the creation of the Lubbers machine in 1903, replacing hand artisans, radically improved glass production. In 1917, the Colburn continuous ribbon process again transformed the industry. Pilkington introduced its float-glass production in 1963, creating another major shift in productivity and transforming the basis of competition in the industry.[4] In his book *Value Migration*, Adrian Slywotzky identified other industries which also experienced a major shift in their value creation processes during the 1980s and 1990s, including steel (vertically integrated to minimills) and airlines (direct flights to hub/spoke systems and back to direct flights again).[5]

The great powers doing business in punctuated equilibrium environments must be able to create fairly stable spheres during periods of convergence, but then shift those spheres rapidly during periods of competence-destroying disruption. In their research on organizational behavior, Michael Tushman and Elaine Romanelli proposed the use of periodic reorientation followed by periodic convergence.[6] The reorientation periods focus on creating or imitating radical new business models, while convergent periods focus on stability and better execution of the new approach. It would be tempting to try to erect walls during the period of stability, but come the next revolution, these walls may become rubble. Therefore, in a punctuated equilibrium environment, successful firms must stay flexible to reorient themselves and not rely on wall-like barriers to entry.

During periods of convergence, great powers often use formal and informal alliances to stabilize the environment, sometimes around a technological or product standard. The alliances also serve to cover the company's bets in case they need to go through another reorientation. The alliances facilitate shifting direction rapidly and can help the firm to absorb, shape, or dampen the next disruption.

In the punctuated equilibrium environment, the greatest opportunity for an insurrectionist to seize supremacy is by initiating one of these disruptive revolutions. If there are many potential revolutions which have not yet shown any evidence of taking off, the great powers will probably opt for one of the counterrevolutionary wait-and-see alternatives. Great powers in a punctuated equilibrium environment need to understand, however, that one revolutionary idea or another will eventually become powerful enough to displace them. Therefore, they must prepare for this eventuality.

In a punctuated equilibrium environment, the best opportunity to make big profits is for the great power to preempt the revolution. Though preemption can be high risk, it can also have the biggest payoff, enabling a great power to gain first-mover advantage, set the new industry standard, and be well positioned for the interim period of stability and convergence. In such cases, a great power often uses an advanced sphere of influence to reroute its resources to seize first-mover advantage in new geo-product zones. Whether you decide to use preemption or a wait-and-see tactic, advanced spheres make it easier to quickly reconfigure the sphere whenever and wherever the next insurrection surfaces.

The Disequilibrium Environment

This environment is characterized by frequent, discontinuous, competence-destroying disruptions. In other words, the insurrectionists have gone wild, and the competitive environment is in a state of near riotous conditions. In *Hypercompetition,* I argued that great powers can only keep their supremacy by constantly changing their geo-product zones through creation of new products and competencies that destroy the old ones. In this way, the great powers actually drive the chaos (outdisrupting the disrupters) so that they can control it and ensure continued supremacy over the disrupters.

Many high-tech manufacturing industries and the world of electronic commerce experience constant and rapid disruptions. Intel uses constant disruption with successive and frequent issuance of new-generation microprocessors to keep the clone manufacturers from gaining supremacy over the market. Intel wants to avoid repeating the mistake it made when Japanese memory chip manufactures imitated Intel chips, sold them for less, and took leadership of the market. Post–Andy Grove, Intel's sphere is now expanding to include non-PC chips, some software development, and other technologies, so its boundaries remain fluid, keeping pace with the rapidly changing computing world.

Only the fluid spheres of guerrillas and marauders can capture the opportunities inherent in this chaotic world before the insurrectionists seize the high ground. Great powers can't rely on barriers to entry and stable core products or core competencies in an environment of disequilibrium, making walled and colonial spheres ill-suited for this environment. Often

advanced spheres are also insufficient because alliances may lock a great
power into the interests of its alliance partners, creating some degree of in-
flexibility. Like advanced spheres, fluid spheres can use alliances but these
alliances must be very short term in nature to avoid any constraints that
prevent frequent shifts in the alliances.

The fluid sphere must develop an internal culture of driving disruption
and pushing the envelope. Great powers in disequilibrium environments
profit mainly by improving and creating customer value, looking for new
opportunities, and shifting their cores whenever those cores are about to
be invaded or destroyed. Therefore, they use nomad and opportunistic
growth strategies when faced with extreme disequilibrium. Frequently,
great powers doing business in such a chaotic atmosphere live close to the
edge of exhaustion and seek to move to a more stable sphere as soon as
possible. Part of the goal of a fluid sphere is to create value leadership so
strong that it endures, thereby providing a core market around which the
firm can build one of the other types of spheres. This, in turn, contributes
to shifting the environment away from a disequilibrium environment.

Patterns of Disruption and Picking Your Paradigm for Power

A great power builds strategic supremacy and improves its chances of successfully weatherproofing its sphere against disruption by adapting its type of
sphere and resource routing pattern. Weatherproofing proactively reduces
the impact of disruption, not by hunkering down to resist the disruption,
but by selecting the paradigm that takes advantage of the opportunities created by the pattern of disruption in the environment (see Exhibit 4-7). As
Netscape founder Marc Andreessen once said, "In a fight between a bear
and an alligator, what determines the winner is the terrain."

If your sphere's paradigm for power is at odds with your competitive
environment's pattern of disruption, can you still survive? Of course, but
this lack of synchronicity can dramatically increase your vulnerability
when an insurrection challenges your power, and it can hurt your chances
of gaining strategic supremacy.

In Chapters 2 and 3, I discussed how the immediacy of competitive

Frequency of Disruption

		Infrequent	Frequent
Type of Disruption	**Competence enhancing or neutral**	Walled spheres	Colonial spheres
	Competence destroying	Advanced spheres	Fluid spheres

Exhibit 4-7: Tailoring the Sphere to the Pattern of Disruption

compression affects your choice of growth strategy and the type of sphere. I also discussed how the type of sphere you should choose depends on how you want to create power and wealth, and on how you want to route resources to growth opportunities and competitive hot spots in your sphere. In addition, the type of sphere you choose is influenced by (and influences) the type of relationships you will have with other great powers (e.g., isolationism, pragmatism, etc.). These are all important short-term factors that must be weighed when choosing your type of sphere.

Now in this chapter, I've introduced a longer-term perspective. The purpose of considering patterns of disruption when choosing your sphere is that it gives you a context in which to ground the more short-term factors discussed in Chapters 2 and 3. The bottom line is, your paradigm for power must be selected to fit as many of the company's strategic needs as possible, not just today, but over time. Often, a company will stick with the same old paradigm because its sphere was successful in the past at projecting power and accumulating wealth. Hence, many companies are reluctant to change, and they choose their paradigm based on the past pattern of disruption. But, all else being equal, the company that recognizes the *future* pattern of disruption is the company that picks the successful paradigm for power, adapting appropriately to the turbulence of the times.

COMPETITIVE COOPERATIVES:
JOINING FORCES WITH OTHER GREAT POWERS

If you can't adapt your sphere to the competitive environment, or you don't have the strategic supremacy to apply effective counterrevolutionary tactics against insurrectionists on your own, then you may need to join forces—pooling your power with that of other great powers. In addition, no matter how much supremacy you have, sometimes the magnitude and frequency of disruption can be so great, you still won't be able to preempt, shape, dampen, absorb, or hedge your way out of trouble by acting alone. This is particularly the case in punctuated equilibrium and disequilibrium environments.

In such situations, great powers find it beneficial to form what I call "competitive cooperatives." By joining forces with rival great powers—at least regarding this mutual cause of dousing disruption and maintaining the status quo hierarchy—great powers can be much more effective at using counterrevolutionary tactics. These competitive cooperatives can take three distinct forms: a *concert of powers, polarized blocs,* or a *collective security arrangement.*

Concert of Powers

In this type of competitive cooperative, the great powers continue to compete with each other but cooperate with respect to the insurrectionists, deciding whether they should jointly dampen or absorb the disrupters (see Exhibit 4-8).

A concert of powers is actually quite common in both the brick and mortar world and cyberspace. For example, the Big Three automakers have formed a concert of powers to promote auto battery innovation and the development of a B2B exchange for auto parts and supplies.

While they continue to compete fiercely for car buyers, they are working together to dampen the impact of potential revolutions in batteries. All three car makers get access to the benefits of a major disruptive technology in batteries, so no single great power benefits disproportionately. Equally important, no upstart such as manufacturers of equipment pow-

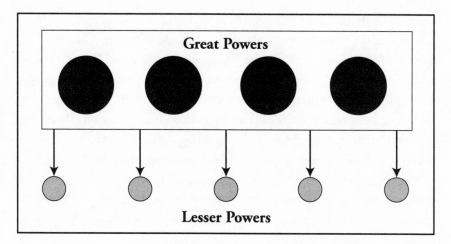

Exhibit 4-8: A Concert of Powers

ered by electric engines (e.g., major home appliances and electric-powered forklifts) will be able to disrupt the Big Three's supremacy. By pooling their resources to keep developing cutting-edge battery technology (which could replace combustion engine vehicles), the Big Three make sure that no one else can enter the marketplace by investing heavily in battery technology, or transferring battery technology from another industry.

The major car manufacturers also block entry into auto manufacturing by cooperating to create their B2B auto supply exchange. As parts get standardized and modularized for sale over the Web, new assemblers could appear using Dell-like virtual networks. Anyone with a distribution network (such as CarMax, AutoNation, rental car companies, Jiffy Lube, or even Sears, which once sold Sears-branded cars back in the 1920s) could brand and distribute "plug and play" cars unless the Big Three anticipate them. By owning the on-line exchange, the Big Three also preempt the rise of a venture-capital-funded auto parts exchange that could cut into their lucrative after-market parts and dealer repair revenues.

Currently, concerts of powers are forming industry by industry around XML (Extended Mark-up Language). XML is the next generation software infrastructure for browsers and Web pages. The great powers in major computer manufacturing (such as IBM), software (such as Oracle), and systems integrators (such as EDS and the Big Four accounting firms) are working with the great powers in several manufacturing and service industries under the banner of the W3C (WorldWideWeb Consortium). The W3C sets standards for the "meta-tags" used in XML, the unique identifier numbers associated with data on prices, parts, finished goods, and equipment. Without a common set of meta-tags, B2B exchanges cannot work because the users can't easily exchange information. By setting and then continually updating the meta-tags, the W3C is a way for industrial and service great powers to delay insurrectionists with killer B2B applications from using their own meta-tags. This benefits the concert of powers by giving them an opportunity to own and operate their own B2B exchanges, and to limit who has access to these exchanges, much the same as the auto industry has done.

Polarized Blocs

In this type of competitive cooperative, great powers continue to compete with each other but they strongly encourage insurrectionists to align with one of the great powers. Typically, the great powers form two, or less frequently more, polarized blocs of companies. Each bloc can contain more than one great power and several lesser powers and insurrectionists.

If the lesser powers and insurrectionists align with a bloc, they benefit from preferred relationships with the great powers within that bloc. If they refuse to take sides or prove disloyal, the blocs ostracize them, working jointly to ignore or weaken the resisters (see Exhibit 4-9). By polarizing the insurrectionists, the blocs make sure no lesser powers or other insurrectionists are able to rise to great power status. In addition, this enforced polarization also prevents the consolidation of lesser powers who could ban together to form a new great power.

In Japan, major players create polarization through informal zaibatsus and formal keiretsus. Japan's most powerful example of this enforced polarization is Toyota's highly successful vertical keiretsu. This keiretsu includes a manufacturing group of suppliers and distributors that provides secure, high-quality, just-in-time parts to Toyota's assembly operations. Toyota has taken significant minority interests in the ownership of many of its keiretsu members, and frequently its members have small stakes in Toyota. In this

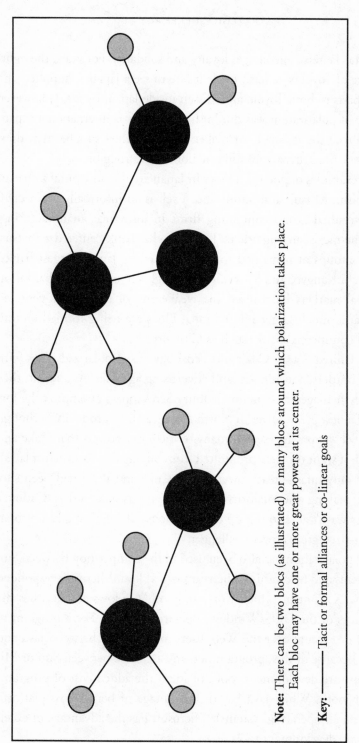

Note: There can be two blocs (as illustrated) or many blocs around which polarization takes place. Each bloc may have one or more great powers at its center.

Key: —— Tacit or formal alliances or co-linear goals

Exhibit 4-9: Polarized Blocs

way, Toyota's keiretsu encourages loyalty and solidarity. For years, the tight-knit nature of Toyota's keiretsu made it rare to see a Japanese supplier who provided parts to both Toyota and Nissan inside Japan. By 2001, however, the degree of polarization was diminishing slightly as international expansion has forced the Japanese car makers to widen their supplier networks. Nevertheless, the keiretsus are still functioning as strong blocs.

Other examples of polarized blocs in Japan are the horizontal zaibatsus of Mitsubishi, Mitsui, and Sumitomo. Each is an informally connected, highly diversified group containing firms in insurance, manufacturing, gas, and chemicals, among others. Japan also has bank-centered zaibatsus, which are groups of firms tied to and financed by Japan's largest banks, Fuji, Daiichi Kangyo, and Sanwa. Interestingly enough, the globalization of financial markets has caused the weakening of these bank-centered blocs because much larger international blocs are being formed around the global commercial banks such as CitiCorp.

In the United States, Coke and Pepsi have used polarized blocs with suppliers, bottlers, consultants, and advertising agencies. As a result, they successfully managed to contain Cadbury Schweppes's attempt at the formation of a new great power in North America and Europe. Even though Cadbury Schweppes aggregated many of the lesser powers that Coke and Pepsi did not want (or were prohibited from buying due to antitrust laws), it reached only quasi–great power status. Coke and Pepsi had been successful at making the majority of lesser powers take sides; Cadbury Schweppes wasn't able to dig up enough "loose change" to add up to an equivalent-sized great power challenger.

Forced polarization has also been used in the competition between Sun Microsystems and Microsoft. When Sun issued Java, Microsoft responded with Active X Control, which works only on Windows and accesses the full resources of the DOS/Windows operating system. For a program to download or execute over the Web, users must choose between Java and Active X. Because of this, programmers must choose between Sun or Microsoft software development tools, or incur the added cost of programming with both. While Java has the advantage of being cross-platform (running on all operating systems), Microsoft has the advantage of excellent software development tools.

Collective Security Arrangements

In this type of competitive cooperative, the great powers form agreements among themselves and with insurrectionists that give a "piece of the action" to everyone. This creates a peaceful co-existence as long as all the players don't get greedy and everyone mutes their competitive instincts within a limited number of product markets (see Exhibit 4-10).

Collective security arrangements are the most difficult of the three competitive cooperatives to pull off because they require the great powers to enhance the security of some portion of their competitors' spheres. In addition, because the great powers rely even less on discipline (than they do with the other two methods) to get the lesser powers to cooperate, they have to offer greater incentives to these lesser powers in order to get them to "buy in" to the collective security arrangement.

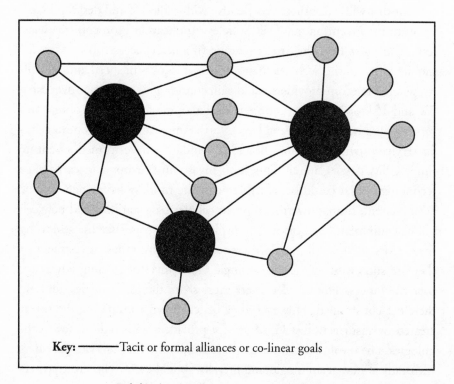

Key: ————Tacit or formal alliances or co-linear goals

Exhibit 4-10: Collective Security Arrangements

Collective security arrangements can be tricky because too much co-operation can be construed as anticompetitive behavior. Nevertheless, it is possible to achieve collective security in ways that government antitrust regulators will accept because the arrangement serves some larger societal purpose. For example, a collective security arrangement can be created to foster innovation, or to create open standards that allow many customers and competitors to benefit from access to the same network or to benefit from other aspects of using those standards.

Consider the mutual interest of wireless telephone carriers in North America and Europe regarding the need to innovate. As the carriers become more of an access point to the Internet, they face many challenges. One is the problem of providing better or different content from other Internet distribution channels, such as cable TV and desktop computers. Another challenge is limited bandwidth—the capacity to move data over the airwaves—so the wireless telephone carriers want to accommodate the richer content that will make them competitive with cable TV and desktop PCs.

With the invention of WAP (Wireless Application Protocol), the wire-less carriers now have the first generation (if not yet successful) software for mobile access to the Web. As such software improves in speed and reliability, wireless telecom providers could gain considerable advantage over cable TV and desktop PCs. In addition, to deal with the cell phone's content and capacity disadvantages, several large North American and European cellular service providers—using the GSM standard—have formed a venture fund, GSM/Argo Capital. This fund invests in startups and early stage technologies that could benefit them all. The fund looks for new mobile Web content, more powerful chips for cellular base stations, and new cell phone equipment (e.g., capable of displaying Web page–like images) using the GSM standard. All the GSM carriers benefit from these investments if they are successful, without any single GSM investor gaining advantage over the others. The GSM carriers must share the technologies, and are therefore constrained. However, they benefit from eliminating the threat created by insurrectionist GSM service providers with radical new tech-nologies. The revolutionaries who would supply the GSM service providers with radical new technologies are literally "bought in." The great powers give these start-up revolutionaries the finances to develop and grow their businesses. And these revolutionaries are happy with faster access to the wireless carrier marketplace because the great power investors are able to deploy the disruptive technologies on a large scale.

Another example of a collective security arrangement is the one being arranged by Bluetooth, the leading designer and manufacturer of chips enabling short-distance wireless connections for PCs, personal digital assistants, printers, cell phones, and any other digital device. By spring 2000, 1,824 companies had agreed to use the Bluetooth standard for their high speed, short-distance radio communications needs, making all their devices and software capable of communicating with each other. These companies included great powers in several industries (such as Nokia, IBM, Intel, Microsoft, Motorola, Toshiba, and Lucent) as well as hundreds of lesser powers (such as Acer, AMD, and Delco) that also reaped the benefits of increased connectivity.

By mid 2001, some cracks in this collective security arrangement began to appear, with Microsoft's announcement that it is dropping Bluetooth support from Windows XP. This points out the difficulty of holding collective security arrangements together when the interests of the players change. Nevertheless, if the Bluetooth security arrangement falls apart, it is likely to be replaced by another collective security arrangement built around 802.11b, a wireless ethernet standard. And, if the two (Bluetooth and 802.11b) build simultaneously competing security arrangements, polarized blocs will result.

Yet another example of a collective security arrangement was the one created by American investment banks in the U.S. government securities (bond) market. In 1996, when the U.S. government issued a bond, a handful of American banks had a lock on its distribution. Deutsche Bank, barely a player in this market, then offered an on-line system, making prices transparent for these securities. This made it harder for the established players to make profits from buying low and selling high to institutions that were unfamiliar with prices in the closed, private market among the established players. The U.S. investment banks responded to this insurrection by forming www.TradeWeb.com. Morgan Stanley, Goldman Sachs, J. P. Morgan, Merrill Lynch, and Salomon Smith Barney, among others, took minority equity stakes in the Web site and co-mingled their pricing information and trading platforms, locking Deutsche Bank out of the trading process. Regulators later forced the opening of the Web site, allowing Deutche Bank and others to distribute and buy bonds on TradeWeb, however, these "nonfounders" could not become owners of the exchange Web site.

Despite the fact that margins declined, the founding U.S. investment banks were able to protect, and even grow in some cases, a fair amount of share that might otherwise have gone to Deutsche Bank. So the great powers managed to hold onto their great power status in this market, and the lesser powers (Deutsche Bank, Chase Manhattan, Lehman Brothers, Barclay's, and Greenwich NatWest) were satisfied because they were able to "wet their beaks" by dipping them into the U.S. government bond market.

KEEPING THE LID ON REVOLUTION

Early Christianity and microbreweries may seem like they are centuries (and miles) apart, but their lessons are similar. By making Christianity part of Roman imperial culture, Constantine harnessed the power of this revolutionary religion to reunite the Roman Empire. Unlike Diocletian before him, Constantine was able to deal effectively with the internal Christian challenge by "absorbing," rather than "dampening," its followers. Through his acceptance and his support of the codification of Christian beliefs, Constantine reshaped Christianity from a mystical passive-resistance movement to an acceptable and established religion. In this way, the Roman Empire (and the subsequent Byzantine Empire which evolved from the eastern half of the Roman Empire) enjoyed hundreds of years of additional life unified and motivated, in part, by the defense of Christendom.

Anheuser-Busch used counterrevolutionary tactics similar to those of Rome when it hijacked the microbrewery ideology. First, Anheuser reshaped the perception of the microbrewers' value proposition by producing one of the top-selling specialty beers, proving consumers will accept a small beer with a big brewer's name on the label. This undermined one of the core tenets of the microbrew ideology (that microbrews have to be made in small breweries by obscure artist-like brewers). Second, it dampened the acceptance of microbrews by exposing the fact that two of the most popular "microbrews"—Pete's Wicked Ale and Plank Road—were made in Stroh's and Miller breweries, respectively. Third and most importantly, the megabrewer used its influence over distributors, its economies of scale, and its deep pockets to gain the advantage over independents, thus dampening the revolutionaries. Even though the microbrew ideology survived, specialty beers failed by a long shot to reach their heady expectations, remaining below 3 percent market share in the first half of 2000. Nationwide, hundreds of brewpubs and breweries have disappeared. In short, due in large part to Anheuser's early and consistent launching of its own craft-style beers, the disruptive ideology introduced by the microbreweries lost its disruptive edge. As a modern business, you may be facing disruptions in hundreds of products in hundreds of countries. Clearly, you can't suppress every revolution everywhere immediately. More importantly, you don't need to.

Your competitive space will always be a boiling cauldron full of revolutionaries and ambitious lesser powers seeking to blow the lid off your leadership. Instead of wasting your energy trying to get rid of all the revolutionaries, you can keep order by staying above the fray, regulating the intensity of the fire, or keeping a tight lid on the cauldron.

Through wait-and-see tactics you can bide your time, watching to see which revolutionaries boil to the top, and then dousing the fire when and how you need to. Through competitive cooperatives, you can tighten the lid if you need to. Through preemption you can fan the flames wherever you need to turn up the heat on rival great powers. And through adapting your sphere to the pattern of turbulence within your cauldron, you can even reshape the lid however you need to. As a result, great powers working alone or together can regulate the degree of disruption brought on by lesser powers and revolutionaries and stabilize their industry structure, maintaining the current hierarchy of powers (see Exhibit 4-11). In short, apparent disorder in the competitive space doesn't necessarily mean the absence of order.

Sitting above the fray, the great powers provide stability and continuity to the competitive space. If they fall into the cauldron, they provide more meat for the stew. So in order to provide order to the disorder, they must douse small disruptions as they surface to the top, and they must remember what Arthur Wellesley, the Duke of Wellington (1838), once said: "There is no such thing as a little war for a great nation."

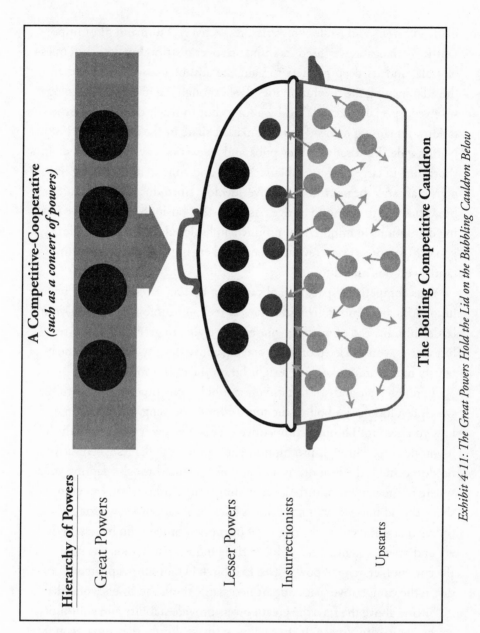

Exhibit 4-11: The Great Powers Hold the Lid on the Bubbling Cauldron Below

Chapter 5

Competitive Configuration

Shaping Great Power Relationships to Gain Preeminence for Your World View

OVERVIEW

How do great powers achieve supremacy over other great powers? The key is to master the art of competitive configuration—*the ability to create an industry structure of great power alliances, targets, and spheres that reflects your world view for the competitive space. Competitive configuration starts by creating* triangles *that reduce the complexity of the space to two clear issues—which great power spheres make the best targets, and which great powers make the most useful (and loyal) allies. The goal is to focus as many triangles as possible on the target. Competitive configuration also includes the use of* signals *and* balanced-deep overlaps *to keep others aligned—or at least in line—as you move against your target. And finally, great powers use a variety of approaches—*divide-and-conquer, assimilator, coordinator, *and* balancer strategies—*to gain influence not only over the current competitive configuration, but over the process of reconfiguration. This ensures that even as your competitive space evolves, your great power status remains great.*

NAPOLEON'S GAME OF RUSSIAN ROULETTE

Napoleon had his hands full. By 1806, the French general, consul, and self-proclaimed emperor had conquered most of Western Europe—with the exception of Britain, which remained indomitable on the high seas. Abandoning the notion of invasion, Napoleon took another tack, instituting the Continental System, which employed a boycott of British goods by all Western European countries under France's control. With the Continental System in place and working, Britain was virtually "walled out" of the Continent. France's triumph over her arch rival—and her elevated position as a great power—seemed virtually assured in the first decade of that new century.

But, as history reveals, Napoleon's grand empire proved a fleeting contender in the parade of global superpowers. What happened to cause Napoleon's downfall? The answer, paradoxically, is inextricably entwined with Napoleon's success. As France emerged as a major global player with a secure sphere under its control, it lost the luxury of competing in a one-on-one power struggle with Britain. Suddenly, Napoleon wasn't facing one superpower rival, but two. Czar Alexander I of Russia had become increasingly leery of France's growing power. To pacify the czar, Napoleon proposed an alliance between their two countries. For Russia, the alliance would bolster its forces against the Ottoman Empire to its south. For France, Russia's support would bolster its forces against Britain. Just as importantly, the alliance would buy Napoleon time, allowing France to put off its ultimate confrontation with Russia.

Russia initially agreed to the alliance, and together the two powers did indeed tighten the noose around Britain's ability to trade in Europe, at one point narrowing England's commerce to a single port of entry in Portugal. But within a few years, cracks began to show in the Franco-Russian alliance. Napoleon balked on his promise to support and recognize the Russian occupation of the Ottoman provinces of Wallachia and Moldavia. France and Russia developed conflicting goals in Eastern Europe because Napoleon feared Russia would tip the balance of power in its favor if Russia captured too much Ottoman territory. Ultimately, the czar—fed up with Napoleon's fickleness and foreseeing the potential gradual constriction of his own empire—decided to curtail his alliance with France and side with Austria as a counterbalance to Napoleon's growing strategic supremacy over Western Europe. From there, things went downhill fast for Napoleon.

By 1812, France was engaged in a two-fronted conflict. To confront the Russians, Napoleon amassed the largest army ever seen. He won a costly victory in Borodino, then marched his weakened forces into Moscow. There, he found nothing but a burning and deserted city. His troops exhausted, his lines of supply critically overextended, and winter nipping at his heels, Napoleon beat a costly retreat back to France. Less than a year later, a coalition of allies consisting of Prussia, Britain, Sweden, and Austria defeated the French emperor at Leipzig, then pursued him into France and took Paris. In 1814, Napoleon was forced to abdicate his throne and was exiled to the island of Elba.

As the story of Napoleon demonstrates, creating a powerful sphere with supremacy over lesser powers is only one critical phase in achieving strategic supremacy. While Napoleon demonstrated his genius at conquering the divided, weaker, or smaller territories of Continental Western Europe, he ultimately failed to weaken or contain France's great power rivals—Britain and Russia—two spheres that pushed against his own.

In business, countless firms that have reached great power status by achieving preeminence within their own spheres have met fates similar to that of Napoleon's empire, because they too have failed to create strategic supremacy over their neighboring great powers. These failed firms faltered at what I call "competitive configuration." Achieving a competitive configuration that tips the power balance in your favor demands that you cooperate with some great power rivals, in order to more effectively compete against a targeted great power. This reduces the complexity of competing in a global marketplace, allowing you to focus on one major rival at a time, knowing that—at least while the configuration is intact—your back is covered from attack by other great powers. If you are successful at configuring enough right alliances against the right target, the result is an industry structure—a competitive configuration—that embodies your firm's "world view" or vision for the competitive space.

RECONFIGURING CYBERSPACE

In today's dynamic business environment, many global firms already understand the value, if not the art, of competitive configuration. The tsunami of global mergers and acquisitions alone reveals a trend of combining once strange bedfellows into a single powerful sphere of influence.

AOL's Steve Case provides but one example of a recent, eye-popping move to reconfigure the players in cyberspace—the $172 billion merger between America Online and Time Warner. This merger combines the world's biggest Internet service provider (AOL) and a massive media empire that includes one of the largest cable TV service providers in America (Time Warner). Like Napoleon's consolidation of Continental Western Europe, AOL's merger with Time Warner creates a sphere of influence with potential supremacy over access to the Internet via graphical user interfaces (for TVs and desktop computers). Because AOL had already corralled Netscape, the deal could help AOL's sphere of influence gain preeminence by eliminating the threat of millions of customers dumping its service for the swifter cable-modem connections offered by companies like Time Warner. It also strengthens AOL's sphere by adding cable distribution of AOL's content and user interface to its existing distribution pipeline as an Internet service provider (ISP).

While the AOL's wooing of Time Warner is intended to secure its sphere of influence in the digital age, it is also a focused strategy for tipping the balance of power *away* from two other great Internet powers—Microsoft and Yahoo! Microsoft now has approximately 90 percent of personal computer operating systems and two-thirds of the browser market, giving Microsoft's MSN portal a significant presence in the Internet access marketplace on desktop computers. Yahoo! competes with AOL and MSN by being a content aggregator and portal site that is independent of desktop operating systems, Web browsers, and distribution channels.

When (and if) AOL's CEO Steve Case successfully integrates Time Warner into AOL's sphere of influence, the balance of power may tip away from Microsoft and Yahoo! because AOL has configured the players in a way that could require Yahoo! and MSN to go through AOL's pipelines to the consumers. When the AOL/Time Warner merger was approved, the government placed some limits on AOL's ability to use its control over cable lines as a competitive weapon. Nevertheless, like Napoleon's Continental System, the AOL/Time Warner alliance could significantly tighten the noose around its rivals' abilities to reach a significant portion of the marketplace.

But, just as Napoleon discovered that France's success in Western Europe brought her in contact with a new player, Russia, AOL will also have to confront new powerful rivals for preeminence in the Internet access market. The invention of numerous Web-connected information appliances—hand-held personal digital assistants like the Palm Pilot and high-end Internet-ready cellular telephones—has created a variety of new software interfaces with the Internet.

AOL has made some alliances with these new rival powers but Microsoft also has tried to accommodate such devices with its Windows CE, a reduced version of DOS/Windows. Fortunately for AOL, Windows CE has not been widely accepted thus far. Part of the reason is that Microsoft and Symbian are now battling over standards for cell phone operating systems and Symbian looks to have the advantage because it is being backed by an alliance of cell phone manufacturers crossing software and hardware, as well as cell phones and computers.

AOL finds itself having to configure new great powers in its efforts to gain preeminence not just over Yahoo! and MSN, but also Palm (which was spun off from 3Com) and cellular service providers. Can Steve Case succeed where Napoleon failed? As of April 2001, the answer rests on whether Case makes Napoleon's mistakes.

Almost two hundred years ago, Napoleon paid a big price for consolidating control over Western Europe. But his conquest wasn't worth the price he paid because he failed to configure Russia and Britain in a way that tipped the balance of power in his favor. Similarly, in this new millennium the AOL/Time Warner merger will only be worth its $172 billion price tag if AOL can configure the great powers in the non-desktop world to tip the balance of power away from Microsoft and Yahoo! Otherwise leadership over cable and ISP access could be superseded by wireless access to the Internet.

Clearly, competitive configuration is a high stakes game. From Napoleon's control of the Continent to Steve Case's influence over cyberspace, the art of competitive configuration has been proven to be key in determining which spheres achieve strategic supremacy over the other great powers. In short, to master this art is to master your future.

MASTERING THE ART OF COMPETITIVE CONFIGURATION

Rarely do great powers compete to wipe out everybody else in the competitive space. Instead, a successful great power configures the other great powers with the goal of gaining preeminence in the geo-product or cyber-product markets that matter most to its sphere of influence. But competitive configuration is about even more than a tussle over turf. Winning geo-product or cyber-product markets is only one tool used in the larger process of creating a strong sphere and influencing the competitive configuration, or industry structure. You must also configure the other great powers in a way that gains preeminence for your firm's world view.

Your world view is your vision for the competitive configuration, including how you would like to define the overall competitive space, how many great powers you want to compete in that space, and the positioning and relative power of each of those players. When considering your world view, several alternative competitive configurations may be equally desirable, in which case you have an embarrassment of riches and you must pick one and pursue it with all the power of your sphere. Otherwise you'll end up with a muddled configuration that doesn't conform to any of your alternative visions for the space.

If you have the strategic supremacy to configure the players the way you want, then that resulting configuration—that structure of alliances, targets, and spheres that you have orchestrated—will reflect your chosen world view. On the other hand, if your rival great power has supremacy, the competitive configuration embodies that firm's world view. And, if no player has achieved strategic supremacy, the current competitive configuration is a compromised version of multiple world views. Or the configuration may simply reflect the "momentary" structure of an industry in flux.

Within any competitive space there are multiple possibilities of competitive configurations, the result of any number of alliance combinations, power balances, cooperative and competitive relationships, and player positions within a competitive space. Even when the competitive space is limited to two great powers—an infrequent and sometimes transient occurrence—competitive configurations can vary greatly. The configuration depends on factors such as whether the relationship between the two powers is competitive or cooperative; whether there is a balance or imbalance of power between the rivals; and whether they are pursuing common, nonconflicting, or conflicting goals.

Competitive configurations become even more complex when there is a third great power (or more) on the scene that can be used to change the relationship between two great powers. Consider the way Napoleon attempted (but ultimately failed) to use an alliance with Russia to gain the upper hand against Britain, or the way AOL is using its acquisition of Time Warner to gain supremacy over Microsoft and Yahoo! Third great powers can be used in a variety of ways. For example, some great powers rally competitors against a preexisting common rival the way Coca-Cola got McDonald's to join forces in its battle against PepsiCo when PepsiCo owned some of McDonald's biggest rivals, including KFC, Taco Bell, and Pizza Hut. Still others configure the players using a tacit agreement against attacking each other. Consider how ABC, CBS, and NBC news are so aggressive at investigative reporting about corporations and their misdeeds, but very rarely do they criticize rival news organizations. The exception to the rule is when they are pushed into a corner, such as when GM's lawyers went to court to prove that an NBC reporter blew up one of its trucks to create a false impression of a vehicle defect. Yet after the initial coverage of the NBC-GM story, the networks quickly dropped it. They refrained from repeatedly mentioning this lapse in moral judgment for months as they typically do when a political figure provides false evidence or even exaggerates the facts.

Because there are multiple possibilities of competitive configurations within the same space, how do you know which one—which arrangement of cooperative alignments and designated targets—makes the most sense for you? The answer comes back to your world view: How do you want to define your sphere and the spheres of your rivals? What do you want your relationships to be with each great power rival? How many rivals do you want in the space? Do you want an equal distribution or an imbalance of power? And once you achieve strategic supremacy, how will you use your position?

With this understanding of your vision for the space, you gain insights into which competitive configuration is the most favorable for your sphere. Then comes the hard part—using your sphere to get other great powers to buy into your world view. And *that* is the art of competitive configuration.

GREAT POWER RELATIONSHIPS: HOW SPHERES INTERACT ONE-ON-ONE

Every competitive configuration boils down to relationships. Therefore, to master the art of competitive configuration, you will first want a clear understanding of the balance of power between your sphere and each great power in the competitive space.

In the previous chapters of this book, I have discussed several factors that go into creating a powerful sphere. For example, your sphere's power is directly related to its structural integrity—how solid is your position in your core and vital interests? How effective are your buffers at insulating you against attack by other great powers? Is your sphere cohesive or are there structural holes, critical zones of interest that you fail to occupy? Does your sphere adhere to a paradigm that maximizes your ability to accumulate wealth?

Your sphere's power is also affected by its success at offensive maneuvering. What impact do your forward positions have on other spheres? Do you use ideological (value) leadership to set the expectations of customers and rivals in terms of quality, price, and performance? How effective are you at creating competitive compression on rivals? How good are you at putting down insurrections by ambitious lesser powers and revolutionaries (especially in your core)?

In addition, the power of your sphere directly relates to its ability to survive and shape the future. What are the growth rates in your sphere's various zones, particularly your pivotal zones—the positions you take that are bets on the future, without any specific rival in mind? How does your sphere counter competitive compression as it grows and evolves over time?

Taken together, these three overarching factors—the sphere's structural integrity, its offensive maneuvering skills, and its ability to shape its future—determine not only the power of your sphere, but also your *relative* power compared to every other major rival in the competitive space. And this relative power, at any given moment in time, can be literally mapped by creating a visual representation of each geo-product space and the many invasions being launched in and out of the spheres.

Below, I've provided a sample of this type of map, using the power relationship between Toyota and General Motors (see Exhibit 5-1). While my example is taken from the automobile industry, the value of mapping relative power relationships is applicable to any competitive environment. A map of a power relationship should depict how forward positions are being used against the main bodies of each sphere (i.e., the cores and their immediate vital interests and buffer zones). It should also show the contests (if any) over pivotal zones and vital interests outside the immediate vicinity of each sphere's core. Once complete, the map will reveal the overlapping elements among spheres of great powers, the degree to which players threaten each other's cores, and the strength of their thrusts.

The story that follows further analyzes the power relationship between Toyota and General Motors. Note how each sphere's structural integrity, its offensive maneuvering skills, and its ability to shape the future play a key role in determining the balance of power between these two rivals, and the growth potential of their spheres.

Toyota vs. General Motors: Driving Each Other to Distraction

The map of the power relationship between Toyota and General Motors in Exhibit 5-1 reveals that General Motors' sphere of influence is centered in North America, while Toyota's sphere is centered in Japan. Yet, more often than not, the world doesn't seem big enough for the both of them. For years, the companies have battled for key zones, with their competing spheres of influence colliding again and again, each with incompatible strategic intentions for the same geo-product zones, particularly in the United States.

As shown in this simplified map, Toyota and GM are clearly engaged in a struggle for occupation of pivotal zones in the geo-product space, as well as in a battle over each other's vital interests. During the 1980s, General Motors used its cash flow from its European stronghold to fund its

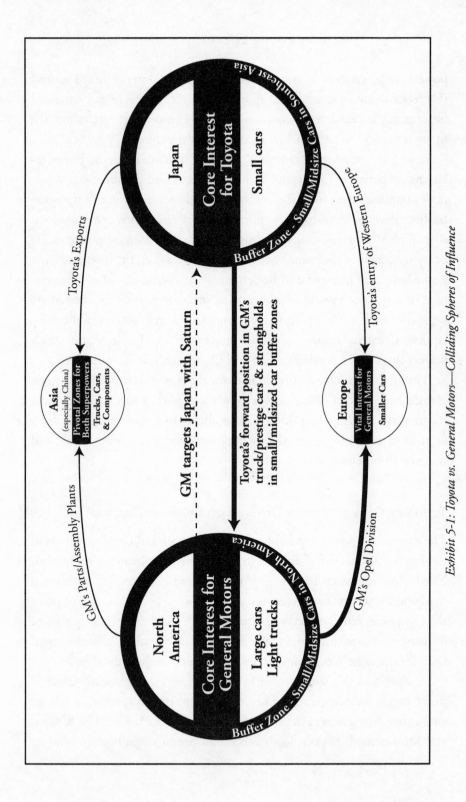

Exhibit 5-1: Toyota vs. General Motors—Colliding Spheres of Influence

battle with Toyota in North America. Toyota used its profits from its stronghold in Japan to fund its attack in North America. For example, it used its efficient plants in Japan to launch an attack in North America on low-end cars in the 1970s, high-end cars in the 1980s, and light trucks in the late 1990s. Each time, Toyota priced its cars well below comparables, leaving lots of money on the table that could have been taken as profit margins.

Over the long haul, we can see from Exhibit 5-1 that Toyota holds the balance of power in its favor even though its core economy is currently weak. Japan's core is still well protected from attack given its strong barriers to entry. When its core economy recovers, it will still have an increasing presence in GM's core. In contrast, GM has made ineffective inroads into Toyota's home turf with the launch of Saturn in Japan in the late 1990s in an unsuccessful attempt to weaken Toyota's sphere. Moreover, GM's vital interest in Europe is maturing and is about to suffer a shakeout as the European Union integrates. Plus, Toyota is in a better geographic position to capture the future growth market in Asia. Finally, Toyota's stronger brand reputation and customer loyalty among American youth and baby boomers position it as the long-term value leader by a wide margin. Thus, Toyota's sphere is the stronger of the two. Exhibit 5-2 summarizes some of the many factors that determine who holds the balance of power in its favor, but Exhibits 5-1 and 5-2 also reveal that the GM-Toyota struggle for industry leadership is not yet over.

Mainland China, for example, may well determine the future balance of power between Toyota and GM. Anyone who wins there will have overwhelming economies of scale in twenty to thirty years, and Toyota does not have Asia locked up yet. By 2000, General Motors was (perhaps temporarily) benefiting from the poor Japanese economy and strong yen, which have undermined Toyota's core in Japan, preventing Toyota from diverting resources from Japan for attacks on GM's vital interests in North America and Europe. Finally, with Opel in Germany, GM's strong position in the European market may well become an asset, despite the maturity of that market. As consumer acceptance of German cars continues to grow throughout Europe and as other barriers fall within Europe, exporting from Germany to large markets throughout Western Europe will become easier and cheaper.

Factors Related to:		
The Structural Integrity of the Spheres	**Offensive Maneuvering**	**The Future**

• Strength of walls and vital interests
• Effectiveness of buffer zones
• Relative size and power
• Effectiveness of resource routing strategy
• Cohesiveness and holes in the spheres
	• Value leadership in the core
	• Power to put down insurrections
	• Ability to create competitive compression
	  – magnitude
	  – key markets
	• Impact of forward positions
		• Growth rates in each sphere's zones
		• Effectiveness of each sphere's pivotal zones
		• Effectiveness of growth pattern
		• Degree and type of compression constraining each sphere's growth

Exhibit 5-2: Several Factors Affecting the Balance of Power between GM and Toyota

Understanding this power relationship helps explain some anomalous behavior between GM and Toyota. For example, despite the fierce rivalry between the two companies, General Motors and Toyota agreed to cooperate in the 1980s with the New United Motor Manufacturing, Inc. (NUMMI) joint venture in California. Each company established a forward position in the other's sphere of influence—NUMMI helped General Motors create Saturn (which has made inroads into Toyota's North American small/midsize car market) and Toyota expanded its forward position in General Motors' home North American territory more quickly. While this joint venture looked like cooperation, it actually served to intensify the turf battle between the firms. It did not create greater stability because each gained a stronger position from which to attack the other. Because Toyota held the balance of power in its favor, it was well positioned to exploit its forward position in GM's core markets. In contrast, GM's historical focus on large cars made it poorly positioned to be a player in Toyota's core small car market. With NUMMI, GM was only playing catch-up in manufacturing and quality. And even with a better car from the NUMMI plant, GM's negative brand image at the time forced it to sell its share of NUMMI's output at a discount. Toyota not only commanded a premium price, but also gained and still holds significant market share in North America. So why would GM risk losing its home markets in a joint venture with Japan's most powerful car manufacturer, when it could have joint ventured with a less threatening high-quality Japanese firm?

One view was GM didn't have much choice due to Toyota's superior power. Although General Motors was a force to be reckoned with, Toyota's supremacy created a dilemma for GM. If GM accepted the offer, it aided Toyota's U.S. expansion. If GM refused, Toyota had the power to push even harder against GM. Plus, Toyota could have used its power to ally with a GM competitor like Ford, giving Toyota even greater superiority over GM. GM would have been in trouble if it accepted, and in trouble if it didn't. GM chose to go along with the deal because at least this way it got something out of the situation. Given Toyota's power, the best GM could have done was to minimize its losses.

Mapping your one-on-one relationship with a great power shows, in black and white, your role in the space, and how that role affects the balance of power. For a broader view of the competitive space—its existing competitive configuration—it is useful to extend this process by doing a map of your sphere's relationship with *each* of the other great powers. Note, however, that a map of an industry's competitive configuration should include *only* the great powers, because the lesser powers are, by definition, less influential. Despite the ability of lesser powers and revolutionaries to challenge the preeminence of a great power within its sphere, a great power can deal with these "disrupters" using the strategies offered in the previous chapter.

GREAT POWER TRIANGLES: INTERACTING ONE-ON-ONE-ON-ONE

In reality, most competitive spaces are multipolar, meaning there are more than two strong spheres of influence within the competitive space. Therefore, while one-on-one maps of power relationships are an important first step in the art of competitive configuration, they provide only a limited perspective of the competitive space. You must also look at the impact of third parties on each pair of great powers. Remember Napoleon, who caught on quickly that you can't afford to focus on a single rival while ignoring other nearby great powers. Do so, and you are essentially handing those third parties an invitation to blindside you.

In politics and business, great powers have addressed the complexities of competing in a multipolar world by creating virtual "triangles" among the players in the competitive space. Each triangle reflects the power relationship among three great powers at any given time. While these great power triangles are only a virtual configuration of the competitive space, they serve a very real purpose in helping you ultimately to tip the balance of power in your favor in two ways. First, you can configure triangles that supplement your sphere and add strength to it. Second, you can configure triangles that weaken a sphere that poses a threat to your power.

Mapping these virtual triangles, just as you mapped the one-on-one power relationships between two spheres, allows you to see many important strategic implications, including:

- Who is vulnerable because they have been targeted by two of the other great powers
- The relative position of your sphere based on the alliances you or your rivals are embedded within
- Whether a web of alliances exist that weaken some players and give others strategic supremacy
- Whether a group of great powers have formed "competitive co-operatives" that exclude some great powers, making those who are excluded more vulnerable to ambitious lesser powers and revolutionaries
- Whether a formal or tacit alliance can be formed with a great power that already shares your interests with respect to a common target

To achieve strategic supremacy over other great powers in your space, you need to understand your role in these triangles *and* how you can manage them. Think of your sphere as one corner of the triangle. Another corner represents a rival's sphere that you have selected to target. The third corner represents a third great power—an alliance partner that supplements your sphere in its move against a target sphere, or a great power that could interfere with your attack on a target.

Because you can't fight in every triangle you're embedded within, your goal is to select one sphere at a time to target—while simultaneously keeping the rest of the players aligned with your interests, or at least in line, while you go after your target.

Consider how triangles affected the maneuvering of great power rivals Johnson & Johnson and Procter & Gamble in their efforts to define and expand their spheres of influence. These two great powers spent years maneuvering one-on-one over parts of the baby market, until the rise of a third party in the disposable diaper market, Kimberly-Clark. When two became three, the balance of power shifted and the borders in the baby and diaper markets were renegotiated.

Changing Diapers: The Shifting Borders in the Baby Market

Before the mid-1970s, the two supermarket superpowers Procter & Gamble and Johnson & Johnson had established an uneasy truce. The two great powers were equally powerful, with strong positions in the super-market, formidable brand names, and reputations for strong innovation. Both spheres shaped competition in their markets. P&G's sphere of influ-ence was centered on controlling soaps and shampoos; J&J's on baby prod-ucts. (They both, of course, had broader spheres, but I've focused on the supermarket competitive space to simplify my examination of the com-petitive dynamics between two spheres with clashing interests.) Both companies got along just fine as long as their spheres of influence within the supermarket channel remained relatively separate.

For years, each company chose to leave the other alone—a standoff at the corporate level—since a potential confrontation could possibly lead to mutual assured destruction in the baby-products aisle. P&G produced adult shampoos but stayed out of J&J's hair, so to speak, by staying out of the baby shampoo business. (P&G most certainly could have entered this zone successfully, given its extensive core competence in the chemistry of soaps and shampoos.) Likewise, J&J left P&G's sphere alone, structuring its own sphere strictly around baby products (see Exhibit 5-3, Diagram A). Then, in the mid-1970s, P&G broke the unspoken truce! Tempted by the size and growth of a power vacuum in disposable diapers, P&G intro-duced Pampers, a move that—from J&J's perspective—could absorb a whole lot more than what its competitor was advertising to parents (see Exhibit 5-3, Diagram B).

For Johnson & Johnson, Pampers presented a serious threat to its baby product core. With P&G's knowledge of soap/shampoo chemistry, its super-market distribution, and its new strong baby-oriented brand name (Pam-pers), the company could potentially take a dangerous share of J&J's core baby market. J&J had no choice but to defend its baby fiefdom by introduc-ing its own brand of diapers. Alas, J&J's counteroffensive failed since J&J didn't share P&G's economies of scale in diaper production or distribution.

This failure left J&J with a dilemma: If it continued to fight in baby di-apers, the company would lose a fortune. If it didn't fight P&G—and P&G were to extend its Pampers brand into J&J's core baby market—J&J could also lose a fortune. Clearly, J&J needed to find another method to hold P&G in check. J&J could, for example, move into adult diapers. From this hypothetical forward position, J&J could use its competitive arsenal to create a credible threat of its own. Using its economies of scale in adult diaper production facilities and its strong brand name, J&J could potentially move into P&G's baby diaper stronghold. But, unfortunately for J&J, Kimberly-Clark moved there first.

Kimberly-Clark's product, Depends, created barriers around adult diapers that J&J could not overcome. Thanks to this third party, P&G was left in a superior position over J&J with respect to its potential for expansion into other baby products. P&G, with its skill in the chemistry of shampoos and the Pampers brand name, could still move easily into J&J's stronghold of baby shampoos (see Exhibit 5-3, Diagram C).

Nevertheless, in the longer run, Kimberly-Clark's presence actually did benefit J&J. While J&J was left with an uneasy set of borders between its sphere and P&G's sphere, J&J knew that P&G would be preoccupied defending its baby diapers against Kimberly-Clark. Kimberly-Clark's stronghold in adult diapers would undoubtedly help it build economies of scale in production and distribution of diapers. Plus, J&J knew that Kimberly-Clark could be a tacit ally against their common rival, P&G.

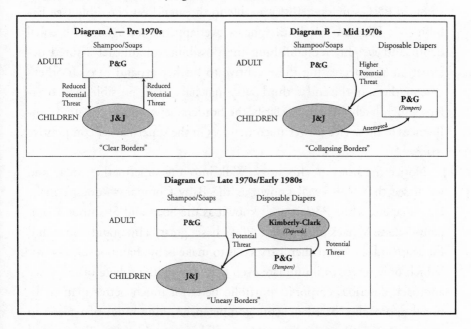

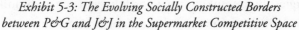

*Exhibit 5-3: The Evolving Socially Constructed Borders
between P&G and J&J in the Supermarket Competitive Space*

The plot thickened in the late 1980s and early 1990s. Profit margins on baby diapers shrank considerably, thanks to the aggressive efforts of Kimberly-Clark operating from its secure base in adult diapers. In addition, the rise of independent private label diaper manufacturers and the entry of large pulp and paper companies into private label manufacturing also hurt margins in baby diapers (see Exhibit 5-3, Diagram D). As a result of these multiple triangles focused on P&G's diaper business, the diaper market became less attractive to P&G and P&G may have felt pressure to look for growth opportunities in other baby products where it could utilize the Pampers brand name. And J&J probably knew this. Consequently, P&G's weakened sphere—thanks to the margin-reducing moves of Kimberly-Clark and private labels in baby diapers—allowed J&J to be more aggressive in protecting its own borders.

To stabilize its borders with P&G, J&J purchased Neutrogena, an adult soap and shampoo company with a specialized "mild soap" niche (a niche that fit with J&J's image of wholesome and gentle products). This move was a foray into P&G's core. Now, through the use of a forward position in P&G's market, J&J was able to threaten P&G credibly (see Exhibit 5-3, Diagram E). Both spheres overlapped once again with equal depth and weight, reestablishing the possibility of mutual assured destruction and decreasing the incentive to further expand in each other's core markets. In the end, a third party may have made possible these overlaps which likely helped to clarify the borders between the spheres of influences of these two powerful contenders in the supermarket competitive space.

Notice the irony of this story. Walk into any supermarket today and you'll see that J&J—well known as the Baby Company—doesn't make baby diapers, while P&G—well known as the Soap and Shampoo Company—does. What's more, while P&G has a great baby brand name, and the soap and shampoo chemistry skills to make baby shampoos, it doesn't. Which only serves to illuminate even further why the sphere of influence approach describes corporate portfolio behavior much better than traditional approaches based on core competencies, economies of scale, and other synergies. By rethinking your portfolio as a sphere of influence and competitive arsenal, the illogical takes on a broader, more meaningful logic.

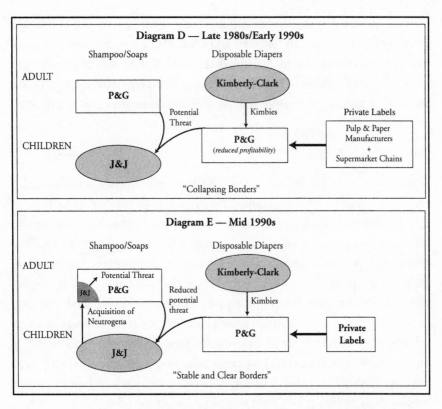

Exhibit 5-3 (Continued): *The Evolving Socially Constructed Borders between P&G and J&J in the Supermarket Competitive Space*

FORMING TRIANGLES:
CHOOSING YOUR TARGETS AND ALLIES

By the mid-1990s, Johnson & Johnson benefited from multiple triangles focused on a single target—Procter & Gamble's disposable diapers marketplace. The consequence was that Johnson & Johnson fell into a configuration of the great powers that ensured its hold on the rest of the baby market.

While the "changing diapers" example demonstrates the formation of naturally occurring triangles, there are many techniques to proactively create triangles that tip the balance of power in your favor. To do so involves two crucial strategic choices: (1) selecting the appropriate target; and (2) selecting the appropriate alliance partner or partners. These choices are made in the context of the overarching goal of getting as many triangles as possible focused on your target. In this way, you concentrate power where you want to apply it. By doing this for an extended period of time, you can change the shape of a rival's sphere of influence. If this is done repeatedly, you have the power to influence the evolution of the overall competitive configuration.

Selecting Your Target

Whom do you target? This is one of the most important questions in the art of competitive configuration. One choice is to take on your biggest threat, the rival who has most deeply penetrated your sphere, posing the most serious danger to your core. Another option is to target the weakest of the great powers in order to reduce it to a lesser power, or take it out of the game by merger or bankruptcy. This has the effect of consolidating the marketplace and consolidating your stronghold over the vacated territory. A third option is to target a rising power in order to prevent it from achieving great power status or even strategic supremacy. And finally a fourth option is to target a competitor who doesn't threaten you directly, but who has such a strong (but unprotected) core that it behooves you to preempt others that might grab this plum before you do.

Any of these targeting choices is reasonable, but the choice often depends on your world view and what is feasible given the current power balance and the opportunities that naturally present themselves over time. Under certain conditions you may want to target the weakest great power if, for example, you're one of many great powers and it's not possible to cover your backside against all of the other great powers. Targeting the weakest great power lets you reserve some of your power just in case your backside gets kicked. Targeting the most threatening great power may make sense if it's putting so much pressure on you that you can't afford to ignore it. This option is especially attractive when your biggest threat is engaged in a multifronted conflict over different zones within its sphere.

Most great powers often prefer to fight smaller battles rather than larger, risky ones, so they target the most vulnerable sphere. However, this choice is not always so clear. When you're number two, and number one is within reach, you might want to take decisive action and target your strongest threat using one or more of the competitive compression strategies discussed in Chapter 2. The key in selecting a target is to look forward to what the configuration will look like after you have eliminated a great power, neutralized its influence over you, turned it into a lesser power, or pinned it down under the weight of several triangles.

Whether you're going after your biggest threat, the weakest great power, a rising great power, or a juicy plum, you'll want to understand the structural flaws in your target's sphere and how the geo-product positioning of your sphere can be applied to the places where these vulnerabilities or "cracks" exist. By recognizing these cracks in the spheres of your potential targets, you can make a more informed choice about both the target and the type of competitive compression strategy to apply. Some of these cracks include:

- *Core woes.* Any sphere with a core that is being challenged by an insurrectionist is a company that may be ripe for gradual constriction. But beware, you may end up owning something rotten in the core, or wasting your energies on a sphere that is going to die a natural death anyway.

- *Incohesiveness.* If a sphere has no presence in a key buffer or vital zone, it may be particularly vulnerable to the toppling dominoes strategy. A sphere with no or few forward positions may be susceptible to managed containment because it has no way to break out past its buffers.

- *Hot spots.* A sphere that is under siege—due to internal unrest and/or external invasions in several important geo-product zones— may be particularly vulnerable to sequential stripping of zones not currently under siege.

- *Overstretch.* Companies that grow too big or too fast often lack the resource reserves to fund their needs across the entire sphere. This makes them more vulnerable to all types of competitive compression.

Spheres are also vulnerable if they suffer from management flaws such as internal disunity. The more diverse and contentious a sphere becomes, the more challenging it is to maintain the unity needed to be responsive to external attacks. This diminished responsiveness is reflected in the sphere's inability to route resources in a timely manner to where the action is. If you have a particularly strong and flexible system for resource routing you can hopscotch your way through this type of target.

Another management flaw is complacency. The longer a company has been on top, the more vulnerable it may be to insurrection in its core because it has failed to keep up with the times. By aiding an insurrectionist in the core of the complacent target, you can wipe that smug look off its face.

One major warning when selecting a target: Avoid escalators at all costs. For more insights into what escalators are, why you want to avoid them, and how to deal with them if you are forced to play chicken with one, see the accompanying discussion, "Playing Chicken with Escalators."

PLAYING CHICKEN WITH "ESCALATORS"

Escalators are rational rivals that may respond to your actions or signals by forcing you to "play chicken" or engage in brinkmanship. The escalator intentionally (or unintentionally) creates riskier and riskier outcomes in order to force you to back down. If you get caught up in the game, both you and the escalator become increasingly threatening until one side eventually "chickens out" or faces disaster.

In history, the Cuban Missile Crisis is a good example of the dangers of brinkmanship. As both the United States and the Soviets escalated the conflict, the threats became so unreasonably high that neither side could afford to lose. This created a winner-take-all conflict that caused both countries to face disaster if they didn't escalate the conflict even further.

In business, the stakes are not nuclear destruction, as they were in the Cuban Missile Crisis, but they can be devastating to the players involved. For example, if an escalator threatens an all-out price war in several geo-product zones of your sphere—and you get caught up in the game—this can seriously affect the overall profitability of both your spheres. The stakes can be even greater if you have an emotional or reputational investment in the process. For example, if you are in a bidding war with an escalator for the acquisition of a target company, you both may raise your offers to avoid losing prestige, or to maintain your reputation of toughness for future takeovers. But by the time one player is willing to back down, you both may have lost. The winner has likely bid too much for the target—and suffered a case of "winner's curse." And the loser suffered the reputation of being a "wimp," which could affect how others bid against the company in the future.

Three factors can influence your success in a battle of brinkmanship. First, choose a weaker opponent, one with smaller resources or a reputation for retreating under pressure. The weakness may be due to a variety of reasons: It may be experiencing financial pressures; its goals for the geo-product market may be in question (e.g., seeking to harvest profits); the company may lack a commitment to or interest in the disputed market; or the CEO may have a reputation for wimpiness and capitulation, and too much concern about short-term profitability and stock market reactions.

Second, if you are the aggressor and can control your own risks while increasing your competitor's, you may compel your competitor to withdraw. This can be done by fighting in markets where you have little to lose and a lot to gain (e.g., places you have low market share), and markets where your rival loses a lot if it responds too aggressively (e.g., with price discounts). In addition, you may be able to avoid escalation if you leave your opponent a face-saving way to back out. This might be done by giving up a less important market or by instigating some aggressive action on a second front that offers a victory to your rival in exchange for backing down in the first (more important) market. A face-saving strategy gives the losing CEO a way to walk away without being fired.

The third factor that can influence your success in a battle of brinkmanship is if you take on the role of escalator. If you appear to be committed to winning—even at irrational costs—your competitor may chicken out quickly, rather than fight a ruthless and unrelenting rival. But, if you do, you must be prepared to escalate if your rival calls your bluff.

Choosing Your Allies

As Oscar Wilde once said, "A man cannot be too careful in the choice of his enemies." But it is also wise to remember that your future will be judged not only by your enemies but also by the friends you keep. Just as every zone in your sphere must serve a specific strategic intent, so too must your allies (see Exhibit 5-4). Alliance partners can supplement and enhance your sphere by playing one of the following roles:

- *Surrogate attackers.* These allies act as forward positions on your behalf. They do part or all of the "heavy lifting" for you so you can add to or reserve your strength.

- *Critical supporters.* These allies play the role of a vital interest, supporting your invasion of a rival's sphere by providing arms and materials.

- *Flank protectors.* These buffers slow the forward advance of a rival into your sphere.

- *Strategic umbrellas.* These allies serve as facilitators for your pivotal zones. If a rival interferes with your freedom of movement into new areas, your strategic umbrellas threaten retaliation.

- *Passive aggressors.* These allies serve as facilitators for your forward positions. Through tacit agreement, they don't interfere with your use of forward positions against the targeted sphere, and they don't attack your sphere.

An alliance partner may be created by formal means—joint venture, long-term contract, or even an agreement to merge with you. An alliance partner may also be a *tacit* ally—a player who has no formal agreement with you but who serves one of your purposes for its own reasons. Tacit alliances may occur naturally, accidentally, or proactively.

In considering allies, either formal or informal, the key to success rests with something Thucydides, the Greek historian, wrote almost twenty-five hundred years ago, "Identity of interests is the surest of bonds." In politics, bonds are forged through common enemies, and, in business, through common targets. In either case, *the enemy of my enemy is my friend* is an apt sentiment. As a great business power, selecting an alliance partner who is already the "enemy of your enemy" allows you to feel more

Type of Alliance Partner	Strategic Impact (How each helps shift the balance of power)	Supplements Your Sphere by Acting as a:
Surrogate attacker	Attacks/weakens the sphere of a rival, especially its core or vital interests	Forward position
Critical supporter	Provides arms and materials to fight longer/harder against a rival	Vital interest
Flank protector	Slows the forward advance of a rival into your sphere	Buffer zone
Strategic umbrella	Threatens retaliation against a rival if it interferes with your freedom of movement into new areas	Facilitator for your pivotal zones
Passive aggressor	Tacitly consents to the weakening of a rival by failing to come to its rescue when needed or by avoiding attacking your sphere	Facilitator for your forward positions

Exhibit 5-4: Supplementing Your Sphere

confident that your chosen ally will remain a loyal friend, at least as long as your interests remain identical.

Typically, the common target approach to tacit alliances in business often manifests in "swarming." Like giant killer bees, the great powers swarm around a common target, each focusing on a different part of the target's sphere. For example, Sears lost its strategic supremacy to swarming when: Wal-Mart and Kmart went after the low end of Sears's sphere; Federated Department Stores and others consolidated a number of high-end retailers to go after Sears mall stores; Circuit City went after Sears's core interests in the home appliance and consumer electronics businesses; and Home Depot attacked Sears's strong position in the hardware and home improvement markets. Unable to swat so many killer bees simultaneously, Sears experienced the business equivalent of anaphylactic shock. Paralyzed, Sears gradually lost its position in its core and vital interests (hard goods) and many of its pivotal positions, such as higher margin soft goods.

Another approach to the "common enemy" model of alliances is to use formal alliances to galvanize the great powers into one massive effort against a single targeted great power. Sun Microsystems attempted to create an "Everyone-but-Microsoft" alliance to support Java, for example. In Chapter 4, "Dousing Disruption," I discussed how competitive cooperatives (concerts of power, polarized blocs, and collective security arrangements) can effectively be used against ambitious lesser powers and revolutionaries. Similar great power alliances can be used to target other great powers, as well.

ALIGNING INTERESTS TO CREATE, EMPOWER, AND MAINTAIN EFFECTIVE TRIANGLES

You've chosen your target and allies. You now have a vision for how you want to configure some of the other great powers. But this vision is just a pipe dream until you can convince your target to be a target and your allies to be allies.

In some instances, your target and allies will fall into place naturally, just as they did in the cases of Sun Microsystems vs. Microsoft, and Johnson & Johnson vs. Procter & Gamble. In the struggle over the diaper market, for example, Procter & Gamble was a *natural* target for Johnson & Johnson because J&J had to defend its core position in the baby market. In addition, Procter & Gamble was a *fixed* target because it couldn't escape J&J's moves into P&G's core shampoo/soap market. Interestingly enough, P&G may even have been a *willing* target. Return for a moment to Exhibit 5-3, Diagram E. If you reconceptualize the relationship between P&G and J&J, you could see how the rivals share an identity of interests. P&G can rely on J&J to avoid intervening in P&G's battles against food and other packaged goods providers, Unilever and Nestlé. And J&J can rely on P&G to avoid intervening in J&J's battles with American Hospital Supply. Ironically, by being a target, P&G accomplished a larger purpose in its effort to configure the other great powers in its space. By being a target, P&G ended up being J&J's alliance partner in different triangles with Nestlé, Unilever, and American Hospital Supply.

Despite the situation with P&G and J&J, most targets certainly aren't willing and they don't often remain fixed. For example, your target might simply sidestep you, giving way to your advances without a fight. Some managers may see this as a positive. After all, you win that piece of geo-product turf without a costly fight. But this is a shortsighted victory because the target, by giving way, denies you the opportunity to weaken its sphere or change its interests in a way that respects the other boundaries of your own sphere. As a result, you fail to enhance or even preserve your own power. Therefore, a better strategy is to align the interests of several alliance partners in order to create multiple triangles that effectively "box in" the target, preventing it from sidestepping your advances.

Like targets, alliance partners are also more often made than born. J&J was fortunate when it came to finding a natural alliance partner, because Kimberly-Clark was already aligned with J&J's interest against Procter & Gamble. But more likely, you will have to *create* allies by *changing* the interests of others. This can be done either by formal agreement, or through informal, unspoken agreements that result from signaling. Both formal and informal agreements reflect each great power's interests in terms of how they will work together to achieve previously unattainable goals, or divide their duties in the pursuit of their joint interests.

Changing the Interests and Goals of Other Great Powers

Verbal signals are a good tool to convince other great powers to align their interests with yours. And combining verbal signals with the use of forward positions is an even better tool to convince other great powers to act the way you want them to, since forward positions put some teeth into the signal. In combination, verbal signals, forward positions, and selective withdrawals from parts of your current sphere can not only achieve conformity with your interests, but also *shift* the interests of other great powers. Verbal signals can take three forms: announcements, threats, and promises.

ANNOUNCEMENTS

Typically, announcements take the form of news releases, speeches at trade shows, and advertisements. But great powers can also announce their interests through actions that speak louder than words, such as test marketing new products, limited product launches, selective market withdrawals, filing for patents, price changes, increased advertising, and boosted investment in plant or R&D. Verbal and action-based announcements allow others to read your intent for different zones within your sphere and your commitment to invasion of specific zones of a rival's sphere. In conjunction with the use of forward positions and selective withdrawals, announcements can shape how targets and allies interpret your actions and, therefore, influence their actions.

Announcements can also serve as "trial balloons" to test the reactions of others and to gather information about their interests. The reactions of others can indicate whether they will aid you, intervene, or stay out of the way during your move against a targeted sphere. Depending on other great powers' reactions to your announcement, you can begin to discern who is friend, and who is foe. Through back-and-forth public announcements, corporations can conduct informal "conversations," without necessarily crossing the line into antitrust violations.

THREATS

The point of threats, which can take the form of statements of intention or actions, is to change the interests of other great powers. Threats either directly attack another great power's sphere of influence, or they can alert potential allies and targets that you will "punish" them if they fail to cooperate. There are two types of threats: compellent threats, directed toward getting your rival to do something, and deterrent threats, focused on preventing your rival from doing something.[1] Threats are not typically a good way to make friends, but they can be used to keep a nonaligned great power "in line," and hence out of the way while you target another great power. To be effective, a threat must be credible, meaning you have convinced the other great powers you can and will carry out the threat. Otherwise, it is likely to be ignored.

PROMISES

These are offers of rewards for those nonaligned great powers that agree to cooperate with your interests. Promises can be used to entice another great power to take action against a common rival's sphere. Or they can be used to deter another great power (even your target) from taking an undesirable action. For example, two great powers can signal promises to each other that help them to agree on avoiding entry of each other's spheres, or the great powers can signal promises that help them agree to attack two different zones of a common rival.

Announcements, threats, and promises can all be used to create alliances that enable you to more effectively target a common rival sphere. But signals can also be used to make sure your sphere doesn't *become* the common target. Such a signal can take the form of being a "lunatic with a hat pin." When lunatics wave their pins, it is anybody's guess what they are thinking. Lunatics brandishing hat pins may not always be able to cause mortal harm, but their reputation for unpredictability helps to ward off potential attackers or warn away potential escalators. Companies such as Intel, Oracle, and Microsoft all make a big deal out of their intent to win at almost any cost. They purposely perpetuate a reputation for near-ruthlessness and winning at any cost, because this appearance of "lunacy"—whether real or contrived—can serve as a mighty deterrent.

Preventing Dysfunctional and Unstable Triangles

To be effective, the alliance within a triangle must reflect Lord Salisbury's statement that, "The only bond of union is the absence of all clashing interest" (see Exhibit 5-5, Diagram A). Nevertheless, even when the alliance partners within a triangle are aligned against a common target, the triangle may still be dysfunctional. After all, every alliance partner is still a rival great power. As partners you may share a common target, but as rivals you may still experience conflicts and infighting that can weaken your collective focus on the targeted sphere (see Exhibit 5-5, Diagram B). Like any dysfunctional relationship, the partners need to build trust so that their fighting doesn't get in the way of their common interests.

It is particularly difficult to build trust with an alliance partner that is growing. Even if you signal your good intentions toward the alignment and make a point to move your sphere out of the way of the ally's growing sphere, this may not be enough to satisfy the appetite of the alliance partner for more turf. Ironically, getting out the way of a growing sphere may not only fail to remove all clashing interests, but may make matters worse.

While excessive conflict among partners can lead to dysfunctional triangles, outside troublemakers can lead to unstable triangles (see Exhibit 5-5, Diagram C). This outside trouble can arrive in the form of interveners, who can destabilize a triangle by coming to the aid of the target. If this happens, the power of the triangle is neutralized, causing the allies to bring in more allies to counterbalance the intervener. Some great powers neutralize the interests of potential interveners by creating another triangle designed to keep the potential intervener pinned down in its own sphere. If this process continues, then the competitive configurations won't remain stable for long because one player will eventually gather more interveners on its side and tip the balance of power in its favor.

So how can you address the challenges that lead to dysfunctional and unstable triangles? One prevalent answer is for great powers to create overlaps between their spheres. These overlaps are achieved through the use of selected forward positions, which give each player a foothold in the other player's sphere. This leads to the possibility of mutual assured destruction, which, in turn, creates incentives for both players to avoid escalating their

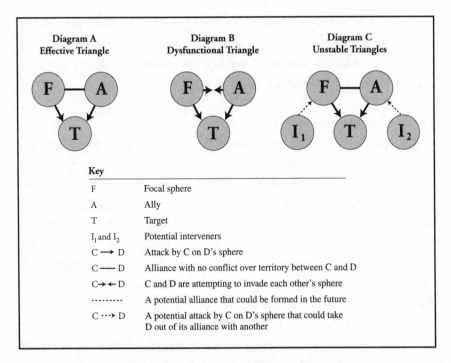

Exhibit 5-5: Effective and Dysfunctional Triangles

conflict. Overlaps can establish and reinforce a pattern of cooperative and confrontative relationships, much in the way struts and braces reinforce the structure of a building. In essence, overlaps can change the interests of allies and interveners because these overlaps threaten others. They can, therefore, help stabilize the borders of everyone's spheres when everyone becomes fearful of retaliation if they attack others. What's more, overlaps create an interesting paradox. Great powers can use them to show a *lack* of respect for each other's borders, in order to *encourage* respect for each other's borders and preserve the uniqueness of each sphere.

Done right, these overlaps can result in mutual forbearance (as J&J did with P&G). But the spheres of many great powers overlap and the result is far from cooperation and stability. Some overlaps constitute an invasion that triggers a major conflagration. Others create little fear of retaliation and hence don't foster mutual forbearance. And still others provoke a series of small retaliations.

Given the challenges inherent in creating overlaps between great power spheres, what makes an overlap work? The key is to achieve balanced-deep overlaps, in which the reciprocal overlaps are equally and deeply penetrating (see Exhibit 5-6, Diagram A).

BALANCED-DEEP OVERLAPS

Overlaps are "deep" if both firms have footholds close to each other's core. The overlaps are "balanced" when both firms have penetrated their rival's sphere with *equal* weight or force, hence creating reciprocal threats of the same magnitude. Deep and balanced footholds provide both firms with the power to inflict damage on the other's core, while incurring only small losses because an unimportant forward position is used as the instrument of threat. Consequently each firm is unlikely to act aggressively toward the other, a pattern of cooperation is encouraged, and an equal "balance of power" exists between the two firms. This balance solidifies the tacit alliance.

When constructing a balanced-deep overlap, you need to be careful to avoid four common pitfalls. The first pitfall is to fail to make the overlaps deep enough (see Exhibit 5-6, Diagram B). Shallow penetration provides less incentive for mutual forbearance because neither firm threatens an important geo-product market of its rival. Consequently, the relationship between the two firms may not be very cooperative, and, if it is cooperative, this relationship will not be as durable as when the overlaps are truly deep, as illustrated in Diagram A.

The second pitfall when constructing a balanced-deep overlap is to fail to make the overlaps equally deep (see Exhibit 5-6, Diagram C). When one firm has established a foothold deep in the sphere of another, but the other firm has established a foothold only in its rival's periphery, the two firms don't pose equal threats. Such an unbalanced (or asymmetric) situation is likely to encourage the first firm to expand its presence in the second firm's core or vital interests. Consequently, in the short run, rivalry is provoked. In the long run, cooperation can be encouraged if the second firm responds by opening a new foothold in the first firm's core.

The third pitfall in establishing a balanced-deep overlap is to fail to give the overlaps equal weight (see Exhibit 5-6, Diagram D). When the

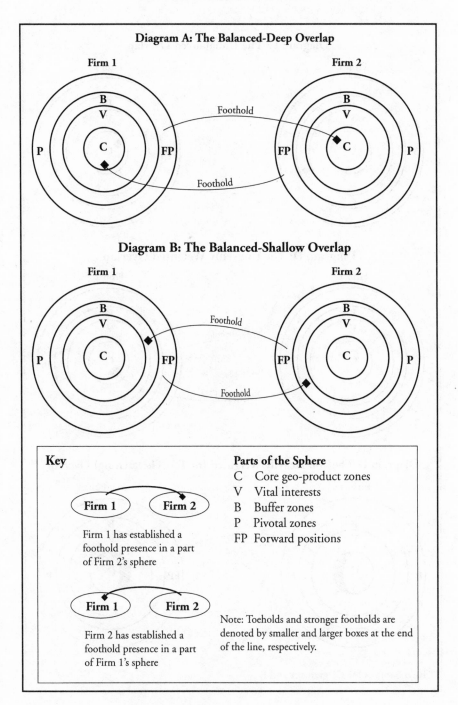

Exhibit 5-6: Alternative Types of Overlaps

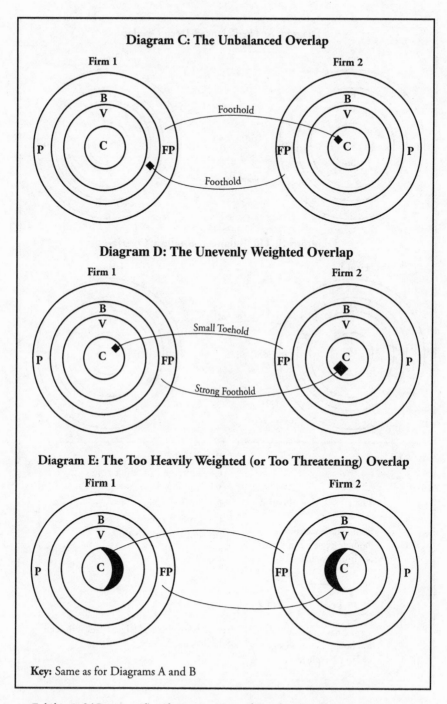

Exhibit 5-6 (Continued): *Alternative Types of Overlaps (continued on page 216)*

first firm holds a large, strong foothold (i.e., a high market share position) in the second firm's core, and the second firm has only a toehold (i.e., a low market share niche) in the first firm's core, the firms don't have the same amount of weight behind their threats. This removes the mutuality of the threats and mutual forbearance is unlikely. Consequently, the first firm is positioned to attack the second firm's core. Confrontation will normally ensue because the second firm must protect its core, while the first firm will be unconstrained in its aggressiveness.

The fourth pitfall is to give the overlaps too much weight, which happens when the firms have taken (or intend to take) too much market share in the rival's core. In this case, the reciprocal footholds are so large or aggressive that both firms are excessively threatened in their cores and vital interests (see Exhibit 5-6, Diagram E). If the companies don't control the growth and aggressiveness of their subunits, then the overlaps can become major invasions. In such a case, the foothold denies the other great power strategic supremacy in its most important marketplaces and substantially weakens the power of the other. When that happens, both great powers are likely to go ballistic.

Because the construction of overlaps is such a delicate task, most overlaps ultimately fail or produce less than ideal results (see sidebar, "When Overlaps Underwhelm"). In addition to the four pitfalls just mentioned, even once effective balanced-deep overlaps can be compromised if certain things change with the spheres. For example, if for some reason one of the two firms gains or loses power (e.g., a sudden decline in demand in one of the firm's cores, or mismanagement of the sphere's resource routing paradigm) the equal balance of power created by the balanced-deep overlap may be disrupted. This could cause the more powerful firm to become more aggressive, which would stop the mutual forbearance. If this happens the rivalry will be very destructive because of how important the zones involved in the overlap are to each firm's power.

WHEN OVERLAPS UNDERWHELM

Balanced-deep overlaps are not always equally effective at creating cooperative bonds between great powers. Studies of several industries (in the transportation, manufacturing, banking, and retailing sectors) have shown that balanced-deep overlaps create more cooperation when two firms:

- hold truly threatening positions
- hold positions that create economies of scale and scope when used
- have roughly equal deep pockets

Having a foothold in the core of a rival in not enough. If two firms each hold a truly threatening position in the other's sphere, then mutual forbearance will be even more strongly encouraged. For example, a foothold will be more effective if it provides a platform from which the rival's core competence can be rendered obsolete or its competitive advantage can be neutralized. Such a foothold creates the requisite fear that guarantees forbearance by the rival.

Mutual forbearance is also more likely if each firm can use its foothold without shooting itself in the foot, so to speak. If pulling the trigger means a firm will harm itself more than the competitor, then that foothold (even if it is in the rival's core) will not create mutual forbearance. It is much better if expanding or being aggressive in the foothold will help the firm capture synergies and economies of integration, scale, or scope.

Deep pockets also make a difference. To be effective, balanced-deep overlaps assume that both firms are equally sized, financed, flush with cash or unused borrowing capacity, and matched in their abilities to use these deep pockets. If one of the firm's spheres can't afford to exploit its forward position in its rival's core, then there is no credible threat and no incentive for its rival to forbear.

Thus, the power of balanced-deep overlaps to cement a cooperative relationship between great powers varies. If the overlap is weakened by a lack of mutual deep pockets, economies of scale and scope, and threatening platforms, two alternatives can compensate for the diminished effectiveness. These are: (1) create an overlap in a new geo-product zone where at least some of the conditions are met; and (2) increase the number of overlaps in enough geo-product markets to cumulatively influence the rival's profitability.

ONE-SIDED OVERLAPS

On the road to creating balanced-deep overlaps between two spheres, someone has to start the ball rolling. Which means that at some point in time, one firm will have to create a one-sided overlap in a rival's sphere. The first firm thus establishes a foothold in the second firm's sphere, but the second firm has no countervailing presence in the first firm's sphere. This creates a threat by the first firm that puts pressure on the second firm to fight back.

A one-sided overlap that is deep within the rival's core (see Exhibit 5-6, Diagram F) creates more pressure than a one-sided shallow overlap (see Exhibit 5-6, Diagram G). The second firm is likely to respond aggressively to a deep one-sided overlap in order to drive the first firm out of its sphere because of the importance of the threatened geo-product zone. What do I mean by "respond aggressively"? I'm talking about a counterattack that is speedy, prolonged, and seriously damaging to the first firm because it involves radical innovation and lower prices, and is usually backed by massive resources.

Generally, a shallow one-sided overlap (i.e., in a buffer zone) provokes a less aggressive response. However, if the first firm leverages its position in the periphery to enter a vital interest or core zone of the second firm, the second firm is likely to respond more aggressively because it wants to preserve its power. The second firm may even respond aggressively at the mere possibility of this situation.

Consequently, although you may start off thinking you are working

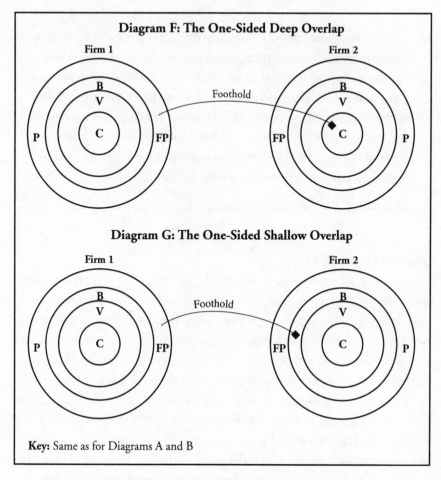

Diagram F: The One-Sided Deep Overlap

Firm 1

Firm 2

Foothold

Diagram G: The One-Sided Shallow Overlap

Firm 1

Firm 2

Foothold

Key: Same as for Diagrams A and B

Exhibit 5-6 (Continued): *Alternative Types of Overlaps*

your way toward a tacit alliance, the other party may think it is more of a target than an alliance partner. This is where announcements, promises, and threats can be helpful in signaling your longer-term intent.

Notice that a one-sided deep overlap can be used as a major invasion, in which case you can expect your target to attempt to create a balanced-deep overlap in order to neutralize your invasion. So if your target isn't willing to be a target, you may end up inadvertently with a tacit alliance partner or with a failed invasion. If you intend to use a one-sided overlap as an invasion, you must be careful to head off the target from hijacking the situation. To prevent the failure of your one-sided deep overlap, you may have to build the relative power of your sphere, especially by beefing up your core or buffers, so that the target can't seriously counterattack your core. So the difference between creating a target and an alliance partner may depend on your buffers and how strong you are. Thus a one-sided overlap can be the first step toward an alliance, or the first step toward a target.

Lock Up Alliances—But Don't Throw Away the Key

In an attempt to show commitment to a tacit or formal alliance, or to an attack strategy, great powers often make "irreversible" commitments that lock them into their promises, threats, overlaps, and other courses of action. Such irreversible commitments are made using long-term contracts, investment in single-purpose plants, and other strategies that are costly to get out of. The result is that competitive configurations can become frozen solid.

In the rapid-change world we live in today, irreversible commitments can be too permanent and too inflexible. Instead, it is often better to negotiate or signal alliances tethered to a fixed-time period or specific goals. This way, you can make it clear that the alliance will be dissolved or renegotiated after those conditions have been met. In other words, because the divorce is planned right from the get-go, this "pre-nup" provides the alliance partners with flexibility regarding their commitment to the current competitive configuration.

Moreover, it is often better to commit to a course of action for as long as it makes sense, rather than become committed to a specific ally. In the software world, for example, the players commit to "standards," not allies. Each player knows that when the standard is replaced, the players will reconfigure based on the new competitive situation. Thus, the commitment is to a course of action, not a permanent marriage of the great powers. So, pay close attention to your use of an ally within a triangle. Otherwise, you may turn out to be the one whom your rivals triangulate into a corner.

STRATEGIES FOR UNFREEZING AND
CONSTRUCTING COMPETITIVE CONFIGURATIONS

If the current competitive configuration has been frozen by a lot of irreversible commitments, then you may need to break the ice. Unfreezing and constructing a new configuration is especially important when the existing configuration promotes a rival's world view, reflects a compromised world view that none of the great powers is happy with, or is just the accidental result of the chaos in your competitive space.

If you're unhappy with the current configuration in your space, you can unfreeze it by actively chipping away at the bonds that hold together the key triangles within the configuration. Using a "divide-and-conquer" or an "assimilator" strategy, you can create new opportunities for new configurations. Once this has been done, you can begin building a configuration using a "coordinator" or "balancer" strategy to encourage others to follow your world view.

The *divide-and-conquer* strategy can chip away at the formation of coalitions by a central player in a network of triangles, thereby throwing the entire coalition into a state of confusion and requiring each member to reassess its desire to remain in the coalition (shown in Exhibit 5-7).

For example, Pepsi had built a number of distribution alliances to challenge Coca-Cola in its overseas markets. Coca-Cola caused many people to question the viability of Pepsi's coalition when it divided Pepsi from its long-time Venezuelan distribution partner, the Cisneros family, and conquered the Venezuela market. For decades, the Cisneros group's control of the soda business in Venezuela has been so complete that—prior to the success of its divide-and-conquer strategy—Coca-Cola was never able to get more than 12 percent of this market. Severing the fifty-year relationship between PepsiCo and the Cisneros family represented a $500 million coup for Coke, one that ultimately resulted in a serious shakeup at PepsiCo International, including the sudden departure of its CEO. What's more, Venezuela was PepsiCo's only dominant market position in the world. In one day, PepsiCo's market share in Venezuela went from 42 percent to zero.

A divide-and-conquer strategy can also be carried out using the legal system. For example, American Express has been actively lobbying the U.S. Jus-

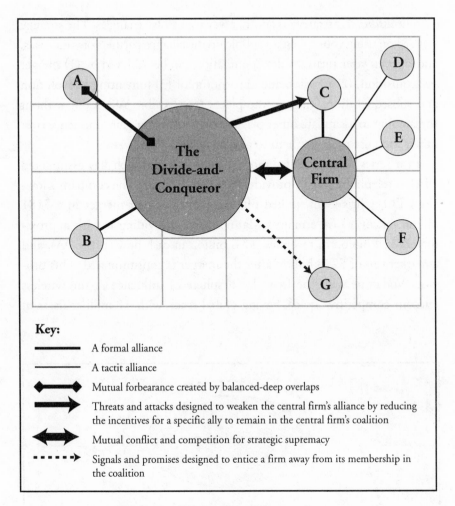

Key:

———	A formal alliance
———	A tactit alliance
◄►►	Mutual forbearance created by balanced-deep overlaps
►►	Threats and attacks designed to weaken the central firm's alliance by reducing the incentives for a specific ally to remain in the central firm's coalition
◄►►	Mutual conflict and competition for strategic supremacy
▪▪▪▪►	Signals and promises designed to entice a firm away from its membership in the coalition

Exhibit 5-7: The Divide-and-Conquer Strategy

tice Department, trying to force banks to decouple from Visa and MasterCard on the grounds that the close partnership between these brands and the banks has reduced competition in the credit card marketplace. If American Express is successful, it will be able to align with some of the banks to target its rivals Visa and MasterCard. This could shift the balance of power in credit cards toward American Express. It would also allow the banks to form new alliances with American Express to form triangles against their rival banks, opening up another avenue for them to gain supremacy over their rivals.

The *assimilator* strategy is another way to dissolve triangles. The strategy is based on using your sphere to gobble up the alliance partners of your rivals, and/or even your rivals' rivals. Assimilation can be achieved by (1) merger or acquisition, (2) invasion and absorption, or (3) fomenting a revolution and subsequently picking up the pieces (see Exhibit 5-8). Even without threatening to assimilate other players, the assimilator gains influence over others, because it causes them to anticipate its next moves.

In a series of spectacular moves, Vodafone Airtouch has assimilated wireless telephone service providers on a global scale. The company's low-key CEO, Chris Gent, pulled off the world's biggest merger in a $181 billion takeover of Germany's Mannesmann, providing it with approximately $24 billion in revenues, $7.8 billion in cash flow (EBITDA), and a market cap of $238 billion after the merger is consummated. This provides Vodafone with the first global sphere of influence in the wireless telecom competitive space, having global reach with 34 million users in

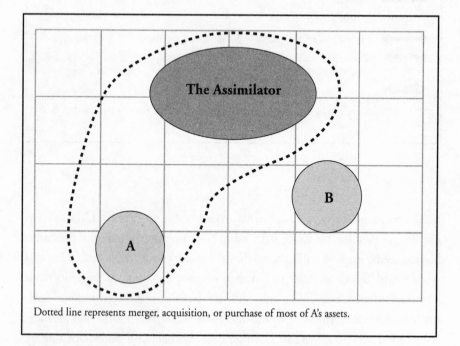

Dotted line represents merger, acquisition, or purchase of most of A's assets.

Exhibit 5-8: The Assimilator Strategy

Europe, 10 million in the United States (including its joint venture with Verizon), and four million users in the rest of the world.

Using this new global sphere as a base, Vodafone now plans to expand its sphere of influence by giving cellular subscribers access to the Internet. Gent hopes that his firm will become the preferred Web tool in the world, superseding PCs. This may seem crazy, but half of Vodafone's customers already use its short messaging system, a truncated form of e-mail for cell phones! And, in 2000, Nokia couldn't fill all the demand for its Internet-ready cell phones, which have a built-in browser that provides pared-down access to Web pages. (Note: Demand for a truly fast Internet-ready phone would still be high in Europe in 2001. However, the slowness of recent models has created a lot of disatisfaction.)

Vodafone's global sphere of influence is also a great base for extending into the broadcast and multimedia businesses. It is within the company's reach to provide access to radio broadcasts and even movie, sports, and video clips over cell phones. Clearly, Vodafone has unfrozen the old competitive configuration dominated by national telephone companies, broadcast networks, and ISPs like AOL. Its assimilator strategy has given Vodafone a head start in building the global competitive configuration of the future for the cell phone, broadcast, and Internet-access competitive space.

The *coordinator strategy* is a method to configure the players by building several triangles with a common purpose. The result is a coalition that could be used for several purposes, including: (1) to reduce the relative power of a common target, or (2) to allow the coalition members to achieve their compatible visions for which spheres will cover which markets. The coordinator uses both the carrot and stick—that is, both promises and threats, as well as formal alliances and disciplinary attacks—to gain the cooperation of several other great powers (see Exhibit 5-9).

For example, Corning has acted as a coordinator, forming joint ventures with many other great powers, including Dow Corning, Dow Owens, and a joint venture with Asahi Glass in Japan. Through its coordination of many great powers, Corning has become the premier high-tech and specialty glass company in the world. Similarly, Airbus is at the center of numerous alliances with European suppliers and governments, making it the only major player to rise up against Boeing in the commercial airliner business.

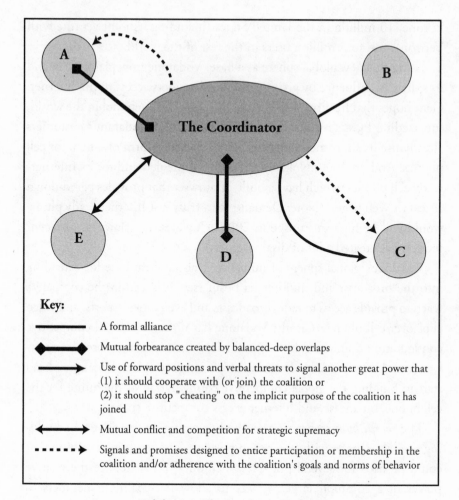

Exhibit 5-9: The Coordinator Strategy

In the cyberworld AOL has become the number one ISP by cutting deals and coordinating relationships with thousands of Web sites. Internationally, AOL is scooping up local content providers. In contrast, Yahoo!, the number one Internet content aggregator, has attempted to lock up local ISPs all over the globe, providing them with a way to hold off AOL. Following up on the AOL story at the opening of this chapter, it is crucial for AOL to win the coordination race with Yahoo! A decisive victory would help AOL solidify a strong core. This, in turn, will enhance

AOL's ability to win the contest for global preeminence in Internet access over MS/MSN, the wireless Internet access providers, and the hand-held device manufacturers such as Palm.

The *balancer strategy* configures the players by keeping them off balance. A balancer throws its weight back and forth between rival great powers in order to tip the scales in whichever direction it wants. In this way, the balancer keeps the other players from gaining too much power and allows the balancer to influence the other great powers' positioning and movement in the competitive space (see Exhibit 5-10).

For example, application software developers can shift allegiance between hardware manufacturers. Apple's position in the personal computer market was further eroded when application software developers began to

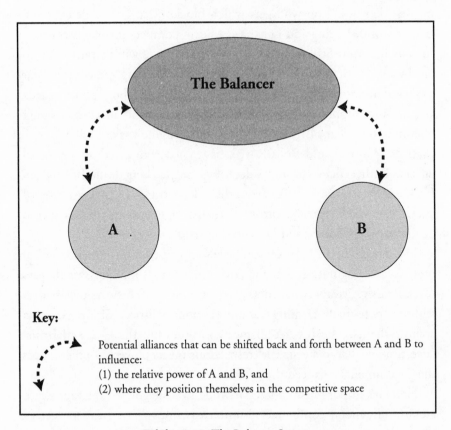

Exhibit 5-10: The Balancer Strategy

focus on applications for IBM PCs first, and then Apple much later. This helped tip the balance toward IBM. The balancer strategy may soon be used in the world of video game software developers. It remains to be seen which of these developers will shift allegiance away from Nintendo or the Sony PlayStation now that Microsoft has introduced the X-box video game system. (In June 2000, Microsoft acquired Bungie, a video game developer that previously developed games for Sony's PlayStation 2, because Microsoft may have feared that other potential software balancers would not tip the scales in Microsoft's direction.)

The balancer strategy must be an ongoing process to be effective. In the pharmaceutical world, blockbuster drug development labs regularly switch allegiance among the major pharmaceutical companies with strong distribution. As a consequence, these labs affect the relative power of the majors, depending on who gets which blockbuster. In the defense contractor world, Boeing and Lockheed Martin compete for major contracts such as the Joint Strike Fighter. This fighter plane will be purchased for use by all the branches of the U.S. military. Winning the contract may well be determined by which of the two giants gains the support of radar and avionics suppliers (e.g., Northrop Grumman) and airframe designer/manufacturers (e.g., British Aerospace). Jet engine makers, such as GE, Pratt & Whitney, and Rolls-Royce, have chosen to avoid acting as balancers. Rather than chosing sides, they are backing both Boeing and Lockheed Martin in order to avoid the risk of losing. In contrast, the balancers can ask for greater profits if their weight can tip the balance of power between Boeing and Lockheed Martin.

In some cases, the balancer can have so much control influence over an industry's configuration that the government steps in. This was the case when British Airways switched its allegiance from US Airways to American Airlines, potentially creating an almost monopolistic position for trans-atlantic flights. The BA-AA alliance continues but the U.S. and British governments placed substantial restrictions on its power. In other words, the governments balanced the balancers.

Here, it's important to note that while I've categorized the four strategies for influencing configurations into two camps—one camp focused on unfreezing the competitive configurations and the other camp focused on constructing them—they don't always play out this way. All four of the strategies can be used to maintain your supremacy over the current configuration by interfering with an ambitious great power's efforts to reconfigure the space according to its own world view. For example, a divide-and-conquer strategy can be used to block the formation of a new coalition by a rising coordinator. Assimilator and coordinator strategies can be used to snatch victims from the jaws of a hungry assimilator. A balancer strategy can be used to jump in and to counterbalance a troublesome great power attempting its own balancer strategy.

In addition, a coordinator strategy can facilitate peace or mobilize a coalition against a disruptive power. If you gain a reputation for excellence at using these four strategies to maintain the existing configuration, you will enhance your strategic supremacy even further. By virtue of your reputation, these strategies can work for you without your ever having to actually apply them. The behavior of other great powers can be influenced because they will anticipate the futility of attempting to destabilize the existing order. As a result, you gain not only influence over the configuration, but also control over the *process of reconfiguration,* as the competitive space evolves.

GENERAL MOTORS REVISITED: ACHIEVING A PREEMINENT WORLD VIEW

Earlier in this chapter, I offered an example of a world divided between General Motors and Toyota in which both of the companies were in conflict over vital, pivotal, and core interests. For the sake of clarity, I presented this scenario as if the two companies existed and competed in a bipolar world. In reality, the competitive space of the auto industry is multipolar. GM, Toyota, and Ford are all great powers vying for strategic supremacy. In addition, the space grew more crowded thanks to the merger that created DaimlerChrysler, which raked in record profits of over $10 billion at the end of the millennium before its financial difficulties in 2000. (See Exhibit 5-11, Diagram A, which shows the difference between a simple bipolar view and the more complex multipolar view of the worldwide auto industry competitive configuration.)

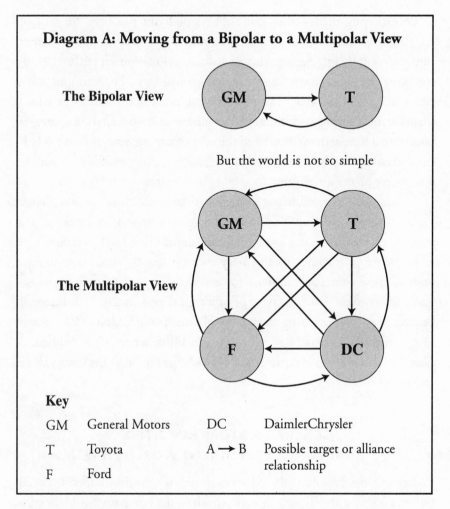

Diagram A: Moving from a Bipolar to a Multipolar View

The Bipolar View

But the world is not so simple

The Multipolar View

Key

GM	General Motors	DC	DaimlerChrysler
T	Toyota	A → B	Possible target or alliance relationship
F	Ford		

Exhibit 5-11: Competitive Configuration in the Global Auto Industry

Let's take a closer look at some of the alternative global competitive configurations that could emerge in the overall automobile industry. In specific, let's look at the issue of competitive configuration from GM's perspective, with a focus on: (1) some alternative world views that might benefit GM; (2) considerations for selecting a world view; (3) how GM could apply some of the strategies for configuring the players discussed in this chapter; and (4) how these strategies must be carefully chosen to construct the competitive configuration that fits GM's selected world view.

In the struggle for supremacy in the North American market, GM and Ford have overlapping cores and vital interests. Historically, these overlaps worked like balanced-deep overlaps. Today, globalization has brought in new competitors who compete aggressively. Toyota continues to gain ground in North America, changing the interests of the traditional great powers there. Consequently, the overlaps between the spheres of GM and Ford no longer facilitate mutual forbearance. In fact, these overlaps can be exploited by third parties that can tacitly align with one of the two overlapping competitors (GM or Ford) to create a common enemy, effectively turning the overlaps into a reason to align with the third party. Given this new environment, the Ford-GM overlaps are so significant that they now look more like major invasions that could threaten the financial viability of both players.

Daimler's purchase of Chrysler has created more uncertainty in GM's sphere because Daimler, a European-centered great power, now has a forward position in the United States targeted against its biggest challengers in Europe, GM/Opel and Ford. This situation may constrain GM's and Ford's movements in Europe out of fear of DaimlerChrysler's reaction in America, especially in years when DaimlerChrysler is enjoying strong financial success.

First, GM needs to simplify its mental map of the multipolar configuration that it is embedded within before it can understand the opportunities presented by this current competitive configuration. GM has to recognize that it is involved in several triangles simultaneously and must dissect this tangle of triangles, taking a GM-centric view in which GM is at the center of numerous bipolar relationships (see Exhibit 5-11, Diagram B). This simplification allows GM to evaluate its relative power in each of these relationships (just as was done in the Toyota vs. GM example earlier in this chapter).

Next, GM should look at alternative views of each possible triangular relationship (see Exhibit 5-11, Diagram C). These views will allow GM to consider the implications of each triangle (just as was done in the Johnson & Johnson, Procter & Gamble, Kimberly-Clark diapers example).

Once GM understands what is feasible given the overlaps and power relationships observed in Diagram C, then it must narrow down the possibilities to a single target. To do so, it should visualize different patterns of alliances that could provide it with the ability to go after one target,

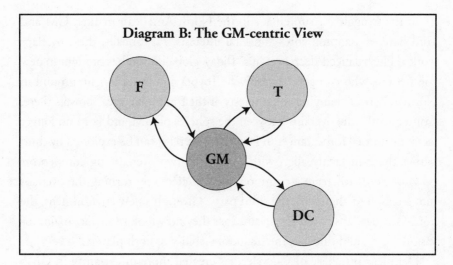

Exhibit 5-11 (Continued): *Competitive Configuration in the Global Auto Industry*

while keeping the rest of the great powers at bay (see Exhibit 5-11, Diagram D). For each of the targeting alternatives GM should consider how and if it is possible to unfreeze and realign the interests of the other great powers to conform with its targeting alternatives. Looking at all these factors, GM may decide it prefers the middle option in Diagram D, because Ford's interests and sphere present the greatest threat to GM's sphere given

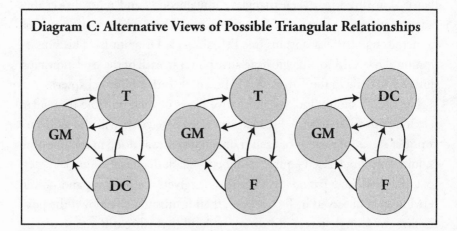

Exhibit 5-11 (Continued): *Competitive Configuration in the Global Auto Industry*

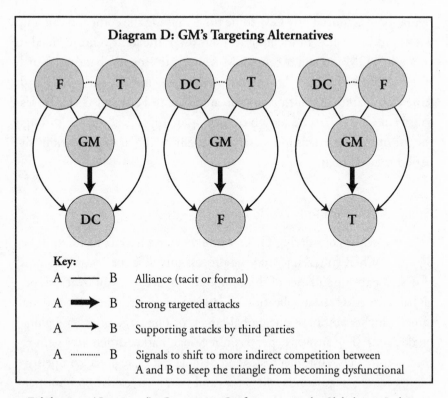

Diagram D: GM's Targeting Alternatives

Key:

A ——— B   Alliance (tacit or formal)

A ➡ B   Strong targeted attacks

A ⟶ B   Supporting attacks by third parties

A ·········· B   Signals to shift to more indirect competition between
                      A and B to keep the triangle from becoming dysfunctional

Exhibit 5-11 (Continued): *Competitive Configuration in the Global Auto Industry*

Ford's invasionary overlaps into GM's core and vital interests (e.g., in luxury and large cars, light trucks, and SUVs).

Going through this process is extremely valuable because it provides insights that wouldn't otherwise immediately come to mind. Let's take a second look at GM's joint venture with Toyota in NUMMI, mentioned earlier in the chapter. Why the GM alliance with Toyota, given the fact that this joint venture helped Toyota expand in America? The answer, in a word, is Ford. At the time of the NUMMI deal, GM saw Ford as the most significant threat to GM's core. GM probably hoped to realign the interests of Toyota—and maybe even encourage some Japanese restraint against GM in the United States—so that it could focus on Ford as its target. GM agreed to share plants and processes with Toyota in order to gain leverage against what its saw as the more serious rival. In the short run, this configuration did indeed buy GM some time, helping the company catch up with Ford in quality. In the long run, however, the joint venture failed to strengthen GM's sphere because GM couldn't tie Toyota's hands in North America. Toyota used NUMMI to make deep inroads into the North American market that ultimately threatened both Ford and GM. The lesson: Had GM done a better job of locking in Toyota's allegiance through the use of more overlaps in Japan, GM might not be in the precarious situation it faces today.

Going Global with Your World View

Thus far, while considering GM's world view, we haven't factored in geography. When you're applying the process just described, you also need to describe the boundaries of the competitive space. Do you treat it as one global market? Or as a collection of regional markets? The answer determines whether you have one global target, or one target in each regional marketplace. The answer depends on regional market differences with respect to products, customer tastes and demographics, regional competitive configurations, regulations and tariffs, and your own relative commitment to the geo-product zones, given the location of your core and the size of your resources.

Returning to a GM-centric perspective, what makes more sense— should the company launch a worldwide effort or a series of more regional attacks? If GM were to pick one global target, its global alliances and targeting strategy might be focused on Ford, which poses the biggest threat to GM's sphere. In the alternative, based on the targeting criteria provided earlier in the chapter, GM could also see DaimlerChrysler as a target. DaimlerChrysler is the more vulnerable target given its smaller size and the problems created by its incomplete, postmerger integration process, including the lack of central information and coordination systems required to use its overlaps effectively. Both Ford and DaimlerChrysler are reasonable choices for GM's global targeting strategy, but given its vulnerability, the sphere of DaimlerChrysler may be the more feasible, less costly choice. (See Exhibit 5-12, Diagram A, which demonstrates how GM must configure the players in order to target DaimlerChrysler globally.)

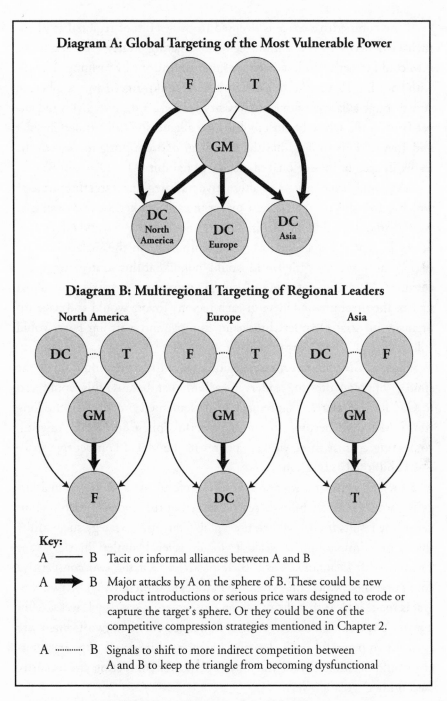

Diagram A: Global Targeting of the Most Vulnerable Power

Diagram B: Multiregional Targeting of Regional Leaders

Key:

A ——— B   Tacit or informal alliances between A and B

A ➡ B   Major attacks by A on the sphere of B. These could be new product introductions or serious price wars designed to erode or capture the target's sphere. Or they could be one of the competitive compression strategies mentioned in Chapter 2.

A ·········· B   Signals to shift to more indirect competition between A and B to keep the triangle from becoming dysfunctional

Exihibit 5-12: Multiregional vs. Global Targeting

If the competitive space is deemed to be a series of regional markets, then GM needs to use a multiregional targeting strategy. For example, GM could target DaimlerChrysler's sphere in Europe by forming alliances with Ford and Toyota. At the same time, GM could target Toyota's sphere in Asia through alliances with DaimlerChrysler and Ford. And GM could target Ford in the United States by forming alliances with DaimlerChrysler and Toyota. This strategy has the advantage of attempting to weaken the leader in each of the regional markets (see Exhibit 5-12, Diagram B).

GM could also consider an alternative multiregional targeting strategy, which is to focus on the weakest player in each market. In this case, GM would target DaimlerChrysler in North America and Asia, and target Toyota in Europe. This alternative seems reasonable on the surface, but it's important to see what the world would look like if this strategy were successful. GM would not achieve strategic supremacy because it wouldn't uproot the preeminent sphere in each region. Toyota would still have supremacy in Asia; DaimlerChrysler in Europe; and a strong Ford would still threaten GM in North America.

Thus, if GM chooses a multiregional world view it should favor the strategy of going after the leaders in each market, because this would lead to GM having strategic supremacy if implemented properly. In the long run, GM would become the most powerful sphere in North America, competing against three weaker spheres in the global competitive space (see Exhibit 5-13, Diagram A).

Now let's compare the results if GM were to use a multiregional targeting strategy successfully (based on targeting the leader in each region) versus the results if GM were to use a global targeting strategy successfully (based on eliminating the weakest global player, DaimlerChrysler). (See Exhibit 5-13, Diagrams A and B, respectively.) Of the two competitive configurations, which one gives GM strategic supremacy? The two diagrams make it clear that the multiregional targeting strategy leaves GM in a better position. Global targeting would place GM in a two-fronted war against two powerful rivals. In contrast, the multiregional targeting strategy would position GM as the only superpower competing against three "second tier" great powers.

Thus, GM's world view ought to be the configuration that would result from multiregional targeting of the regional leaders. GM should re-configure the players to look like the multiregional triangles shown earlier in Exhibit 5-12, Diagram B. Note that this means that GM would be al-lied in one location with its target in another location.

To achieve this world view, GM would have to provide powerful in-centives to unfreeze the existing configuration by aggressive use of divide-and-conquer and assimilator strategies. GM would then have to construct a new regional configuration using regional coordinator and balancer strategies, as well as overlaps, announcements, promises, threats, and other

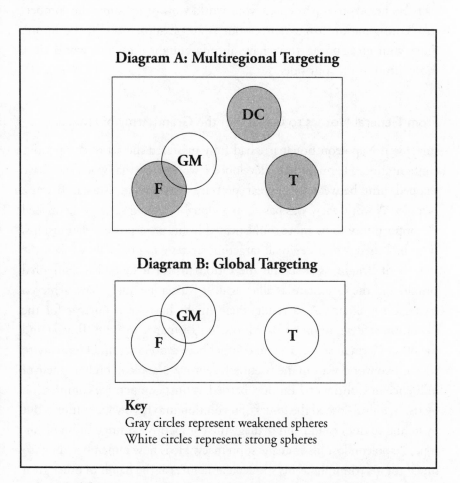

Exihibit 5-13: Long-Run Results of Multiregional vs. Global Targeting

methods to align the interests of potential alliance partners with GM's world view. To protect its backside, GM would also use the same methods to create tacit agreements among the other great powers to be less aggressive in GM's vital or core interests in each region. This world view becomes all the more feasible for GM if the other great powers have not built the organizational capabilities to see and capitalize on the big picture of the global competitive configuration.

While it's unclear whether GM has these capabilities, it is crucially important for your business to build them. If your world view becomes embodied in the current competitive configuration, then that configuration will also help you to perpetuate your world view or to adjust the competitive configuration to guarantee your strategic supremacy in the future. Since your great power rivals have already bought into your world view, momentum is on your side.

From General Motors to General of the Grand Army of France

Imagine if Napoleon Bonaparte had fully mastered the art of competitive configuration. He might have developed a world view that would not have trapped him between two great powers, Britain and Russia. Because Napoleon's world view was based on a global targeting strategy, he missed the opportunity to be more sophisticated in his great power relationships. If he had used a multiregional targeting strategy to gradually weaken the spheres of Britain, Russia, and the Ottomans, or if he had reconfigured Britain and the Ottomans as allies against Russia, he might have achieved strategic supremacy. As a result, there might have been no czar for the Communist Revolution to overthrow, no Bismarck to unify Prussia and the other German states, and no conflict between France and Germany to trigger two world wars in the twentieth century. Napoleon built a sphere of influence in Continental Europe, battled against competitive compression by rivals, and absorbed the forces of revolution into his own ambitions. But by failing to understand and manage the competitive configuration of Europe, Napoleon lost his strategic supremacy. He is now remembered not so much for his triumphs as his spectacular failures at the hands of other great powers. As he himself said, "Glory is fleeting . . . but obscurity is forever."

Chapter 6

Global Power Systems

Intervening in Your Industry to Stabilize or Transform the Distribution of Power

OVERVIEW

In any industry, there is a global power system *at work—a combination of spheres, structure, and dynamic processes that influence the power hierarchy among firms. As a great power with strategic supremacy, you can and must proactively intervene in your industry's power system by selectively using your power—by applying* competitive pressure—*to keep the balance of power in your favor. By looking at* pressure maps *you can predict the way your industry will evolve. You can pressure the status quo by employing* stabilizing mechanisms *to achieve* dynamic stability. *Or you can intervene in the system in more dramatic ways, conquering chaos through putting pressure on selected rival spheres, rapidly rebalancing to absorb sudden power surges, or using* pressure cascades *to guide the evolution of a system in transition. Each of these strategies employs a particular form of co-opetition—the right balance and pattern of competition and cooperation to ensure the power system in your industry continues to work for you.*

WAR AND PEACE

The Bourbons of France, the Hapsburgs of Austria, the Hohenzollerns of Prussia, and the Romanovs of Russia reigned for centuries in Europe, until

Napoleon came along. Prior to Napoleon, these great dynasties had experienced comparatively minor disruptions of their territorial boundaries. The ruling dynasties traded territories—including subjects who had no concept of nationalism—but maintained a relatively stable order among themselves. In this dynastic power system, power was distributed and redistributed among the dynasties, and their territorial spheres were reconfigured frequently. But despite these fluctuations in territory and power, the dynasties shared strategic supremacy over Europe's evolution. This continued for centuries, with more and more territory in continental Europe coming under the control of the Bourbons, the Hapsburgs, the Hohenzollerns, and the Romanovs. Napoleon inspired the people of France (and over time, Europe) to see themselves as citizens of a nation-state, rather than subjects of a king with the "divine" right to rule. Millions of citizens were rallied to fight by a sense of patriotism and nationalism, rather than loyalty to the king. Napoleon destroyed the stable order among the great powers. Napoleon was ultimately defeated at Waterloo, but the power of the great dynasties of Europe was shaken. They needed to find a new way to restore the stability of their relationships and protect their interests.

First, the European nations developed the concept of a "Concert of Powers." Originally organized by Prince Klemens von Metternich from the Hapsburg Austrian Empire, from 1814 to 1848, this Concert of Powers intervened in several minor wars to ensure that no one power gained supremacy over the other dynasties. During this period, the restored French kings reestablished France's powerful role in the European power system, and France joined the Concert of Powers.

But between 1848 and 1878, the Concert of Powers began to break down and a new strategy was needed to ensure stability. The European powers stopped cooperating and pursued their own self-interests during the revolutions of 1848–49, the Crimean War, and the Russo-Turkish War. While these disruptions threatened the peace, they never rose to the intensity of a Napoleonic-style war, and did not threaten the supremacy of the dynasties. The disruptions resulted only in minor shifts in the distribution of power.

These "fluctuations" in the stability of the dynastic system could easily have escalated to the level of a Napoleonic-style war, if not for the creation of stabilizing alliances by Otto von Bismarck, foreign minister to the king of (Hohenzollern) Prussia. Bismarck established alliances with Russia and Britain to isolate France and prevent her from forming her own alliances that could tip the balance of power on the Continent in her favor. By 1870, the relationship between France and Prussia had seriously deteriorated, threatening numerous smaller Germanic states and resulting in a war that Prussia won. Bismarck balanced the growing power of France by helping to unify these numerous states into Prussia, creating the German Empire under the domination of the Hohenzollern dynasty. The actions of Bismarck held France in check and averted another major European-wide war until the early 1900s. The use of the Concert of Powers and Bismarck's counterbalancing alliances helped ensure relative stability in Europe between the end of the Napoleonic era and the start of World War I.

Business Bismarcks and Modern-Day Metternichs

Just as the great European powers operated in a global power system, corporations also operate within their own industry's global power system. If you could perch yourself far above your competitive space for a moment, viewing your own company and those of all your rivals from the stratosphere, you would see this system at work.

A global power system describes the power relationships among a set of great and lesser powers. The system is defined by:

1. *Its basic building blocks*—the variety and number of spheres within the competitive space; i.e., the number of walled, fluid, colonial, and advanced spheres

2. *Its structure*—i.e., a competitive configuration, competitive cooperative, or power hierarchy

3. *Its dynamic processes*—the mechanisms and activities that perpetuate or transform the existing structure and its building blocks; i.e., growth processes in the face of competitive compression, processes for countering revolutionaries, and processes for reconfiguring great power triangles

Taken together, these components create a dynamic system of interdependent, powerful players that influence each other's spheres through the patterns of competition and cooperation they establish. The global power system includes the ongoing creation, use, distribution, redistribution, preservation, and stabilization of power of those within an industry. It also includes the cooperative use of power, and the competitive use of power directed against targeted spheres.

A stable distribution of power results when the great powers have no way left to increase their power by reconfiguring the players. Stable systems usually involve an equal distribution of power among the players with strategic supremacy, and they involve a mechanism to prevent or make it difficult for any of the great powers to shift that balance of power. Recall Metternich's Concert of Powers and Bismarck's stabilizing alliances.

The great powers in a stable power system typically avoid direct conflict over a specific piece of territory held by another great power. Instead, they compete indirectly by doing a good job at selecting and executing their paradigm for power, and by moving into power vacuums and pivotal zones faster than the other players. For example, during Bismarck's day, the European great powers were competing indirectly for colonies well outside the European arena. No matter how much some of the great powers may want stability, there is always an underlying struggle for power and strategic supremacy because of this indirect competition. And, if one great power is better at these indirect methods than the others, a power imbalance will occur and the structure of the system destabilizes.

Even stable power systems are constantly evolving. Because cooperation engenders new forms of (indirect) competition, and because competition engenders new forms of cooperation, every global power system in every industry has a natural evolutionary cycle that alternates between periods of stability and transformation. This cycle occurs because of inevitable major shocks to the system—such as the rise of Napoleon in Europe—or the results of unconstrained indirect competition. For example, one of the factors that ultimately contributed to the end of the dynastic global system in Europe was the heightened "competition" between France and Prussia, which resulted from France's growing wealth and power garnered from her overseas empire. France's "power surge" meant that Germany had to unify in order to rebalance the distribution of power with France, and to isolate France to prevent her from forming alliances with England or Russia that could target Germany. Thus, the stage was set for World War I.

Whereas nations use methods of war and diplomacy to intervene in the system, corporations use different forms of competition or cooperation, called co-opetition, to intervene in their industries' global power system. These forms of co-opetition vary depending on the balance and pattern of competition and cooperation applied by the great powers. Using strategies from the previous chapters—such as triangulation and balanced-deep overlaps—firms with strategic supremacy can create cooperative relationships with some great powers, in order to focus competition against others. Different forms of co-opetition are used to either stabilize the existing power hierarchy, or to guide the redistribution of power in the system during periods of transformation.

PRESSURE MAPS: SEEING THE "INVISIBLE HAND" THAT SQUEEZES THE COMPETITION

You can't see power but you can see how deeply and how heavily rivals are exerting pressure in markets that are part of your sphere of influence. By measuring the competitive pressure each player is putting on the others, we can develop a picture of the power usage, and hence relationships, among different players in an industry. As I discussed in Chapter 5, deeper and heavier overlaps apply more pressure on the invaded player. So, if you can measure the depth and weight of overlaps, you can see invisible patterns of competitive pressure (i.e., the use of power) and how those patterns of compression change over time.

How can we assess this competitive pressure? Pressure is applied when one great power takes footholds in the sphere of a rival. Two factors affect the strength of this competitive pressure from a given foothold: size and depth. First, the pressure created by a single foothold increases when the *size* of the foothold is greater. The size of the foothold might be assessed by using the market share of the invading power in the particular geoproduct zone where the foothold is achieved. The second factor that affects pressure is the *depth* of the incursion—how important the geo-product market is to the invaded firm (i.e., deeper in the sphere). Pushing deeper into the sphere, closer to the core, increases the pressure felt by the invaded sphere. This importance can be assessed by using the percentage of the invaded firm's revenues generated in the invaded geo-product market divided by the invaded firm's total revenues. Thus the pressure created by each foothold in a rival's sphere can be measured as follows:

$$\boxed{\text{Pressure}} = \boxed{\text{Size of Incursion}} \times \boxed{\text{Importance of Incursion}}$$

| On the invaded firm in the invaded geo-product market | Market share of the invader in the invaded geo-product market | Percent of the invaded firm's total revenues provided by the invaded geo-product market |

A given great power may have a number of footholds in its sphere, so the total pressure on that firm is the sum of the pressures of the individual footholds in its sphere. By adding up all the pressures from all the footholds from different firms separately, you can see just how much each of the other spheres is threatening the invaded sphere.

Airlines: Dogfights and Diplomacy

The airline industry offers a long-term, detailed perspective on the use of competitive pressure among the carriers. The major carriers and a host of minor ones have engaged in a shifting set of overlapping routes, alliances, and dogfights that have shaped the pattern of competitive pressure in the industry. The availability of detailed FAA data presents an opportunity to explore the shifting pressure systems in some detail, demonstrating mapping techniques that can be applied to your industry.[1] The creation of these "pressure maps" provides insights into the forces that are shaping the industry's evolution.

FAA data offer a snapshot of the competitive pressures major airline carriers were applying to rivals in 1989, as summarized in Exhibit 6-1.

	AA	AO	AS	BN	CO	DL	EA	HA	AW	MW	NW	PA	PI	TW	UA	US	SW
AA		0.00	0.01	0.02	0.08	0.20	0.04	0.00	0.02	0.00	0.08	0.03	0.01	0.09	0.26	0.12	0.02
AO	0.00		0.00	0.00	0.00	0.00	0.00	0.99	0.00	0.00	0.00	0.00	0.00	0.00	0.01	0.00	0.00
AS	0.18	0.00		0.00	0.02	0.10	0.01	0.00	0.10	0.00	0.09	0.01	0.00	0.01	0.33	0.14	0.00
BN	0.14	0.00	0.00		0.10	0.19	0.04	0.00	0.05	0.01	0.11	0.01	0.01	0.10	0.12	0.07	0.05
CO	0.13	0.00	0.00	0.02		0.16	0.06	0.00	0.02	0.01	0.08	0.02	0.02	0.04	0.27	0.13	0.04
DL	0.22	0.00	0.01	0.03	0.11		0.16	0.00	0.03	0.01	0.08	0.02	0.03	0.06	0.10	0.12	0.03
EA	0.11	0.00	0.00	0.02	0.09	0.36		0.00	0.00	0.01	0.04	0.15	0.03	0.06	0.04	0.11	0.00
HA	0.02	0.87	0.03	0.00	0.01	0.02	0.00		0.00	0.00	0.02	0.00	0.03	0.00	0.06	0.00	0.00
AW	0.08	0.00	0.00	0.02	0.05	0.10	0.00	0.00		0.00	0.03	0.00	0.01	0.03	0.08	0.16	0.40
MW	0.05	0.00	0.00	0.02	0.09	0.06	0.02	0.00	0.01		0.25	0.00	0.00	0.04	0.08	0.10	0.28
NW	0.16	0.00	0.01	0.03	0.10	0.15	0.03	0.01	0.02	0.05		0.01	0.01	0.07	0.21	0.09	0.03
PA	0.15	0.00	0.01	0.01	0.06	0.08	0.30	0.00	0.00	0.00	0.03		0.02	0.16	0.10	0.09	0.00
PI	0.06	0.00	0.00	0.01	0.06	0.12	0.06	0.00	0.01	0.00	0.02	0.02		0.01	0.04	0.09	0.01
TW	0.21	0.00	0.00	0.03	0.06	0.13	0.06	0.00	0.03	0.01	0.08	0.08	0.01		0.17	0.06	0.08
UA	0.28	0.00	0.03	0.02	0.17	0.10	0.02	0.00	0.03	0.01	0.10	0.02	0.01	0.07		0.13	0.02
US	0.16	0.00	0.01	0.01	0.10	0.13	0.06	0.01	0.06	0.01	0.06	0.02	0.15	0.03	0.15		0.04
SW	0.08	0.00	0.00	0.02	0.07	0.08	0.00	0.00	0.38	0.08	0.04	0.00	0.00	0.10	0.05	0.10	
Total Pressure Applied*	**2.03**	**0.87**	**0.11**	**0.26**	**1.17**	**1.98**	**0.86**	**1.01**	**0.76**	**0.19**	**1.11**	**0.39**	**0.31**	**0.87**	**2.07**	**2.00**	**1.00**

AA - American Airlines
AO - Aloha Airlines
AS - Alaska Airlines
BN - Braniff
CO - Continental Airlines
DL - Delta Airlines

EA - Eastern Airlines
HA - Hawaiian Airlines
AW - America West Airlines
MW - Midway Airlines
NW - Northwest Airlines
PA - Pan American World Air

PI - Piedmont Aviation
TW - Trans World Airlines
UA - United Airlines
US - USAir
SW - Southwest Airlines

Note: The focal firm (a) is listed in the first column, while its competitors (b) are listed across the top of the table.
Source: This table is a modification of a table appearing in Ming-Jer Chen, "Competitor Analysis and Interfirm Rivalry: Toward a Theoretical Integration," *Academy of Management Review* 21.1 (1996): 100–134.
*As seen from the perspective of the target companies

Exhibit 6-1: Magnitude of Pressure Data for U.S. Air Carriers in 1989

(For further explanation of the measurement methods used in this chapter see Appendix B, "Pressure Measurement in the Airline Industry.") For each of the firms listed in the left-hand column, the table shows the competitive pressure generated by each of the carriers listed across the top of the table. The higher the number, the greater the pressure. For example, reading the first row, the pressure felt by American Airlines (as the focal company) is coming primarily from overlaps with United (0.26) and Delta (0.20), with US Airways (0.12) as the third most threatening competitor. Reading down the first column, the table also indicates that American (as the invading competitor) is putting the most pressure on United (0.28), Delta (0.22), and TWA (0.21), with Alaska Air (0.18) and US Airways (0.16) being in fourth and fifth place, respectively.

Drawing a Pressure Map

On the surface, pressure measures show the obvious (airlines compete with each other for passengers in some markets and not others), but by using the data from this table to create a "pressure map," we can gain a deeper understanding of the power relationships in the airline industry. This map reveals a lot about *patterns* of power usage and whether power is being used to transform or stabilize the system. For example, the maps can tell you much more about how the specific pattern of pressure is affecting the mixture of competitive and cooperative relationships in the system.

Using the measures in Exhibit 6-1, we can generate the simplified pressure map shown in Exhibit 6-2. For simplicity, it shows only three super-carriers—American, Delta, and United—and only registers pressures greater than or equal to 0.20. This lets us focus on the great powers that have (or almost have) achieved strategic supremacy. The 0.20 cutoff was used because it is enough to be felt as more than a toehold that could be ignored. (This cutoff may vary in other industries, depending on the baseline level of pressure prevalent in the industry.)

What does this map show us? It reveals the pattern of interdependencies among the great powers in the airline industry. The map visually displays: (1) whose profits and growth depend upon the forbearance of others; (2) which spheres have been violated the most deeply by several rivals; (3) which

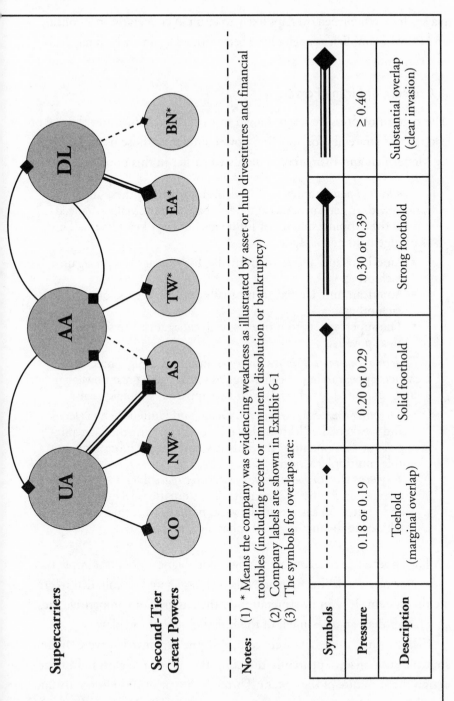

Supercarriers

**Second-Tier
Great Powers**

Notes: (1) * Means the company was evidencing weakness as illustrated by asset or hub divestitures and financial
troubles (including recent or imminent dissolution or bankruptcy)

(2) Company labels are shown in Exhibit 6-1
(3) The symbols for overlaps are:

Symbols			
Pressure	0.18 or 0.19	0.20 or 0.29	0.30 or 0.39	≥ 0.40
Description	Toehold (marginal overlap)	Solid foothold	Strong foothold	Substantial overlap (clear invasion)

Exhibit 6-2: The Pressure Map for the U.S. Supercarriers in 1989

players have established overlaps likely to result in cooperative relationships; and (4) what implicit triangles have been formed against which targets.

A Concert of Airline Powers

The pattern of pressure usage shown in this exhibit illustrates the use of cooperative strategies for applying power similar to those used in Europe by Metternich and Bismarck, as discussed earlier in this book:

1. *A concert of powers* appears to have been formed by these supercarriers, with American at its center. It is based on mutually balanced-deep overlapping spheres of influence between key players. This arrangement encourages:

   - American and Delta to mutually forbear aggression against each other.
   - American and United to mutually forbear aggression against each other.
   - The supercarriers to move aggressively against the second-tier great powers.

2. *Targeting and tacit alliance strategies* among the Big Three supercarriers appear to have been designed so that each great power can target a limited set of rivals with two apparent strategic goals:

   - *Targeting the weak.* American, Delta, and United each targeted and weakened at least one player, perhaps with the tacit purpose of consolidating the industry to create a more manageable multipolar world.
   - *Targeting specific parts of the competitive space.* Delta focused on carriers in the east, American on international launch pads, and United on carriers in the west, perhaps with the goal of establishing distinct regional spheres of influence.

The appearance of a concert of powers or alliances does not imply that the major carriers deliberately or explicitly cooperated or colluded to create this system. It is an interpretation of the patterns of competitive pressure rather than an assessment of the intent of any of the players.

Clearly, when these data were compiled, the supercarriers were sharing strategic supremacy, apparently directing the use of their pressure to redesign the structure of the system. Through the use of this temporary and unstable configuration, they were creating a favorable world around themselves and redistributing power in a way that allowed each to gain strategic supremacy over unique geographic markets and over the lesser powers operating within these geographic spheres of influence.

There is also an Achilles' heel that is apparent in this power system. Despite the cooperative relationships formed within the presssure system in Exhibit 6-2, this system contained one major flaw that undermined the concert of powers among the three supercarriers. Delta and United had not exchanged significant footholds. Although some minor toeholds existed, these weren't enough to provide the two firms with compelling incentives to avoid attacking the other's sphere. When the two acted against each other, their moves rippled through the entire Big Three, and inadvertently triggered responses that spilled over to American's sphere of influence. Consequently American was caught in the crossfire, forced to defend its interests, and often required to use disciplinary actions to keep the others in line.

As the apparent "enforcer" of the tacit supercarrier concert of powers, American was frequently pegged as "the problem" and assigned the blame for causing numerous price wars. Yet many of American's actions more likely resulted from the structural flaw in the entire power system, which required American to act to settle the other supercarriers down. The Big Three could not attain a true concert of powers until they completed the loop with balanced-deeper overlaps between Delta and United.

Three Tiers for the Airlines

If we look beyond these three supercarriers to the smaller players in the airline industry, we see other sources of disruption in the power system. A more detailed pressure map in Exhibit 6-3 illustrates the complete pattern of power usage created by the airlines listed in Exhibit 6-1. The interaction of these small, large, and supercarriers has a significant impact on the broader evolution of the industry.

This map shows how the supercarriers were putting pressure on the second-tier great powers, and how the second-tier great powers were putting pressure on the lesser powers in the third tier. This *cascade of pressure* increased the intensity of competition within the industry in the short

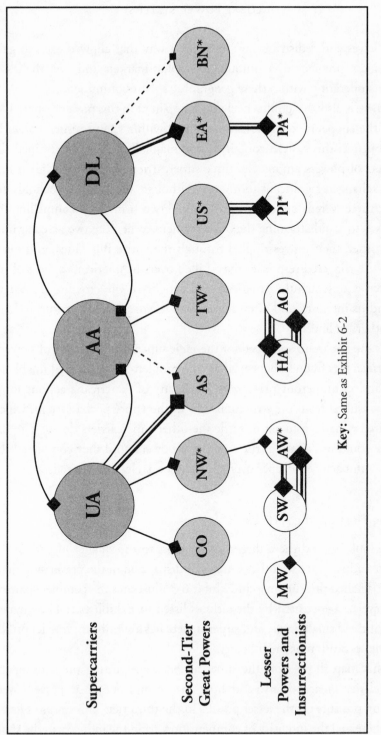

Exhibit 6-3: The Pressure Map for the Overall U.S. Air Carrier Industry

Key: Same as Exhibit 6-2

run. Competition also prevailed over cooperation because some of the regional airlines were still attempting to stake out unique cores and viable spheres. This struggle for survival was played out by Hawaii and Aloha Airlines, as well as America West and Southwest. These lesser powers had taken much more than footholds in the spheres of their competitors.

Great powers sometimes intervene in these struggles among the smaller carriers. In the struggle between America West and Southwest, Southwest's use of direct flights, low service, only one type of airplane, alternative airfields, and low-cost labor was the most disruptive business model in the industry. Northwest might have dampened this disrupter, but instead it attacked the sphere of America West, tipping the balance of power in Southwest's favor. Despite being the lowest cost hub-and-spoke airline, America West was caught in a no-win, two-fronted war that caused significant financial difficulty. In the meantime, Southwest was virtually ignored by the supercarriers while it was still getting off the ground, allowing it to become a larger and more disruptive influence in the industry. (Similarly, the map shows that the great powers ignored U.S. Airways in 1989.) The airline example proves an old military maxim: It is a lot better to be flying high with air supremacy than to be on the ground feeling the pressure from above.

Understanding the Flight Path

The form of co-opetition used by the Big Three airlines (as shown in Exhibit 6-3) reveals that they were actively driving the transformation of the power system in the airline industry. Another perspective on the power system can be gained by examining and mapping the pressure data by tiers. This offers insights into the reasons for the redistribution of power among the airlines and insights on the probable flight path of the industry. Exhibit 6-4 shows the aggregated data for the pressure exerted on and felt by each tier of the 1989 airline industry and Exhibit 6-5 maps these pressures to indicate how the power hierarchy was shifting over the longer run.

Using this aggregated map, you can actually anticipate how the pattern of pressure used may drive the evolution of the power hierarchy over the

	Pressure Exerted by the Supercarriers[a]	Pressure Exerted by the Second-Tier Great Powers[b]	Pressure Exerted by the Third-Tier Lesser Powers[c]
Pressure Felt by the Supercarriers			
A	0.46	0.47	0.05
DL	0.32	0.59	0.10
UA	0.38	0.56	0.08
Subtotal	1.16 ①	1.62 ④	0.23 ⑦
Pressure Felt by the Second-Tier Great Powers			
AS	0.61	0.28	0.10
BN	0.45	0.43	0.12
CO	0.56	0.35	0.09
EA	0.51	0.47	0.03
NW	0.52	0.34	0.12
PA	0.33	0.66	0.02
TW	0.51	0.37	0.13
US	0.44	0.29	0.26
Subtotal	3.93 ②	3.19 ⑤	0.87 ⑧
Pressure Felt by the Third-Tier Lesser Powers			
AO	0.01	0.00	0.99
HA	0.10	0.03	0.87
AW	0.26	0.32	0.41
MV	0.19	0.52	0.29
Pl	0.22	0.76	0.02
SW	0.21	0.33	0.46
Subtotal	0.99 ③	1.96 ⑥	3.04 ⑨
Overall Total	**6.08**	**6.77**	**4.14**

Key:
[a] Based on the sum of the measures in columns AA, DL, and UA in Exhibit 6-1.
[b] Based on the sum of the measures in columns AS, BN, CO, EA, NW, PA, TW, and US in Exhibit 6-1.
[c] Based on the sum of the measures in columns AO, HA, AW, MW, PI, and SW in Exhibit 6-1.

Note:
All carrier abbreviations are the same as in Exhibit 6-1.
①...⑨ refer to Exhibit 6-5.

Exhibit 6-4: Pressure Exerted on and Felt by Each Tier in 1989

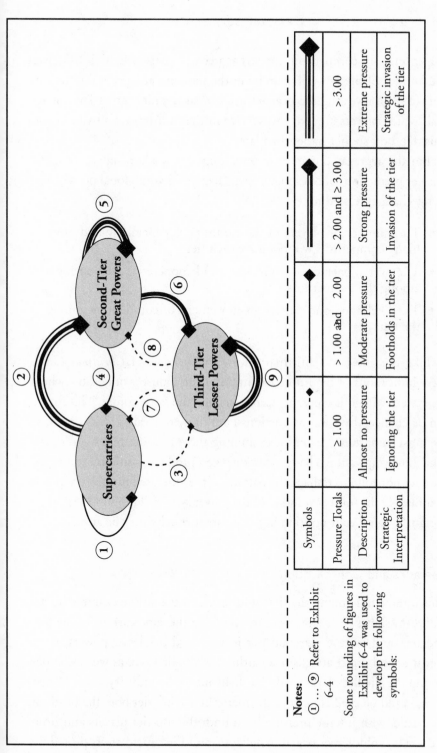

Symbols	- - - - ◆	───◆	══◆	══◆
Pressure Totals	≥ 1.00	> 1.00 and 2.00	> 2.00 and ≥ 3.00	> 3.00
Description	Almost no pressure	Moderate pressure	Strong pressure	Extreme pressure
Strategic Interpretation	Ignoring the tier	Footholds in the tier	Invasion of the tier	Strategic invasion of the tier

Notes:

① ... ⑨ Refer to Exhibit 6-4

Some rounding of figures in Exhibit 6-4 was used to develop the following symbols:

Exhibit 6-5: The Pattern of Pressure among the Tiers

longer term. In comparison, the less aggregated map in Exhibit 6-3 gives you an idea of the power hierarchy in the industry at a given moment in time (1989), revealing the near-term future at the nitty gritty level. It reveals which players are likely to survive in the near term, and whom you must fend off sooner rather than later.

But the aggregated map provides a longer view, allowing you to make smarter predictions about longer-term changes in your global power hierarchy, changes related to:

- The number of players in the future power hierarchy and how many competitors will populate each tier
- The overall balance of competitive and cooperative relationships among the competitors
- The likelihood and pattern of movement of competitors among the tiers

Like the ghost of Christmas Future in Dickens's *A Christmas Carol,* these indications of the future evolution of the industry only show where the system will go if everyone keeps pursuing the same course. This future can be changed by your own actions (and those of rivals). This is perhaps the most important reason for examining these pressure maps—to determine how you want to change your own geo-product positioning and geo-product portfolio to reshape the pattern of pressure used in the system and to influence the future evolution of the power system. This is especially important because your position in the future hierarchy may be at stake.

Cascades and Consolidation

This interaction among the tiers, illustrated in the airline example in Exhibit 6-5, shows the cascade of pressure from the supercarriers to the second tier, and from the second tier to the third-tier lesser powers. Price pressures and direct attacks from airlines in the first tier, as well as battles among the smaller players, led to a shakeout in the industry.

As could be predicted from the map, the second tier bore the brunt of the battle, with intense pressure from both the top-tier players and from peers. This middle tier began to collapse, and the supercarriers picked up the remnants of the second-tier players who failed due to the price wars and selective triangulation by the supercarriers.

As the hierarchy consolidated into two tiers, the power system moved toward a more stable hierarchy composed of two concentric circles—an "inner circle" of ever more powerful supercarriers, ringed by a few great powers without strategic supremacy. The airlines in the outer ring filled in the domestic territories not occupied by the inner circle, avoided significant presence in the spheres of the inner circle, or they established a position in the less-traveled foreign routes to Asia or Latin America.

While the Big Three carriers had not yet created a stable structure within their top tier, they were moving toward a more stable system. They were using the pattern of power in 1989 to create a pattern of cooperation and competition that would drive the industry toward a world that would favor them and give smaller pieces of the sky to the members of the outer circle.

There was significant short-term pain in the fierce price skirmishes that the smaller and weaker carriers were unable to endure. During the airline industry's transition period of the early 1990s, the industry lost over $14 billion (net profits). In the long run, however, the imminent collapse of the three-tier hierarchy meant that the structure of the power system was moving toward a more favorable world for the players with strategic supremacy. Increased stability appeared to be on the horizon.

Insights from Pressure Mapping

The airline industry's power system in 1989 teaches some great lessons about system dynamics. Even in a "competitive" industry, there are always cooperative power relationships. The goal of strategic supremacy is to manage the global power system's balance and pattern of competitive and cooperative relationships using spheres, competitive compression, paradigms for power, counterrevolutionary tactics, competitive cooperatives, selective targeting, signals for realigning interests, and balanced-deep overlaps.

Satisfied competitors with strategic supremacy will seek more cooperation than competition and will use cooperation to create indirect competition. Dissatisfied competitors with strategic supremacy will seek more competition than cooperation, and will use cooperation to compete more aggressively. Dissatisfied competitors will use selective targeting and new spheres of influence to create new orders. Such structures typically distribute power equally among those with supremacy and use stabilizing mechanisms to hold the other players in check.

In particular, the airline example illustrates how dissatisfied great powers with strategic supremacy can use a pressure cascade. Pressure cascades encourage cooperation among some competitors so that more intense competition can be directed toward other competitors. The use of a pressure cascade from one tier in the power hierarchy to the next lower tier can exert enough pressure to change the number of building blocks (spheres) in the power system and flatten the tiers in the hierarchy. This is one of the ways that hundreds of industries have consolidated over time and conquered chaos.

This process of pressure mapping can be used to answer many questions in your own industry, including:

- What does the power hierarchy look like?
- How have the great powers with strategic supremacy specifically divided up their duties as members of a concert of powers? And why?
- Who is doing the "heavy lifting," putting the most pressure on whom? And why?
- How will the current pattern of pressure usage encourage some competitors to retriangulate, and what does this mean for the competitive configuration of the future?
- Who will be squeezed out by the pressure? Who will rise in the power hierarchy?

With answers to such questions, you can then decide on strategies for intervening in the system to either maintain or shift the current distribution of power. Such decisions include:

- What changes in the competitive configuration are needed to redirect the pattern of pressure usage in the direction you want?
- How should the division of duties (with respect to targeting the lesser powers) be reassigned or realigned among the great powers with strategic supremacy to suit your purposes?

- How should the burdens of heavy lifting be redistributed to keep individual great powers from gaining or losing too much power?
- Where and when should new struts and braces be placed to stabilize the structure within the system?
- Where is it possible to divide and conquer a competitive cooperative to redistribute power within the system?
- How can you shape and select your future competitors by shifting where power is being used—without leaning on any of them yourself?
- Where and when should you (acting alone or collectively) stabilize the power hierarchy by dampening the potential rising powers of the future?

Power and Competitive Configuration Are Reciprocal

The airline example drives home the point that an industry's power distribution and its competitive configuration have a reciprocal relationship. The distribution of power influences who owns what geo-product territories and hence shapes the spheres of competitors. But the geo-product location of spheres also influences the distribution and usage of power. For example, America's sphere of influence during the Cold War included NATO. This configuration gave the United States more power against the Soviet Union. At the same time, America's power over the Soviets helped the U.S. convince NATO members and others all over the globe to join the American sphere of influence.

The relationship between power and configuration is even more complex than mere reciprocality. Sometimes the configuration may lag behind the changes in the power distribution, or vice versa. But the two will catch up with each other eventually. The mismatch between a competitive configuration and the power distribution sometimes occurs because not all power redistributions are derived from competitive reconfiguration, and not all aspects of the competitive configuration derive from the power distribution. In addition, time lags can occur because the magnitude of the power shift isn't large enough to warrant the great powers yielding their current spheres and status.

The lag may also occur because of the ability of the established great powers to dampen changes and create structures that resist transformation when the shift in power is relatively small. The use of competitive cooperatives and balanced-deep overlaps can freeze a configuration, but only up to the point when a rising or declining great power reaches or loses strategic supremacy. For example, the Soviet Union held onto its sphere of influence in Eastern Europe even after it had lost a lot of its economic power and even after the war in Afghanistan revealed the weakness of its conventional military power. The eventual disintegration of the Soviet Union's sphere of influence reflected the new balance of power in the world, but it was not a simultaneous shift.

The point is that you shouldn't assume that the causal relationship between power and configuration is linear. It's reciprocal. Power and configuration are two perspectives on the same phenomenon—each yielding insights about the other. Today's industry leaders spend far more time on selecting their geo-product positioning strategy, and hence their competitive configuration, than they do considering the long-term effect on the distribution and redistribution of power. By recognizing the need to look at the pattern of power usage in your industry, you can then see the power of the invisible hand that squeezes the competition.

Even more importantly, you should recognize that the complex relationship between competitive configuration and the distribution and use of power is one of the causes for the evolution of a global power system. In Chapter 5, I discussed how shifts in the competitive configuration can be used to shift the distribution of power among the great powers. Thus far, in this chapter, I have discussed how others adjust their territory or behavior to satisfy aggressive, powerful players using powerful pressure. Now we turn to the continuation of this process, where others in the industry reconfigure to counter an aggressor's power and stabilize the distribution of power in an industry. If the proper pattern of pressure is established, the balance of power shifts away from the aggressor(s), and the period of transformation is over. A new and stable competitive configuration emerges.

DYNAMIC STABILITY: USING POWER PLAYS TO
ABSORB PRESSURE AND POWER FLUCUATIONS

Once the competitors with strategic supremacy are satisfied with the distribution of power (or unable to improve their situation further), they will often seek to stabilize that power system. But the reality is that there will always be some fluctuations in the distribution of power because the geo-product positioning of the players is constantly changing and the cohesiveness of their spheres fluctuates with changes in the profitability of their core and peripheral markets. Some of the many other reasons for fluctuations in geo-product positioning and the cohesiveness of the sphere include:

- *Shifting strategic purposes.* Depending on the nature of the competition, you may need to create a new set of alliances or surrogates better suited to your new strategic intent. Alternatively, you may need to shift your targets because of what Napoleon once said: "Do not fight too much with one enemy, or you will teach him all your art of war."

- *Shifting threats.* For example, a great power may grow disproportionately and need to be constrained. Or you may experience increased threats in your core arising from insurrectionists.

- *Expanding boundaries of the competitive space.* New boundaries may bring in new competitors.

- *Rising powers.* A new player with strategic supremacy may emerge in your competitive space as a result of a revolutionary new ideology or a series of mergers.

- *Shifting power patterns.* Suddenly you may no longer be a target of the great powers because they face a new entrant or rising power, requiring new alliances to confront this new challenge.

- *Declining or exiting great powers.* Management problems or overstretched resources may cause a competitor to pull back, creating a power vacuum that others want to pursue.

In many cases, these changes result in fluctuations that are not important enough to trigger a major transformation in the global power system. Because of these continuous "minor" fluctuations, the best that great powers with strategic supremacy can do is to achieve a "dynamic" stability. The essence of dynamic stability is to maintain the current favorable distribution of power by countering, absorbing, accommodating, or riding out the fluctuations. This dynamic stability can be achieved for at least some period of time.

Even though dynamic stability is temporary it is critically important because it allows you to regroup by consolidating the cohesiveness of your sphere, improving or adjusting your paradigm for power, or bolstering and prepositioning your alliances to prepare for the next transformation that you want to drive.

Stabilizing Mechanisms

A global power system will drift due to random fluctuations in the distribution of power, or the evolution of the power distribution will be driven by a great power seeking supremacy. Therefore dynamic stability doesn't happen by itself. You must proactively intervene in the system.

How do great powers that are satisfied with the current power hierarchy work to stabilize the system? They use a variety of "stabilizing mechanisms" to absorb inadvertent power fluctuations and discourage active power struggles (but not necessarily competition). The great powers with strategic supremacy must work together in both a competitive and cooperative fashion to distribute the power equally among those with strategic supremacy, enforce norms of behavior that discourage entry of each other's spheres, and redistribute or counter shifts in power if anyone gains or loses too much power for any reason. Alliances may be formed either explicitly through contracts or tacitly through the use of balanced-deep overlaps. Pressure is used to mold the behavior and spheres of rivals. And these actions may be pursued by one influential sphere or several acting collectively without formal coordination. The particular mechanisms that work depend on the system of great powers—whether you are competing in a multipolar (more than two great powers), bipolar (two great powers), or unipolar (sole supremacy) world.

Dynamic Stability in a Multipolar World

If there are more than two great powers in a competitive space, three types of mechanisms can be used to temporarily preserve the status quo: *checks and balances, tit-for-tat,* and *shared power.* All of these mechanisms are designed to stabilize the hierarchy of powers by preventing any great power from ascending to a position of strategic supremacy over the other great powers and the overall competitive space (see Exhibit 6-6).

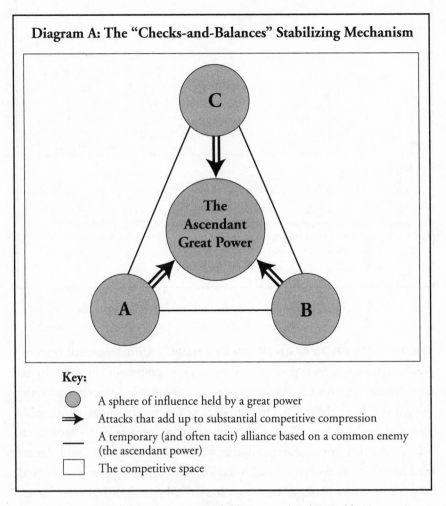

Diagram A: The "Checks-and-Balances" Stabilizing Mechanism

Key:

- A sphere of influence held by a great power
- ⟹ Attacks that add up to substantial competitive compression
- A temporary (and often tacit) alliance based on a common enemy (the ascendant power)
- The competitive space

Exhibit 6-6: Dynamic Stability in a Multipolar World

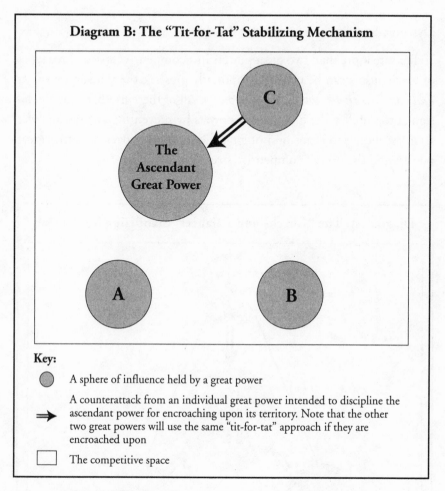

Key:

🔘   A sphere of influence held by a great power

➡   A counterattack from an individual great power intended to discipline the
    ascendant power for encroaching upon its territory. Note that the other
    two great powers will use the same "tit-for-tat" approach if they are
    encroached upon

⬜   The competitive space

Exhibit 6-6 (Continued): *Dynamic Stability in a Multipolar World*

THE CHECKS-AND-BALANCES MECHANISM.   Using competitive compression strategies, great powers hold ambitious competitors in check by either containing, constricting, stripping, or undermining the sphere of the rising power (see Exhibit 6-6, Diagram A). The League of Nations, as originally proposed by Woodrow Wilson, was intended to operate as a checks-and-balances mechanism to prevent another world war. The checks-and-balances mechanism is based on norms of behavior that encourage everyone to hold down or prop up a player whose power has shifted significantly. In most cases, the players gang up on an overly ambitious power. A never-ending process of

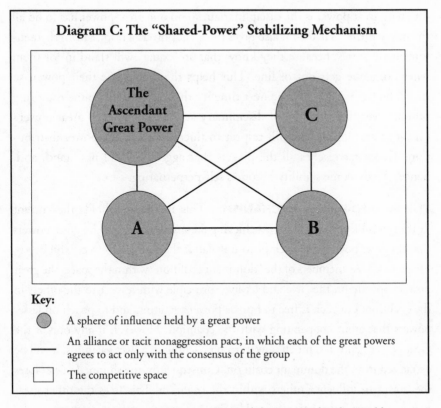

Diagram C: The "Shared-Power" Stabilizing Mechanism

Key:

⬤   A sphere of influence held by a great power

—   An alliance or tacit nonaggression pact, in which each of the great powers agrees to act only with the consensus of the group

▢   The competitive space

Exhibit 6-6 (Continued): Dynamic Stability in a Multipolar World

reconfiguring the relationships among the great powers works to sustain the overall mechanism by rebalancing the distribution of power whenever anyone threatens the status quo. After a while, each great power realizes that there is no incentive to create a war, invade another's sphere, or unbalance the power distribution in any way, ensuring a self-perpetuating dynamic stability.

TIT-FOR-TAT MECHANISM. Instead of the continuous collective pressure used in checks and balances, the tit-for-tat mechanism relies on individual great powers to take turns disciplining a rising power as soon as the rising firm threatens the current distribution of power (see Exhibit 6-6, Diagram B). Wherever and whenever the ambitious power appears, the threatened power assesses the degree of threat, and the most threatened player acts quickly to counter, discipline, and diminish the rising firm's power. In each instance, a different great power is the disciplinarian, so no one great power has to do all the heavy lifting. Tit-for-tat also gives the great powers a respite from their enforcement duties, because they know that an "equal" will stand in for them when someone gets out of line. This helps them conserve their power, so they'll be fresh and ready the next time it's their turn to discipline the rising power. Over time, the use of disciplinary actions signals each great power's tolerance and limitation with respect to fluctuations in the power distribution. Tit-for-tat teaches all the players that aggression will not stand, and, hence, the dynamic stability becomes self-perpetuating.

THE SHARED-POWER MECHANISM. This mechanism holds the current distribution of power steady by achieving a consensus among the great powers that no great power will attempt to unbalance the status quo (see Exhibit 6-6, Diagram C). As members of the "dominant coalition" within the space, the great powers operate on the "live and let live" principle with respect to the others in the coalition, but each is free to pursue power vacuums, and to poach on lesser powers that aren't cooperating with the coalition. However, if any one of the great powers gains too much power from poaching or power vacuums, it will be ostracized from the dominant coalition. Consequently, the shunned player loses the power to influence others within the coalition. This frees the other great powers to assist insurrectionists and lesser powers in their efforts to diminish the ostracized power. Through the use of these third parties, the other great powers can avoid direct aggression, while teaching the disruptive great power a lesson. In this way the disrupter is motivated to rejoin the coalition and can be welcomed back into the fold without hard feelings, vendettas, and mistrust. Self-perpetuating dynamic stability is achieved because the coalition remains intact, even though individual members drop out temporarily and are welcomed back.

Dynamic Stability in a Bipolar World

If there are only two great powers with strategic supremacy, two mechanisms can be used to achieve dynamic stability: the *loose bloc* and the *tight bloc* mechanisms (see Exhibit 6-7). In both mechanisms, each great power forms a coalition of lesser powers, or a bloc, around itself. This is similar to the strategy used by both the United States and the Soviet Union during the Cold War.

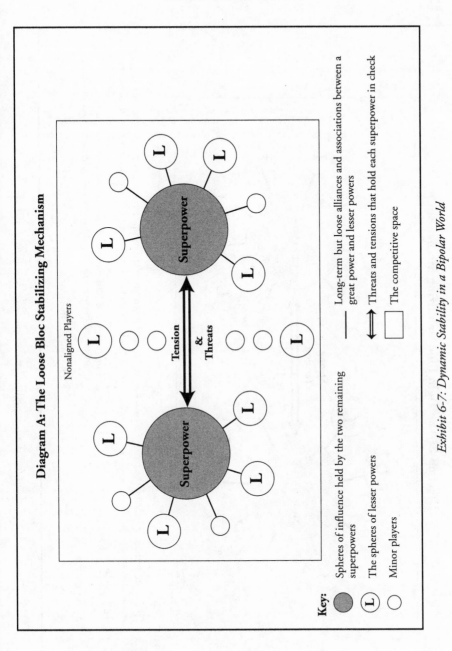

Diagram A: The Loose Bloc Stabilizing Mechanism

Nonaligned Players

Superpower

Superpower

Tension
&
Threats

Key:

⬤ Spheres of influence held by the two remaining superpowers

Ⓛ The spheres of lesser powers

◯ Minor players

— Long-term but loose alliances and associations between a great power and lesser powers

⬍ Threats and tensions that hold each superpower in check

▢ The competitive space

Exhibit 6-7: Dynamic Stability in a Bipolar World

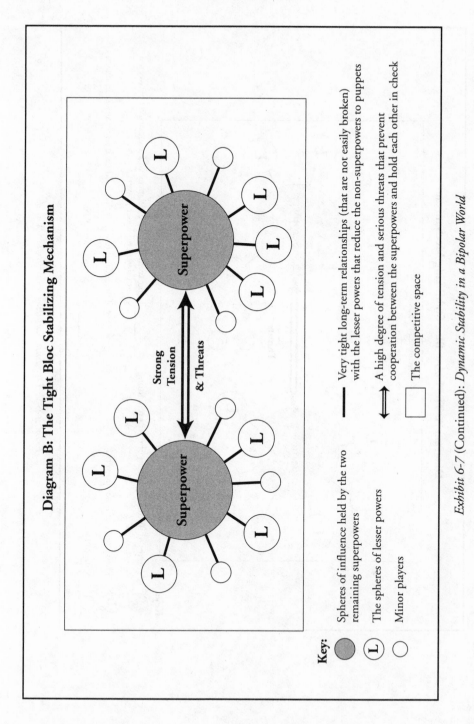

Diagram B: The Tight Bloc Stabilizing Mechanism

Strong
Tension
& Threats

Key:

⬤ Spheres of influence held by the two remaining superpowers

Ⓛ The spheres of lesser powers

◯ Minor players

—— Very tight long-term relationships (that are not easily broken) with the lesser powers that reduce the non-superpowers to puppets

⇕ A high degree of tension and serious threats that prevent cooperation between the superpowers and hold each other in check

▢ The competitive space

Exhibit 6-7 (Continued): Dynamic Stability in a Bipolar World

In the loose bloc mechanism, the coalition of lesser powers is loosely linked (see Exhibit 6-7, Diagram A). When the great power attains superpower status because of its centrality and leadership within the coalition, then the coalition becomes a power "bloc." The superpower is the first among supposed equals, coordinating the usage of power by the bloc. The lesser powers can move in and out of their bloc and even defect to the other bloc. The blocs tolerate neutrality of some players. Neutral parties can sometimes mediate conflicts and facilitate partial cooperation between the two blocs. The two superpowers also hold each other in check by keeping an equal distribution of power through competition for the unaligned lesser powers. Direct conflict is avoided because of the devastating impact of a major power struggle between two superpowers. Because of mediation, constant rebalancing, and the fear factor, the dynamic stability that is achieved becomes self-perpetuating.

In contrast, in the tight bloc mechanism the two superpowers take a more commanding leadership role over their blocs and engage in an "arms race" (see Exhibit 6-7, Diagram B). The superpowers dictate most major policies for their blocs and a clear hierarchy of power exists within each bloc. The lesser powers form tight, unbreakable linkages with their superpower, so membership in the bloc is rigid. Defections and neutrality are not tolerated. Consequently, a proactive power struggle between the two diametrically opposed blocs exists, making any type of cooperation between them unlikely. The two blocs compete to develop power through better execution of their paradigms. Each races for more power. Neither can afford to let the other win the race, and they don't trust each other enough to slow down the race. In this way, an equal distribution of power is preserved and dynamic stability becomes self-perpetuating.

Dynamic Stability in a Unipolar World

If there is only one great power with strategic supremacy, it can perpetuate its supremacy through directive and nondirective mechanisms, as a "world cop" or "world leader," respectively (see Exhibit 6-8). Obviously, with only one central great power, these mechanisms aren't needed to hold other great powers in place, but they can be effective in preventing a lesser power (or group of lesser powers) from rising to great power status. The two mechanisms differ with respect to how the central power influences the lesser powers, but both preserve the power hierarchy.

The directive mechanism contains the lesser powers to a lower tier, primarily through the use of disciplinarian actions, but also incentives (see Exhibit 6-8, Diagram A). The central power realigns the interests of the lesser powers so that they focus on core markets that don't provide them with the opportunity to challenge the existing power hierarchy. However, the central power also provides benefits by actively dampening conflicts among the lesser powers and protecting them from other lesser powers that want to expand into their turf. The central power also grants them a form of "citizenship rights" if they comply with its rules and norms of behavior. These rights include preferred treatment and potential financial aid during times of trouble. If citizenship is spurned, the great power is quick to use disciplinary actions to elicit loyalty.

In contrast, the nondirective mechanism takes a more benevolent, although powerful approach (see Exhibit 6-8, Diagram B). The central power acts more as "world leader," rather than "world cop." It distributes rewards to encourage cooperation, building consensus among the constituents.

With both the directive and nondirective mechanisms, the lesser powers may move up and down the hierarchy (depending on the will of the central power). Nevertheless, the central power effectively uses discipline and incentives to keep the players from coalescing into a combined power that could challenge the hierarchy; hence a self-perpetuating dynamic stability is achieved.

Dynamic Stability in the Airline Industry

The airline industry seems to provide an example of two of these mechanisms at work—shared power and checks and balances. Earlier, I discussed how the industry's 1989 three-tiered power hierarchy was transforming into an inner circle of three supercarriers ringed by an outer circle of lesser powers (such as Northwest and Continental). By 1995, this transition to a new power hierarchy was complete and the industry had settled into a

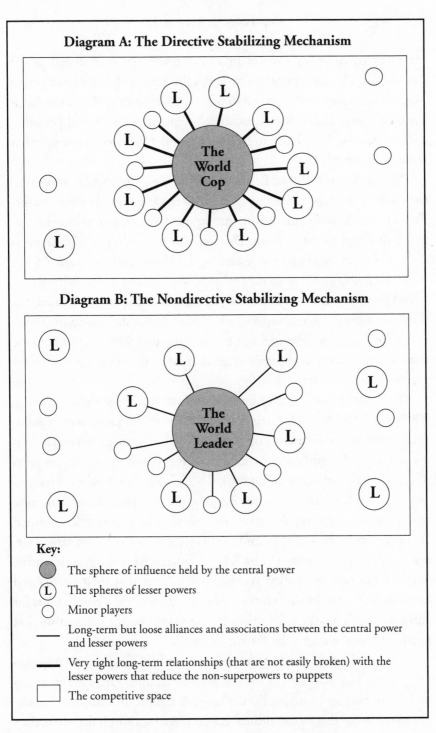

Diagram A: The Directive Stabilizing Mechanism

The World Cop

Diagram B: The Nondirective Stabilizing Mechanism

The World Leader

Key:

- The sphere of influence held by the central power
- (L) The spheres of lesser powers
- ◯ Minor players
- Long-term but loose alliances and associations between the central power and lesser powers
- Very tight long-term relationships (that are not easily broken) with the lesser powers that reduce the non-superpowers to puppets
- The competitive space

Exhibit 6-8: Dynamic Stability in a Unipolar World

period of dynamic stability maintained apparently by a shared power mechanism. This dynamic stability lasted through the late 1990s, a period when the industry earned over $16 billion (in net profit). An equal distribution of power among the supercarriers—American, Delta, and United—resulted because Eastern, Braniff, Pan Am, and TWA were bankrupted or reduced to minor players.

During the early 1990s, Eastern's bankruptcy, in particular, appears to have helped the Big Three supercarriers to achieve roughly equal market shares in the domestic market by turning the leadership of several important hub airports over to them. Delta gained the leading market share in Atlanta. American gained the leadership in Miami and San Juan. Meanwhile, United continued its expansion in the western states. With a tacit shared power mechanism apparently in place in the domestic market, the three supercarriers were able to focus on growth that did not conflict with each other's spheres. Through this mechanism, they were able to keep the status quo distribution of power in the domestic market for a period of approximately four years.

The shared power mechanism that seems to have been used in the late 1990s was based on each carrier's clearly defined, unique sphere of influence centered on different city hubs, as well as enough balanced-deep overlaps to make sure those in the inner circle stayed out of certain parts of each other's turf (see Exhibit 6-9). This mechanism probably emerged as a tacit result of the elaborate signaling and geo-product maneuvering that took place during the transition phase. The supercarriers learned about the economies of scale and profitability associated with large market shares in their various hubs. They also learned from experimenting with the boundaries of their competitors' spheres that their profits and losses were affected by the tolerance or intolerance of their competitors for entry into their markets. In this way, the shared power mechanism was tacitly and legally shaped by the supercarriers.

The shared power mechanism created a self-perpetuating dynamic stability in the U.S. domestic market, and both the inner circle supercarriers and the outer ring of major airlines enjoyed significant improvements in domestic profits due to the airlines' economies of scale in hubs where they held leadership. Simultaneously, they were able to compete indirectly over

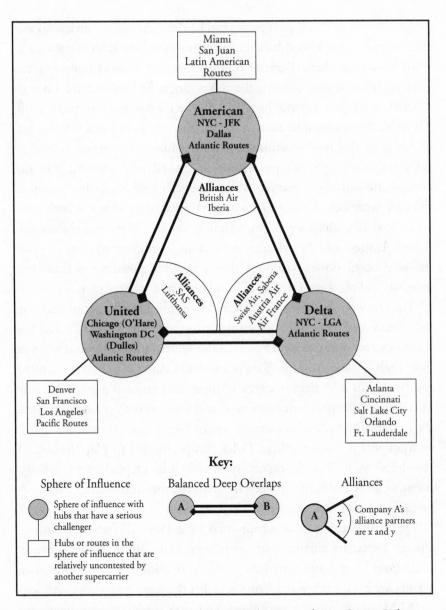

Exhibit 6-9: The Late 1990s Shared Power Mechanism in the Air Carrier Industry

pivotal zones and power vacuums in international markets—a growing high-margin market that was fragmented among many foreign carriers who were typically much smaller than the U.S. Big Three.

In addition to this shared power mechanism, the major carriers appear to have used a checks-and-balances mechanism to help achieve stability in international markets. Because of their indirect competition over the growing international market, the supercarriers had to be careful not to upset their delicate balance of power. In the transatlantic routes, the Big Three held roughly equal market shares, preserving an equal distribution of power in this market. Alliances with the European carriers helped to maintain this rough balance. However, United held leadership in the transpacific and Asian market, while American held leadership in routes to Latin American. Because Delta held only minor positions in both markets, the delicate balance of power among the Big Three was threatened. If both United and American generated an inordinate amount of profits—and hence power—through their leadership positions in these two international markets, Delta could find itself in a squeeze play.

The lesser powers appear to have reduced this threat by supplementing the checks-and-balances mechanism among the Big Three. Two of the lesser powers appear to have balanced out United's and American's power from their leadership in the Pacific and Latin American markets. United and American were held in check in these international markets because of serious challenges from Northwest and Continental, respectively. And the power of the two supercarriers was further tempered by Delta. With its footholds in both markets, Delta was positioned to play the role of "balancer" by having the capability to switch its emphasis and fare discounting back and forth between the markets, thus influencing which supercarrier would make money in those markets.

Delta's balancer role was supported by a loose alliance that formed around Delta. Its alliance with Northwest and Continental potentially could hold United and American in check. In addition, Delta formed an alliance with Air France and Continental at the same time that Continental, KLM, and Northwest were allied. Therefore, Delta could influence international routes, schedules, and prices at Continental that, in turn, could influence Northwest. Consequently, Delta could contain United's and American's positions in the Pacific and Latin American markets respectively through its surrogates. The result of all these checks and balances was an equal distribution of power in all four markets: domestic, Atlantic, Pacific, and Latin America. Peace at last!

GLOBAL POWER PROJECTION:
CO-OPETITION IN ACTION

One company's peace is another company's problem. When dynamic stability is created by firms with strategic supremacy in a given geo-product market, it frees them to project their power into new geo-product markets. As we saw with the Concert of Powers in Europe, nations turned their energy from the stable system of the Continent to opening new territories around the world. Peace at home frees great powers from the threat of a two-fronted confrontation, allowing them greater freedom to pursue a new growth initiative in other areas. This stability provides companies that have global ambitions, or that have already gone global but wish to expand further, with a safer platform from which to fund and launch new growth initiatives.

In the airline industry, peace and consolidated market share at home allowed the supercarriers to gain share from their foreign rivals. A recent study found that the increasing concentration of the U.S. domestic market resulted in major strategic gains in the international market and that the U.S. economy gained more wealth from this global supremacy than it lost due to any minor increases in domestic prices.[2]

The international effects of dynamic stability and concentrated power in the domestic market were substantial. As the industry boiled down to a small number of equally powerful supercarriers, the increased concentration created barriers to entry by limiting the availability of U.S. gates for sale to foreign carriers, and by creating economies of scale in domestic operations for the Big Three. With concentration, the supercarriers' gates and ground operations were utilized more heavily, creating greater efficiency. This resulted in lower costs that put many foreign rivals, especially the European carriers burdened with higher labor costs and smaller economies of scale, at an extreme disadvantage. Because the supercarriers had a lot of influence over access to their hubs, and because they had lower costs, foreign rivals had increased incentives to ally with them. The strength of the Big Three also contributed to their negotiating power with foreign airlines. Foreign carriers wishing an alliance with one of the Big Three had to grant U.S. access to airports in their homelands. In this way, the dynamic stability and equal power distribution created by the Big Three allowed them to project their domestic power into foreign markets.

The results were significant. When looking at the twenty-one nations with which the U.S. exchanged the most international traffic, researchers found international share grew substantially with domestic consolidation[3] (see Exhibit 6-10). There was a very big financial effect resulting from the consolidation of the airlines and the dynamic stability achieved in the power system. In 1995 alone, members of the International Air Transportation Association reported record earnings of $5.2 billion on international sales of $129.6 billion.

Some critics have argued that this wealth was created at the cost of reduced service levels for U.S. passengers; however, this viewpoint ignores the service and cost benefits of the global alliances that were created. United and Lufthansa integrated their operations (see Exhibit 6-11), and

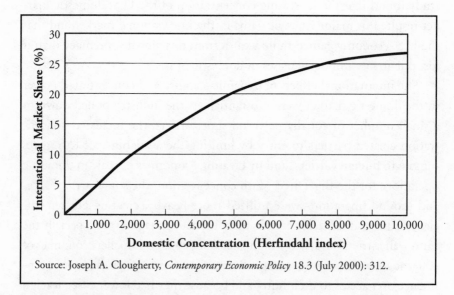

Source: Joseph A. Clougherty, *Contemporary Economic Policy* 18.3 (July 2000): 312.

Exhibit 6-10: The Effect of Domesstic Consolidation on International Market Share

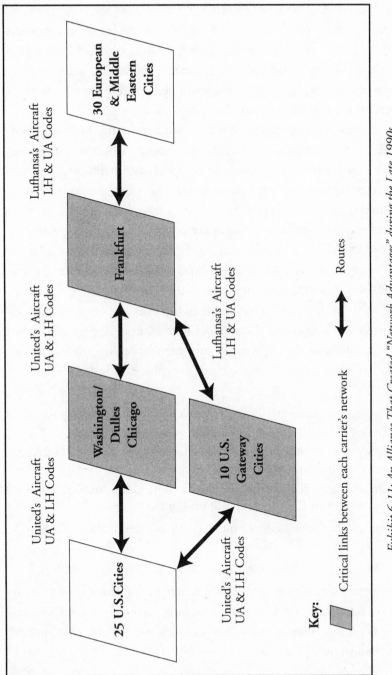

Exhibit 6-11: An Alliance That Created "Network Advantages" during the Late 1990s

by doing so set off a chain of beneficial effects for both the companies and their passengers. United was able to replace its smaller, more expensive overseas hubs and high-cost direct flights to Europe with Lufthansa's hubs and flights. Consequently, Lufthansa's capacity utilization led to reduced costs which, in turn, led to both higher margins and lower fares for U.S. travelers on international flights.

The integration of operations also channeled more traffic through United's domestic network, creating better capacity utilization, which in turn reduced costs, increased margins, and lowered fares for domestic travelers. The integration also improved service, making it easier for passengers to reach more global destinations, and to make connections at more hubs. In sum, the effect of United and Lufthansa's integrated operations was to create a larger network of flights and hubs, and to push more traffic through that network. The resulting "network effects" included better load factors (seats filled) and, consequently, better yields (fares per passenger mile).

The moral of the story: Dynamic stability does not have the same effect as collusive oligopolies. Companies with strategic supremacy do not necessarily profit at the expense of customers. *The New York Times* reported the following results of the battle for spheres of influence:[4]

- On average, fares are down 27 percent from the old regulated prices, after correcting for inflation.
- Eighty percent of passengers are paying less than they would have under the older government-set prices.
- The number of domestic passengers more than doubled, from 254 million in 1978 to over 520 million.
- The number of passenger miles has skyrocketed from 183 billion in 1978 to over 480 billion.

Unfortunately, the very success of the sphere of influence system in airlines has caused overcrowding and taxed the capacity of many airports, especially those that serve as major hubs in an airline's sphere. This problem has resulted from:[5]

- The federal government's failure to deregulate airports and air traffic control at the same time as it did the airlines
- Local governments' failure to build or approve the construction of new airports
- The failure of airports to restrict small planes from landing during peak periods, or to adjust their landing fees to discourage arrivals during peak delay periods because of regulation

Had the government built more flexibility into the air transportation system, everyone would be better off.[6] (Note: By 2001, the FAA had recognized the problem of overcrowding at key airports causing delays throughout the system. It has begun exploring several solutions, but none has been employed.)

In fact, spheres of influence can promote win-win outcomes for both the company and its customers. A large sphere of influence can increase a firm's profitability because of economies of scale and scope, as well as from network effects (discussed earlier in this chapter). Customers can benefit from the better service and cost savings passed along to them (provided the government takes proper regulatory precautions). In fact, the bigger the sphere of influence, the greater the economies of scale, scope, and networks and, hence, the bigger the benefits to both customers and companies. In addition, you can find win-win strategies based on growth into new geo-product territories that add value to both customers and shareholders. And you can increase the reliability and trust that comes with knowing that a company will be around long enough to meet its obligations to customers and creditors. The idea that self-perpetuating dynamic stability means monopolistic or oligopolistic profits is an oversimplification created by those who do not understand the nature—and many forms—of co-opetition that exist in all industries.

On the Razor's Edge

Dynamic stability is inherently fragile, as great powers walk a razor's edge between competition and cooperation. The airline industry reveals the challenges of balancing competition and cooperation, and simultaneously maintaining an equal distribution of power. Given the delicate relationships involved, it is striking that the global power system within the airline industry didn't drift out of dynamic stability for such a relatively long period of four years.

All of the stabilizing mechanisms require cooperation among the great powers or among the great and lesser powers. If the mechanisms get too far out of sync then the existing equal distribution of power becomes unbalanced, thus triggering a transformation of the global power system. The use of stabilizing mechanisms—in any industry—creates a mixture of tacit (and legal) cooperation in some markets, coupled with competition in other markets. The resultant global power system also involves tacit limits on the degree of competition in the competitive markets, and tacit limits on the degree of cooperation in the cooperative markets. Otherwise, the companies in the system won't be able to avoid self-destructive price wars, and antitrust problems for collusion.

This is the paradox of dynamic stability—the simultaneous co-existence of competition and cooperation, and the legal balance of limitations on both. No matter what industry you are in, it seems the natural tendency of global systems is to favor competition over cooperation. So you need to use strong medicine like balanced-deep overlaps to sustain cooperation. Yet, as balanced-deep overlaps are strengthened or used more frequently it is easy to slip over the line into collusion. Pure collusion is not only illegal but can actually interfere with the functioning of many of the stabilizing mechanisms. Consider the checks-and-balances mechanism (shown earlier in Exhibit 6-6, Diagram A). This mechanism fails if the other powers with supremacy cooperate with (rather than discipline) the rising power that threatens the dynamic stability of the power system.

Too many strong balanced-deep overlaps can drive this stabilizing mechanism out of sync, because they undermine the checks and balances in the system. On the one hand, balanced-deep overlaps can cause the checkers and balancers to become complacent, so they lack freedom and can neither check nor balance a rising power. On the other hand, a clever rising power can proactively use balanced-deep overlaps to realign the interests of some of the checkers and balancers, causing the checks-and-balances mechanism to deteriorate or convert to a tight or loose bloc mechanism (see Exhibit 6-12). If some of the checkers and balancers realign with the rising power, the rising power can create a bloc around itself, opposed by the other great powers still acting as checkers and balancers.

Thus, cooperative relationships, especially those established through balanced-deep overlaps, can interfere with the bigger picture—the ability to stabilize the status quo. Stabilizing the status quo often requires that you quickly convert some cooperative relationships to confrontational ones. Therefore, the use of balanced-deep overlaps and cooperation must be considered as a means of executing an effective stabilizing mechanism, and preserving the current power hierarchy. Overlaps and cooperation are not goals in and of themselves. They are means to a more important end.

POWER SURGES AND REBALANCING STRATEGIES

No matter how good you are at creating self-perpetuating dynamic stability, no power system can be stabilized permanently. Major shocks to the system and "power surges" will inevitably occur, overwhelming your stabilizing mechanisms. Major shocks include uncontrollable changes or events that selectively weaken the power of some of the great powers, without diminishing the power of others with supremacy. For example, these major shocks may take the form of a significant drop in demand as a result of shifting customer tastes or demographics, or widespread labor unrest that raises costs, interrupts delivery, or diminishes the quality of products or services.

Similarly, the system can destabilize when one player in the system gains a significant amount of power. For example, the voluntary actions of a rogue firm can enable it to overtake other powers with strategic supremacy. This kind of power surge can be created by adopting a revolutionary new technology. Power surges also can be created through indirect competition such as better execution of the firm's paradigm for power, or by capturing pivotal zones and power vacuums which circumvent the stabilizing mechanisms and give one firm a disproportionate piece of the power pie.

In the case of major shocks and power surges in a system, the established great powers can succumb and undergo a protracted period of transformation such as the one felt by the airline industry from 1989 to

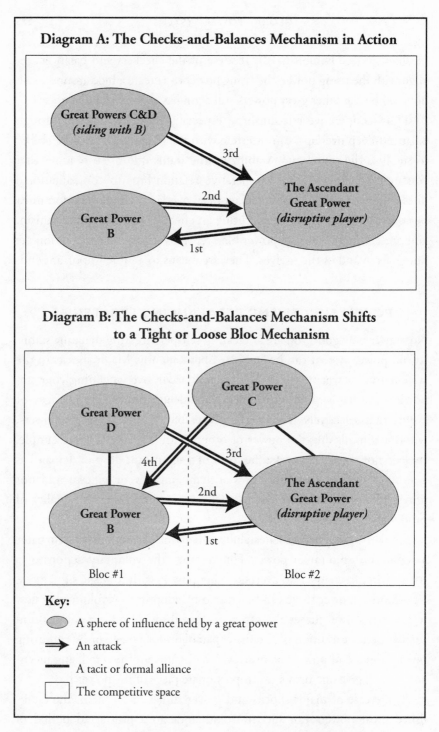

Diagram A: The Checks-and-Balances Mechanism in Action

Great Powers C&D
(siding with B)

3rd

Great Power
B

2nd

The Ascendant
Great Power
(disruptive player)

1st

**Diagram B: The Checks-and-Balances Mechanism Shifts
to a Tight or Loose Bloc Mechanism**

Great Power
C

Great Power
D

4th

3rd

Great Power
B

2nd

The Ascendant
Great Power
(disruptive player)

1st

Bloc #1

Bloc #2

Key:

A sphere of influence held by a great power

⟹ An attack

—— A tacit or formal alliance

The competitive space

Exhibit 6-12: The Malfunctioning of Stabilizing Mechanisms

1994. Or they can install a sort of circuit breaker—a set of "rapid rebal-ancing" strategies that allow the great powers to create a new and equal distribution of power. This helps avoid the trauma of a protracted period of transformation.

In Chapter 4, I discussed several methods for dousing disruptions caused by revolutionaries and other lesser powers. But if the disruption is caused by another great power who already has strategic supremacy, or if the disruption has already gone so far as to weaken one of those great pow-ers with supremacy, those methods may not be enough.

Great powers with supremacy typically respond to a major shock or power surge through rapid rebalancing strategies, which include major re-alignments of alliances and/or a wave of mergers and acquisitions. A merger wave can result in a whole new set of building blocks (spheres) and structure in an industry's power system. Through this process of realign-ment and assimilation of other spheres, the great powers with strategic su-premacy search for a new, feasible, and equal distribution of power.

When a feasible solution exists, the process balances off the shift in power experienced by the firm gaining or losing power. In other cases, re-alignment and assimilation may not immediately suggest a feasible solution. Government regulations, incompatibility between top management teams of potential merger partners, or an inability to convert competitive relation-ships to cooperative ones (or vice versa) can all delay a rebalancing effort. Nevertheless, the rise or loss of power by a firm may become so great—giving one player such a disproportionate amount of power, or threatening the very survival of a player—that the government and managers are ulti-mately convinced to set aside any resistance to a feasible solution.

In general, there is an inherent tendency for the global power system in all industries to move toward an equal distribution of power and to proac-tively seek out a new dynamic stability whether in the short or long run. As Woodrow Wilson once said, "Only peace between equals can last."

Please Fasten Your Safety Belts: Turbulence Ahead

In the airline industry, United experienced a major shock in 2000 that threatened the equal distribution of power among the Big Three (shown in Exhibit 6-9). Even though United was firmly entrenched as one of the Big Three supercarriers, it was destabilized by external threats and unrest from within—ominous threats related to softening demand in its Asia-Pacific routes, and serious labor and service problems. These problems contributed to increased canceled flights and decreased on-time arrivals. As a result, United was perceived as the worst performer of the Big Three, and was even compared unfavorably to some of the second-tier airlines. United's problems contributed to a substantial decrease in its net profits and stock valuation, as well as slowed revenue growth.

If this trend continued, United would soon be the least among the Big Three "equals." United responded to this shock by attempting to make up for its potential loss of power through an ambitious proposed merger with US Airways. If approved by the government, the combined entity would be the only nationwide network, with a market share of 28 percent, far ahead of American (with 19 percent market share) and Delta (with 17 percent market share).

This move by United, which would destabilize the power balance among the Big Three carriers, was expected to lead to reactions by competitors seeking to rebalance the system. Wall Street speculated about some of the rapid rebalancing strategies that the carriers might adopt in response to this proposed merger. Analysts generated five likely merger scenarios and the rebalanced market share associated with each one (see Exhibit 6-13). Note that none of the scenarios includes an American-Continental merger because their combined market share in the Latin American market (a whopping 71 percent) would definitely cause antitrust authorities in the government to reject it out of hand. The five remaining scenarios are:

- *Scenario one:* American merges with Northwest. This leaves Delta the odd airline out—i.e., with low enough market share to lose its supercarrier status.

- *Scenario two:* Delta merges with Continental. This leaves American the odd airline out. Because Delta and American undoubtedly don't want to lose their supercarrier status, the first two scenarios look more like stepping-stones toward a more feasible solution such as scenario three.

Merger Scenario	Resulting Market Shares (%)			
	American	Delta	United	Other
1. American & Northwest	30	17	28	
2. Delta & Continental	19	27	28	
3. Delta & Continental and American & Northwest	30	27	28	
4. Northwest & Continental	19	17	28	21 for NW & CO
5. Delta & Northwest	19	29	28	

Note: Market shares are based on 1999 available seat miles

Exhibit 6-13: Likely Merger Scenarios in Response to the Proposed United–US Airways Merger

- *Scenario three:* Combining the first two scenarios, this enables Delta and American to remain supercarriers with roughly equal market shares and nationwide networks competitive with the joint United/US Airways carrier. This equal distribution of power would allow the reestablishment of a shared power mechanism.

- *Scenario four:* Northwest merges with Continental. This suggests that a new great power would be created with the number two market share in the industry, leaving Delta most vulnerable because it would end up with the lowest market share of the four.

- *Scenario five:* Delta merges with Northwest. This creates two great powers, leaving American at risk with the lowest market share of the three.

Because neither Delta nor American would want to be the most vulnerable player among the big players, scenarios four and five would likely create a long period of transformation designed either to dismember or shore up the vulnerable players. Eventually, the transformation would end up with a roughly equal distribution of power among the stronger players, or with one player grabbing total strategic supremacy by scooping up the lion's share of the weakened players' spheres. Because scenarios four and five would drag out a costly transformation, the players may want to avoid them.

If antitrust regulators decide to interfere with the natural process of power redistribution in the system, they could reject any and all mergers including the United–US Airways merger and the scenarios in Exhibit 6-13. Or they could accept the United–US Airways merger but reject all the subsequent merger scenarios to prevent further consolidation of the industry. In the first case, the government preserves the current distribution of power. In the second case, the government forces American and Delta to grow organically until they catch up with United's postmerger market share. If American or Delta can't do so, the industry will move toward a bipolar world because one of them would probably fail in its attempt to grow given that the other would be fiercely attempting to do the same.

In part because of this possibility, American surprised the industry by announcing its intention to purchase TWA in bankruptcy (January 2001) and the Justice Department approved the takeover in March. In addition, American signed a side deal with United in 2001 to buy a portion of the

US Airways assets (including 50 percent of the valuable US Airways Shuttle) for $1.2 billion and $300 million in aircraft operating leases. In a separate deal with founder Robert Johnson, American agreed to acquire 49 percent in the startup DC Air (to be spun out of US Airways if the United deal is okayed by the Justice Department). As of June 2001, the Justice Department was still silent about the United–US Airways deal, and many believed it could be dead. But, if it does go through, American and United have insured that the balance of power between them will continue, and Delta is actively considering merging with Continental to ensure Delta's place in the triumvirate.

Of course, in all the scenarios described above, many things could go wrong. As Yogi Berra once said, "If the world was perfect, it wouldn't be." Nevertheless, even if the scenarios don't play out exactly as predicted, the system's natural response seems to be to establish a new equal distribution of power fairly quickly through the use of mergers and by moving into the power vacuum left behind by self-destructed firms. Even if a quick and effective response to the shock is not feasible, the system would redistribute the power until one of the stabilizing mechanisms could be employed after a longer period of transformation.

USING STRATEGY TO SHAPE THE FUTURE

Even during times of chaos, industry leaders can measure and map the patterns of pressure in their industry to reveal the "hidden order" behind the chaos. The hidden order within any global power system follows a natural evolutionary cycle that moves from chaos to dynamic stability, to disruptions that undo that stability, to rapid rebalancing or protracted transformations, to a new dynamic stability. In times of both chaos and stability in your industry, understanding the hidden order gives you the vision you need to navigate your firm successfully through turbulence that throws you off your flight path and achieve midflight corrections that reestablish your stability.

Strategy is the intervention in this natural evolution of the global power system. The airline industry exemplifies how firms with strategic supremacy can use their understanding of the "hidden order" to intervene in the global power system, even as their industries experience major shocks to the system. Consider the turbulence created in the airline industry by the Internet revolution. Priceline.com was a revolutionary company based on a radical model of auctioning off discount airline tickets that threatened to redistribute power in the airline industry by driving all ticket prices down. Priceline could have changed the power distribution away from the major airlines by making their marketing muscle less important because Priceline could market anyone's tickets, even those of new entrants and unknown carriers with lower costs than American, United, and Delta. This could have destroyed the existing power hierarchy and triggered a long period of transformation in the industry's power system.

The Big Three intervened in the hijacking of their industry. They formed cooperative agreements to launch their own Web sites and a common Web site to sell only their last-minute unfilled seats at a deep discount via the Web. Most of the other major carriers have joined this effort and followed the same policy of selling only last-minute unfilled seats via the Web. This had the effect of restricting Priceline's power and holding the discounting to the limited, last minute, non–business traveler segment. They doused the disruption caused by the Priceline shock, thus maintaining their position in their power hierarchy.

In fact, instead of destroying the supercarriers' profitability, the Internet has actually improved loads (capacity utilization) as well as revenues and profitability of the major carriers. Business travelers never warmed up to using Priceline, preferring the convenience of travel agencies. The actions of the Big Three did, however, make it easier for price-conscious consumers to find the best deals directly from the airlines, without paying a markup to Priceline. The supercarriers' actions also resulted in more choice for price-conscious travelers. Because consumers could shop around at more Web sites, this put pressure on prices in this segment.

The Big Three were able to intervene in the evolution of the system successfully because they had established strategic supremacy in their industry and had put in place effective stabilizing mechanisms. With strategic supremacy, they were able to restructure the patterns of cooperation and competition to influence the balance, sharing, distribution, redistribution, and pursuit of power. In short, strategic supremacy made the difference between watching a new economy emerge and the preservation of the old economy with a new technology.

Still, history reminds us that while dynamic rebalancing can sustain and rebuild power systems, it cannot ensure they will last forever. Ultimately, the great dynasties of Europe were replaced by a new power system called democracy. Austrian Prince Metternich's Concert of Powers and German Chancellor Bismarck's stabilizing alliances were only able to preserve the power of the ruling dynasties of Europe until World War I. Because of that war, the centuries-old reign of dynasties was over. As historian Robert D. Kaplan wrote, "Bismarck's genius, as well as his great flaw, was the same as that of another outstanding nineteenth-century politician of the German speaking world, Prince Klemens von Metternich. Both men were artificers, able to hold off the future by building a fragile present out of pieces of the past."

Final Thoughts

Dynamic Strategic Supremacy

Throughout history one thing is certain: If you don't achieve strategic supremacy, someone else will. But is strategic supremacy the destination or is it the journey itself? Do you have strategic supremacy if you are on top? Or do you have supremacy if you have the ability to shape the future evolution of competition? The answer is both. As Euripides said in 412 B.C., "None can hold fortune still and make it last."

Dynamic strategic supremacy is the ability to continually create, use, share, distribute, redistribute, preserve, stabilize, counter, circumvent, and direct the pattern of power in your industry. Dynamic strategic supremacy includes the power to expand into new space without resistance, the power to quell local rebellions without a heavy hand, and the power to influence the evolution of your competitive space. From this power comes profits, stability, growth, and lasting wealth for shareholders.

Good Guys Finish First

Friends come and go but enemies accumulate. While the pursuit of power is inevitable, the abuse of it is not and should be guarded against vigilantly. Many powerful firms have failed to gain or keep strategic supremacy because they relied on brute force. They abuse their power by attempting to charge customers higher prices for lower quality goods because their customers had no choice in the firm's core market. They also abuse their power by bullying competitors illegally in order to get them to cave in to their world view. These firms may temporarily achieve monopoly power through these measures but they cannot achieve strategic supremacy and sustain it over the long run. Sooner or later, customers revolt, competitors make a break for it, or the law catches up to them.

As the principles discussed in this book have demonstrated, there are more legitimate and effective methods for gaining and using strategic supremacy. Great powers with strategic supremacy get the world to accept their spheres by a combination of rewards, cooperation, fair competition, and offering great value to customers. Customers must wholeheartedly believe they will be rewarded for their loyalty with better value. Otherwise, a leading firm's core markets will be lost to revolutionaries or invaders. Rivals must also wholeheartedly believe they should live within the borders of the system defined by those with strategic supremacy. They must truly accept the spheres of others and want to abide by their borders because this acceptance allows them to focus their resources on serving customers better than any competitor could. This focus allows them to create value for their shareholders by creating value for their customers.

Envisioning the Future

In many ways the global playing fields of the future will be very different from those of today. What's more, it is almost a given that your company's sphere of influence cannot be maintained in its present form. But, as your sphere evolves in new directions, adding or dropping zones, or perhaps even undergoing a metamorphosis right down to its core, your firm's supremacy can still be sustained. As a leader in your industry you will want to open up new windows of opportunities. You will want to take advantage of progress, from virtual organizations to new information technology.

No global firm can afford to navigate the present, let alone the future, without the benefits of a real-time strategy and competitor analysis information system. Like being in an electronic command center or NORAD-like facility, you will need to visually monitor and map competitors' market shares in each geo-product zone of the competitive space and their maneuvering to reconfigure that space. These capabilities may seem like something out of a sci-fi movie. Yet they are very much in the realm of possibility, considering that a modern GameBoy has more computing power than the Cray supercomputers used by the U.S. Strategic Air Command to control all the strategic missiles in the United States during the Cuban Missile Crisis and the Vietnam War. Only the firms that invest in the coming generation of advanced, real-time strategic information systems and mapping tools will be able to stake out their spheres of influence, see and mold the spheres of others, and signal and realign the interests of others, all to the end of conquering chaos and fashioning a favorable world.

"Seek What They Sought"

From Caesar to cyberspace, history shows that no great power can slavishly follow in the exact footsteps of those who have come before. You need to find your own way. But, while the times are changing, the timeless principles of strategic supremacy remain constant. Therefore, it is always wise to remember what seventeenth-century Japanese poet Matsuo Basho so eloquently said: "Do not seek to follow in the footsteps of the men of old. Seek what they sought." Strategic supremacy.

A Self-Assessment: Will You Make History . . . or be History?

How high is your firm's strategic supremacy quotient? For every YES answer you check off in the following informal assessment, your strategic quotient goes up a notch, offering a glimpse of where your company stands today—and where it may be headed in the future.

Yes No

Sphere of Influence

❑ ❑ Do you have a cohesive sphere of influence located where you would like to be in your competitive space?

❑ ❑ Have you assigned a strategic intent to every zone of your sphere?

❑ ❑ Are you the preeminent sphere in the marketplace?

❑ ❑ If you are not the preeminent sphere, are you actively using your sphere to gain strategic supremacy?

❑ ❑ When power vacuums arise, are you the one who secures the market first?

❑ ❑ Do you understand the logic and positioning of your rivals' spheres of influences?

❑ ❑ Do you know what kind of competitive compression your sphere is experiencing? Do you have a plan to circumvent it?

❑ ❑ Do you have a weatherproofing strategy for your sphere?

Value Leadership in Your Core

❑ ❑ Will customers drive further, pay more, wait longer, and accept no substitutes for your product or service?

❑ ❑ Are competitors using your success as a benchmark and following your lead?

❑ ❑ Is your company or brand name synonymous with the product or service?

❑ ❑ Do you continually evolve your value proposition to meet the shifting competitive environment?

❑ ❑ Are you leveraging your value leadership into new markets?

Mapping Tools and MIS

❑ ❑ Do you have the geo-product market share data to map the system of overlapping spheres in your competitive space?

❑ ❑ Does your MIS and enterprise-wide resource planning system have real-time capability to monitor movements in the geo-product positioning of your company and competitors?

❑ ❑ Do you have the ability to synthesize how the global competitive configuration and balance of power are shifting?

❑ ❑ Do you have the real-time capability at headquarters to monitor whether mutual forbearance is working?

❑ ❑ Do you have the ability to predict where a competitor's sphere is moving in the future?

❑ ❑ Do you have the ability to coordinate actions in one geo-product market to influence other geo-product markets?

❑ ❑ Do you have the real-time ability to prevent one of your divisions from accidentally triggering retaliation by a well-coordinated rival in another market?

Competitive Configuration and the Global Power System

❑ ❑ Do rivals accept your definition of the competitive playing field?

❑ ❑ Are you working to create competitive collectives such as a concert of powers, polarized bloc, or collective security arrangement?

❑ ❑ Are you using balanced-deep overlaps between spheres to influence the competitive configuration?

❑ ❑ Do you actively work to realign the interests of your rivals to structure effective triangles?

❑ ❑ Does your global power system have stabilizing mechanisms in place?

❑ ❑ Do you know if you want an equal or unequal balance of power?

❑ ❑ Do you know which arrangement of cooperative alignments and designated targets makes the most sense for your sphere?

❑ ❑ Do you have a strategy for co-opetition that is more than just a series of one-off alliances?

❑ ❑ Can you predict how the power hierarchy will change in the future?

❑ ❑ Do you know what world view you want others to buy in to? Do you know how you want to define your sphere and the spheres of your rivals to make that world view happen?

Appendix A

August 26, 1998

Dear Rich,

Thank you for your kind and highly valued letter after your seeing *Saving Pvt. Ryan.* For many years I spoke very little about my past in World War II. Just recently people have become interested in the part that I played in helping to win the war. I still am reluctant to answer questions when I am asked about the war.

I was undecided about going to see the movie, but your letter encouraged your mother and me to go see it that night.

It has been over fifty years since the invasion of Europe occurred, but I will make an honest effort to recall some of the important events that I went through at the time. Your mother has a log which she has kept with dates, places, and events which happened to me during the war.

On June 27, 1943 I became 18 years of age and received my 1A draft status and a notice to report to the Allston Armory (Boston, MA) for a physical exam on September 2nd. I passed the Air Corp Cadet exam to be a pilot and was waiting to be called. As circumstance would have it the Army got me first and on September 23rd I was inducted into the U.S. Army.

I waited at Fort Devens for four months for an opening in the Cadet Corp, but time ran out, and I was sent to Fort McCullen in Alabama for basic training. After three months of basic training I was sent overseas as a replacement in the 9th Infantry Division 359 Regiment 1st Battalion Company.

Spielberg does an excellent job of directing and capturing the flavor of the invasion.

On to D-Day 1944. It is a day inculcated in my memory, as well as the weeks immediately following. War is so very unpleasant, disturbing, and distasteful. I was very young, indestructible with youthful courage and little fear of dying, and my mind-set was patriotism, so I did what I had to do. The young can do these things without thinking in the belief that they can do anything without repercussions. However the horror and death were certainly not without repercussions.

It was D-Day on what I was told was Omaha Beach—there was a lot of confusion because bad weather caused the landing crafts to go where they were not supposed to be. I landed as part of the second or third wave (I can't remember which). However, I do remember the fear, the prayers, the nervousness, and the uncertainty of what was about to happen when the gate of the landing barge opened. It certainly became hell with all the bodies drowning and dying on the beach. It is a scene that one tries to forget but can never forget.

As the landing barge approached the shore we encountered cement barriers under the water. When the barges hit these barriers the gate opened, we jumped out in the cold water over our heads. Many GIs drowned because of the sixty-pound pack on their back and others could not swim. Reaching the beach at the base of the cliff was a difficult task with barbwire strung all over the beach, and the Germans firing all they had at us.

The beach from cliff to waterline was only about twenty feet, and when the tide came in we were standing in two to three feet of water. Unlike the film, the beach battle was not over in twenty minutes. I was on the beach with those who were alive, wounded, and dead for about eight hours before the Army Corps of Engineers could blast a road through the steep cliff. With a road accomplished we were able to get men, tanks, guns, and other equipment on the land.

Everyone around me did an excellent job. The Navy kept up the barrages for hours upon hours. The Air Force bombarded the Germans from above, but most of all the medics did a Yeoman's job in helping the men who were hurt and getting them out of danger. The dead were picked up after we left the beach.

The first night on top of the cliff was one big explosion. The only savior was to dig slit trenches in the hard ground. It was exciting to see our Commanding General Manton Eddy up there with us, giving everyone encouragement. It was two or three days later that we were able to move out, but this was accomplished only after the Air Force and Infantry cleaned out the pillboxes.

I remember the hedges along the roads that divided the fields. I remember vividly one of our soldiers lying dead over one of the hedges. I also remember the dead cows lying on their backs with their legs straight up in the air after rigor mortis had set in.

Our objective was to take Cherbourg and establish a supply depot. This took four weeks to accomplish. We were given a week's rest before we were ordered to St. Lo. The Battle of St. Lo was a long terrific terrible bloody battle. In this battle you either got killed or wounded, not too many survived. In my seventh week in from the beach I was wounded by shrapnel on my right outer thigh above the knee. The shrapnel still remains in my leg. The fighting was so fierce that I didn't notice I was wounded until someone told me to get help.

The medical treatment from the evacuation hospital to the general hospital was more than efficient. So efficient that they had me back on the front lines within four to five weeks. I was shipped back to my division which, at this time, was located in Liege, Belgium. From there we went to Aachen, Germany where I got hit by shrapnel again, in the elbow. This wound landed me in the hospital for about six months. The elbow was operated on once or twice, I just can't remember. I could not move my fingers; my forearm was numb with nerve damage. However, after physical therapy, I was able to move my fingers again.

The Army doctors in their wisdom declared me limited service and, with that, I became a clerk typist assigned to the Air Force. From the Air Force I was sent to the 303rd Bomber Group at Air Transport Command in French West Africa for six months, and ultimately discharged honorably on November 23, 1945 from Fort Devens.

When I flew home in a military transport plane, the pilots played a trick on us. They rolled the airplane left and right while rolling empty beer cans into the main cabin. We feared we had miraculously survived the war only to die in a drunken, meaningless crash. But it was just a joke and I got back to the States alive.

At that time no one had cars and as a result I had to hitchhike home. I was awarded the Purple Heart and oak leaf cluster for wounds received in action. I also was awarded the Infantry Combat Badge for being in battle. I might have received more medals, but all my officers were killed, replaced, and killed again so quickly that there was no one to report what happened.

It was a unique experience. One that can't be repeated or explained unless you were there. I never would want to go through it again or have anyone else go through it.

It gave me an insight into how bad and sad war is. I did what I had to do to stay alive. I thank God that I survived and married and became the father of six wonderful children.

I don't consider myself a hero. I was able to go on to college on the GI Bill, work, and be a good citizen, marry, have children and support them.

Your mother and I are now in our senior years, and as we look back we are proud of all our children, for who they are and what they have accomplished. We are in hopes that our children will be as proud of us as we are proud of them, and hope we are surrounded in our golden years by you all.

I have always had the faith that our children would carry on and do us proudly in this great U.S. of A.

Love,
Dad

Pressure Measurement in the Airline Industry

Competitive compression is the strategic type (i.e., constriction, stripping, etc.) of "pressure" that the focal firm (a) experiences from a specific competitor (b) in the geo-products market where the competitor (b) overlaps with the focal firm (a). The *magnitude* of this pressure can be measured as follows:

$$M_{ba} = \sum_{i=1}^{n} [(S_{ai}/S_a) \times (S_{bi}/S_i)]$$

Where M_{ba} = the magnitude of the pressure felt by focal form (a) from its overlaps with competitor (b). Conversely, this can also be seen as the magnitude of pressure that competitor (b) puts on focal firm (a).

S_{ai} = dollar (or unit) sales of focal firm (a) in geo-product market i.

S_a = total dollar (or unit) sales of focal firm (a) across all its geo-product markets.

S_{bi} = dollar (or unit) sales of competitor (b) in geo-product market i.

S_i = total dollar (or unit) sales of all competitors and the focal firm in geo-product market i.

i = a geo-product market among the n geo-product markets served by both focal firm (a) and competitor (b).

The first team (S_{ai}/S_a) is a measure of the geo-product market importance to focal firm (a). The second term (S_{bi}/S_i) is a measure of the size of the presence of competitor (b) in that same geo-product market. The products of these two terms for all overlapping geo-product markets are summed to get the overall measure of pressure that focal firm (a) feels from competitor (b). The larger the overall measure, the deeper and heavier the threat is from competitor (b) to focal firm (a), pushing closer to the focal firm's (a's) core and vital zones with larger footholds.

Three general methodological points are critical to remember:

1. *The definition of a geo-product market* can be broad or fine-grained. A single geo-product market could, for example, be broadly defined as personal care products in Europe or more narrowly defined as soaps in Southern France. Obviously, finer-grained definitions of geo-product market will yield more accurate results. However, fine-grained data are often costly to collect or unavailable. Therefore, the smallest reasonable geo-product market definition should be used, and the market definitions should have approximately the same degree of "fine graininess" for all the spheres and markets being studied, if possible.

2. *The number of overlaps* can be too extensive to measure. In the equation above, *n* represents the number of geo-product markets where the focal firm (a) and competitor (b) overlap. However, when this extends to thousands of markets, many of the overlaps may be trivial—in absolute dollars or units sold, or in relative size compared to the focal firm's (a's) overall sphere. Therefore, it is often reasonable to eliminate the trivial markets using some decision rule, such as limiting the analysis to the top 1,000 overlaps or to overlaps in markets that are at least 1% of the focal firm's (a's) total sales. The cutoff is always a judgment call and the number of markets included in the analysis should be increased if these "small" or "trivial" overlaps cumulatively add up to an important percentage of the focal firm's (a's) total sales.

3. *The pressure measures (M_{ba}) should be* scaled such that their sum across all of a given focal firm's competitors will be equal to one. (This means the sum of the items in each row of Exhibit 6-1 should equal one.) Doing this provides a better predicator of each player's behavior, because it depicts pressures relative to each other as they appear to each focal firm, and the heaviest relative pressure ordinarily gets the quickest or the strongest response. Of course, it is sometimes useful to use unscaled pressure measures to determine who in an industry is subject to the most absolute pressure, and who is dishing out the most. Absolute pressure measures can tell you who may be eliminated or reduced to a trivial player, and who is taking the strongest offensive posture. But relative pressure measures often yield the same conclusions.

Exhibit 6-1 shows the scaled, calculated pressure measures for the airline industry in 1989, a time of intense competitive rivalry. The markets are defined as routes between cities. The analysis was limited to the two thousand largest routes served by each pair. "Units sold" was the number of passengers served. The data were from Department of Transportation sources, including Form 41 Reports, the Service Segment Database, and the Ticket Price Origin and Destination Survey. Note, however, that the methods described in this Appendix can be applied to any industry.

INTRODUCTION

1. Peter Brabeck and Suzy Wetlaufer, "The Business Case against Revolution: An Interview with Nestlé's Peter Brabeck," *Harvard Business Review,* Vol. 79, No. 2 (2001), pp. 113–119.
2. Charles Gray, "Corporate Goliaths: Sizing up Corporations and Governments," *Multinational Monitor,* June 1999, pp. 26–27.
3. Based on data from the *World Competitiveness Yearbook 2000,* published by IMD International, and *Fortune Magazine* Global 500 list, July 24, 2000, p. F1.

CHAPTER 1. THE SPHERE OF INFLUENCE

1. Raymond W. Goldsmith, "An Estimate of the Size and Structure of the National Product of the Early Roman Empire," *The Review of Income and Wealth,* published by the International Association for Research in Income and Wealth, New Haven, Conn., 1984, pp. 263–282.
2. Tarun Khanna and Jan W. Rivkin, "Estimating the Performance Effects of Business Groups in Emerging Markets," presented at the Strategic Management Society Meetings, Vancouver, November 2000 (Harvard Business School working paper, July 27, 2000). The study looked at data from over 800 widely diversified business groups containing almost 5,000 affiliates in 14 countries. The study found that affiliates of business groups had higher rates of return than their competitors in six of these 14 countries. The most positive effects were experienced by members of groups in India, Indonesia, and Taiwan. Positive effects were also experienced in Israel, South Africa, and Peru. The study also found no evidence of a diversification discount in 11 of the 14 countries. Being a member of a group was positively correlated with three measures of capital market efficiency, casting doubt on conventional wisdom that unrelated diversification is a response to inefficient capital markets.
3. Speech, March 1, 1848.
4. Rita G. McGrath, Ming-Jer Chen, and Ian MacMillan, "Multimarket Maneuvering in Uncertain Spheres of Influence: Resource Diversion Strategies," *Academy of Management Review,* 1998, Vol. 23, No. 4, pp. 724–740.
5. Winston Churchill, Speech at Harvard University, September 6, 1943.
6. Roy C. Macridis, *Contemporary Political Ideologies* (Boston: Little, Brown, 1986), p. 2.

7. Quoted in Charles W. Kegley Jr. and Gregory A. Raymond, *Multipolar Peace: Great Power Politics in the Twenty-First Century* (New York: St. Martin's Press, 1994).

8. H. Ma and David B. Jemison, "Effects of Spheres of Influence and Firm Resources and Capabilities on the Intensity of Rivalry in Multiple Market Competition," unpublished working paper, Bryant College, Rhode Island (1994); J. E. Martinez, "The Linked Oligopoly Concept: Recent Evidence from Banking," *Journal of Economic Issues,* Vol. 24 (1990), pp. 589–595; Heather A. Haveman and Lynn Nonnemaker, "Competition in Multiple Geographic Markets: The Impact on Growth and Market Entry," *Administrative Science Quarterly,* Vol. 45 (2000), pp. 232–267.

9. I. Jans and D. I. Rosenbaum, "Multimarket Contact and Pricing: Evidence in the U.S. Cement Industry," *International Journal of Industrial Organization,* Vol. 15 (1997), pp. 391–412.

10. P. M. Parker and L. H. Roller, "Collusive Conduct in Duopolies: Multimarket Conduct and Cross Ownership in the Mobile Telephone Industry," *Rand Journal of Economics,* Vol. 28 (1997), pp. 304–322.

11. J. F. Porac, H. Thomas, F. Wilson, and S. Kanfer. "Rivalry and the Industry Model of Scottish Knitwear Producers," *Administrative Science Quarterly,* Vol. 40 (1995), pp. 203–217.

12. H. G. Broadman, "Intraindustry Structure, Integration Strategies, and Petroleum Firm Performance," Ph.D. dissertation, Department of Economics, University of Michigan (1981).

13. J. A. C. Baum and H. A. Haverman. "Love Thy Neighbor? Differential and Spatial Agglomeration in the Manhattan Hotel Industry," *Administrative Science Quarterly,* Vol. 42 (1997), pp. 304–338.

14. Chris Zook with James Allen, *Profit from the Core: Growth Strategy in an Era of Turbulence.* (Boston: Harvard Business School Press, 2001).

CHAPTER 2. LEADING THE EVOLUTION

1. Oliver Wendell Holmes, New York Trust Co. v. Eisner, 256 US345, 349 (1921).

2. "Poor Ken," *Newsweek,* February 24, 1997, p. 10.

3. S. Coe. "Networks Off to Strong Start in New Season," *Broadcasting,* September 23, 1991.

4. Mark Landler, "The Too-Wide World of Television Sports," *Business Week,* No. 3191, December 10, 1990, p. 200.

"CBS Earns Last Laugh on Monday," *Advertising Age,* February 12, 1990, Vol. 61, No. 7, p. 41.

James P. Forkan, "TV Nets See Merit in Theme Nights, Program Blocks: CBS Tries All-Comedy Monday," *Television-Radio Age,* November 13, 1989, Vol. 37, pp. 34–36.

Judith Grahm, Marcy Magiera, "Monday to Be TV's Prime Battleground," *Advertising Age,* September 18, 1989, Vol. 60, No. 40; Midwest Regional ed. p. 69.

5. Yumiko Ono, "Toys 'R' Us Learns Give-and-Take Game of Discounting with Japanese Suppliers," *Wall Street Journal,* October 8, 1991, p. A-18.
6. *Fortune,* October 25, 1999, p. 37.
7. "This Russian Family Feud Is an All-American Tale," *Business Week,* March 26, 1990.
8. "One Hungry Tyke," *Barron's,* April 8, 1996, p. 22.

CHAPTER 3. PARADIGMS FOR POWER

1. Pankaj Ghemawat and Fariborz Ghadar, "The Dubious Logic of Global Megamergers," *Harvard Business Review,* Vol. 78, No. 4 (July–August 2000), pp. 64–72.
2. Ibid.
3. "Glass with Attitude," *The Economist,* December 20, 1997, p. 114.
4. Ibid.
5. Andrew Maykuth, "Diamond Cartel Is Besieged," *Philadelphia Inquirer,* October 14, 1996, p. A-1.
6. Leslie Kaufman, "As Biggest Business, Wal-Mart Propels Changes Elsewhere," *New York Times,* October 22, 2000.
7. P. F. Drucker, "Entrepreneurial Strategies," *California Management Review,* Vol. 27 No. 2 (1985), pp. 9–25.
8. Kathryn Kranhold, "Utilities' Quiet World Is Shaken Up as Enron Moves on Philadelphia," *Wall Street Journal,* January 7, 1997, p. A-1.
9. S. Brull, "The Wave of New Gizmos Coming Soon from Japan," *Business Week,* November 25, 1996, pp. 62–68.
10. C. K. Prahalad and Gary Hamel, "The Core Competence of the Corporation," *Harvard Business Review,* May–June 1990, p. 89.
11. Michael Porter, *Competitive Strategy: Techniques for Analyzing Industries and Competitors* (New York: Free Press, 1980).
12. Richard D'Aveni, *Hypercompetition: Managing the Dynamics of Strategic Maneuvering* (New York: Free Press, 1994).

CHAPTER 4. DOUSING DISRUPTION

1. Christine Oliver, "Strategic Responses to Institutional Processes," *Academy of Management Review,* Vol. 16, No. 1 (1991), p. 152.
2. Michael Tushman and Elaine Romanelli. "Organizational Evolution: A Metamorphosis Model of Convergence and Reorientation," *Research in Organizational Behavior,* Vol. 7 (1985), pp. 171–222.
3. Philip Anderson and Michael Tushman, "Technological Discontinuities and Dominant Designs: A Cyclical Model of Technological Change," *Administrative Science Quarterly,* Vol. 35 (December 1990), pp. 604–633.
4. Ibid.

5. A. J. Slywotsky, *Value Migration* (Boston: Harvard Business School Press, 1996).
6. Tushman, Romanelli, op. cit.

CHAPTER 5. COMPETITIVE CONFIGURATION

1. Avinash Dixit and Barry Nalebuff, *Thinking Strategically* (New York: Norton, 1991), p. 125.

CHAPTER 6. GLOBAL POWER SYSTEMS

1. Javier Gimeno and Carolyn W. Woo, "Hypercompetition in a Multimarket Environment: The Role of Strategic Similarity and Multimarket Contact in Competitive De-Escalation," *Organization Science,* Vol. 7 (1996), pp. 322–341; Javier Gimeno, "Reciprocal Threats in Multimarket Rivalry," *Stategic Management Journal,* Vol. 20 (1999), pp. 101–128; S. Borenstein, "The Dominant Firm Advantage in Multiproduct Industries: Evidence from the Airline Industry," *Quarterly Journal of Economics,* Vol. 20 (1991), pp. 344–365; W. N. Evans and I. Kessides, "Living by the 'Golden Rule': Multimarket Contact in the U.S. Airline Industry," *Quarterly Journal of Economics,* Vol. 109 (1996), pp. 341–366.
2. Joseph A. Clougherty, "U.S. Domestic Airline Alliances: Does the National Welfare Impact Turn on Strategic International Gains?" *Contemporary Economic Policy,* Vol. 18, No. 3 (July 2000), pp. 304–314.
3. Ibid.
4. Virginia Postrel, "Don't Blame Deregulation for the Airline Problems. Blame Not Enough Deregulation," *The New York Times,* as reprinted by permission in *Continental,* January 2001, pp. 77–78.
5. Ibid.
6. Ibid.

RICHARD A. D'AVENI is Professor of Strategic Management at Dartmouth's century-old Amos Tuck School of Business Administration. The Wall Street Journal recently named the Tuck School as the number one MBA program in the world. He holds a Ph.D. (Columbia), a bachelor's degree (Cornell), and is both an attorney and CPA. His bestselling book, *Hypercompetition,* has been translated into eight languages.

Likened to the ancient master of strategic arts, Sun Tzu, by *Fortune* Magazine, D'Aveni advises executives on how to be a revolutionary, and others on how to create order out of the chaos that revolutionaries cause. Professor D'Aveni was the winner of the prestigious A.T. Kearney Award and credited with developing a new paradigm for strategic thinking. *Wirtschafts Woche* (the German equivalent of *Business Week*) named D'Aveni one of America's leading management thinkers for the future.

He has been frequently quoted or written about in major publications including *Business Week, The Financial Times of London, Fortune, Newsweek, The Los Angeles Times, The New York Times, Time Magazine,* and over two hundred newpapers in the United States, Asia, Europe, and Latin America. *The Financial Times of London* has praised Professor D'Aveni for rejecting "formulaic management techniques in favour of a more fluid approach. Once executives realise there are no set rules, they might be more willing to discard conventional ways of thinking. It is a good time to be a maverick, they say, since old ideas have never been as useless as they are in today's business environment."

Professor D'Aveni has consulted and spoken at more than seventy-five global and *Fortune* 500 firms, including: AGFA, Arthur Andersen, AT&T, Bayer AG, Cargill, Citicorp/Salomon Smith Barney, Corning, Dun & Bradstreet, Fininvest Italia, General Electric, General Motors, John Deere, J.R. Simplot, Merrill Lynch, Motorola, PepsiCo, Pfizer,

Schering-Plough, and US West. He is a regular speaker at CEO forums and professional societies in Asia, Europe, and North and South America.

He was appointed a Forum Fellow by the World Economic Forum and has spoken at its annual gathering of prime ministers, billionaires, CEOs and other global leaders in Davos, Switzerland.

His hobby is helping to start MBA programs in emerging and industrializing nations including India, Israel, Mexico, and Vietnam. He lives and writes in Hanover, New Hampshire, and St. Petersburg, Russia.